Schriftenreihe
„Studien zur Politischen Soziologie"

herausgegeben von

Prof. Dr. Andrew Arato,
The New School for Social Research, New York

Prof. Dr. Hauke Brunkhorst, Universität Flensburg

Dr. Regina Kreide,
Goethe-Universität Frankfurt am Main

Band 2

Bev Clucas | Gerry Johnstone | Tony Ward (Eds.)

Torture: Moral Absolutes and Ambiguities

 **Nomos**

Die Deutsche Nationalbibliothek verzeichnet diese Publikation in
der Deutschen Nationalbibliografie; detaillierte bibliografische
Daten sind im Internet über http://www.d-nb.de abrufbar.

Die Deutsche Nationalbibliothek lists this publication in the Deutsche
Nationalbibliografie; detailed bibliographic data is available
in the Internet at http://www.d-nb.de .

ISBN 978-3-8329-4077-5

1. Auflage 2009
© Nomos Verlagsgesellschaft, Baden-Baden 2009. Printed in Germany. Alle Rechte,
auch die des Nachdrucks von Auszügen, der fotomechanischen Wiedergabe und der
Übersetzung, vorbehalten. Gedruckt auf alterungsbeständigem Papier.

Acknowledgments

We are very grateful to Daniel Metcalfe for his able assistance in editing the chapters for this volume, to the School of Law and Faculty of Arts and Social Sciences, University of Hull, for supporting the conference at which earlier versions of these papers were presented, and to all our colleagues and friends who helped to make the conference a success. Thanks also to Silke Baumann at Nomos for her patience in preparing the book for publication.

Hull, England
December 2008

Bev Clucas
Gerry Johnstone
Tony Ward

Contents

Introduction

Tony Ward, Gerry Johnstone and Bev Clucas

In November 2007 a conference was held at the University of Hull to discuss the permissibility of torture. The very fact that such a conference should seem worth holding is symptomatic, as Massimo La Torre remarks in his chapter, of a significant shift in the terms of political and philosophical debate since 2001. The chapters that follow are based on papers presented at that conference.

It should be said at once that none of the contributors to this book disputes that torture, in the great majority of instances in which it is actually practiced, is morally abhorrent. But some our contributors disagree passionately on questions such as the following:

- Are there *some* circumstances, however rare, in which torture is morally permissible or even required?
- If so, should the legal prohibition on torture be subject to defences which cover such exceptional circumstances?
- Should government agencies prepare their officials to respond to such circumstances?
- What are the terms of acceptable public discourse about the circumstances in which torture is permissible?

A. The ethics of exceptional cases

The case which best illustrates these questions is, perhaps, one to which Uwe Steinhoff refers in his chapter. On 27 September 2002, the 11-year-old son of a senior German bank executive was kidnapped and a million Euro ransom was demanded for his release. Three days later, a law student called Magnus Gaefgen was arrested after collecting the ransom. Under questioning he would not say where the boy was or whether he was alive. The day after the arrest, Wolfgang Daschner, the senior police officer leading the investigation, authorized his officers, in writing, to extract information 'by means of the infliction of pain, under medical supervision and subject to prior warning.'[1] Gaefgen was duly warned what was in store for him if he continued to withhold information. According to Gaefgen, he was told 'that a spe-

---

1   F. Jessberger, 'Bad Torture – Good Torture? What International Criminal Lawyers May Learn from the Recent Trial of Police Officers in Germany' *Journal of International Criminal Justice* 3 (2005): 1059-73, p. 1061; P. Finn, 'Police Torture Threat Sparks Painful Debate in Germany' *Washington Post* 8 March 2003.

cialist was being flown by helicopter to Frankfurt who "could inflict on me pain of a sort I had never before experienced".[2] Whatever the exact words used, arrangements really were made for a helicopter to bring a police martial arts trainer[3] who 'knew the areas of the body that are particularly sensitive to pain and [could] purposefully attack those areas',[4] to Frankfurt. In the event, the threat was sufficient to induce Gaefgen to admit that the child was dead and reveal the whereabouts of the body.

Gaefgen was convicted of abduction and murder and sentenced to life imprisonment. The officer who threatened him was convicted of coercion (*Nötingung)* and Daschner of instructing a subordinate to commit a criminal offence *(Verleitung eines Untergebenen zu einer Straftat).* The Regional Court rejected the defences of self-defence or defence of another *(Nothilfe)* and justificatory emergency *(rechtfertigender Notstand).*[5] To allow either defence on the facts of the case would infringe an absolute constitutional prohibition on violations of human dignity:

> Respect for human dignity is the basis of this state, which is based on the rule of law. The framers of the Constitution have deliberately put such notion at the outset of the Constitution. In contrast, the right to life and to physical inviolability is only laid down in Article 2 paragraph 2 of the *Grundgesetz.* The motivation behind that lies in the history of this state. Documents relating to the origin of the German Federal Republic make it absolutely clear that the members of the Parliamentary Council had very much in mind the cruelties of the National Socialist regime. They pursued the fundamental purpose of preventing anything similar from recurring and clearly to bar any such temptation through the drafting of the *Grundgesetz.* The human being was not to be treated for the second time as somebody having information that the state would wring out of him, even if for the purpose of serving justice.[6]

One aspect of the 'cruelties' to which the Court refers is discussed by Alison O'Donnell and her colleagues in Chapter 9 – and the unimaginable pain inflicted, for example, on concentration camp inmates in the course of medical experiments would clearly constitute torture under the legal definition discussed by Tsvetana Kamenova in Chapter 5. But do these contingent historical circumstances afford a basis for a *morally* absolute prohibition of torture at all times and in all circumstances? The court stopped short of that conclusion, acknowledging that there were 'theoretical borderline cases' which the facts of the case – where the police had not, in the court's view, exhausted all options short of torture – did not require it to decide. Uwe Steinhoff argues in Chapter 2 that self defence or the defence of others

2   J. Hooper, 'Germans Wrestle with Rights and Wrongs of Torture', *Guardian* 27 February 2003.
3   Finn, 'Police Torture Threat', p. A19.
4   Regional Court *(Landgericht)* of Frankfurt am Main, 'Decision of 20 December 2004. *Daschner Wolfgang and E.* Case', excerpts translated as 'Respect for Human Dignity in Today's Germany' *Journal of International Criminal Justice* 4 (2006): 862-5.
5   Jessberger, 'Bad Torture – Good Torture?', p. 1064.
6   Regional Court Decision, p. 863 (paras. 23-4).

provides both a moral and a legal justification for torture in cases like Daschner's, although for reasons that he has stated more fully elsewhere,[7] he opposes any institutionalization of torture or training of torturers. Hauke Brunkhorst (Chapter 4), by contrast, insists that the legal, as distinct from the moral, prohibition on torture must remain '*notstandfest*' – firm whatever the emergency.

Though Daschner and his colleague were convicted, the court found there were 'massive mitigating circumstances' and imposed only nominal penalties (reprimands and suspended fines).[8] Was this simply a merciful response to two people who had acted wrongly under overwhelming stress? Or was the court, as Francesco Belvisi's analysis (Chapter 3), might suggest, conscious of the difference between its own position as the guardian of the law and that of a state official who might have to answer to the public or to the victim's family? Belvisi would maintain the absolute legal prohibition against torture yet endorse torture as morally right in extreme cases – a sort of civil disobedience by the state against its own laws.[9] Hauke Brunkhorst takes a somewhat similar position, but while Belvisi thinks it is the role of the philosopher to consider what a state official should do in these extreme circumstances, Brunkhorst leaves the decision to the individual conscience of the official.

In a contribution to the conference which is not included here because it has been published elsewhere,[10] Michael Moore put forward a different defence of Daschner: that even if torture was absolutely wrong, it was not necessarily wrong to *intend* to torture. Intending to torture, or failing to prevent torture, or preventing others from preventing torture (among other examples) were, he suggested, easier to justify on consequentialist grounds than torture itself. Moore's major contribution to the debate on torture, however, remains his article 'Torture and the Balance of Evils' first published in 1989.[11] Here he argues that although torture is *prima facie* always wrong, it may sometimes be justified on grounds analogous to self-defence, or even in very extreme cases where that analogy (always a debateable one – see the chapters by La Torre and Steinhoff) clearly does not apply. As he put it at the Hull conference: 'If I can locate and defuse a nuclear device at 42nd Street only by torturing the innocent child of the terrorist who planted it there, I torture.'[12]

---

7   U. Steinhoff, 'Torture – The Case for Dirty Harry and against Alan Dershowitz', *Journal of Applied Philosophy* 23 (2007): 337-353

8   Regional Court Decision, p. 864; Jessberger, 'Bad Torture – Good Torture?', p. 1065.

9   Cf. H. Shue, 'Torture', *Philosophy and Public Affairs* 7 (1978): 124-43, p. 143.

10 M. S. Moore, 'Patrolling the Boundaries of Consequentialist Justifications: The Scope of Agent-relative Restrictions', *Law and Philosophy* 27 (2007): 35-96.

11 M. S. Moore, 'Torture and the Balance of Evils' *Israel Law Review* 23 (1989): 280-344, revised and reprinted as chapter 17 of Moore, *Placing Blame: A General Theory of the Criminal Law* (Oxford, Oxford University Press, 1997). Professor Moore kindly suggested that we reprint the article again in this volume, but in view of its length relative to the other contributions we decided not to include it.

12 Moore, 'Patrolling the Boundaries', p. 44.

Moore's article remains a classic illustration of the philosophical dilemma posed by torture. A simple consequentialist approach makes torture seem too easy to justify. On the other hand, the deontologist who insists that torture is absolutely impermissible will always be faced with more and more extravagant examples – like Moore's 42nd St. bomb or the imaginative scenarios in Uwe Steinhoff's chapter – in an attempt to force her to admit that torture will *sometimes* be justified. Once that concession is made, 'any prohibition on torture faces significant dialectical pressure toward balancing tests and the unwelcome consequentialist conclusion that interrogational torture can be justified whenever the expected benefits outweigh the expected costs.'[13]

Moore's own attempt to resolve this dilemma appeals to what he calls 'threshold deontology'.[14] Otherwise absolute moral rules like 'don't torture the innocent' give way at some – unspecifiable[15] – point where the consequences of adhering to them become overwhelmingly terrible. Rather than seek to give legal effect to this view, Moore argues for 'acoustic separation'.[16] If the aim is to ensure that officials torture only in the extremely rare case where it is justi-fiable to avert catastrophe, the best way to achieve it may be to prohibit *all* torture (or, as Moore advocates, all torture of 'the innocent')[17] and assume that officials will break the law when the threshold of horrendous consequences is reached. Such cases can then be dealt with by an exercise of clemency. Again this is a possible interpretation of the Daschner decision – that the exercise of clemency was based on a secret rule that people like Gaefgen *should* be tortured, a rule that could not be publicly announced for fear that it would encourage terror in cases where it was *not* appropriate. Such an interpretation raises troubling questions: as the originator of the 'acoustic separation' theory acknowledges, 'the sight of law tainted with duplicity and concealment is not pretty'.[18]

Whatever the merits of his solution, the way Moore poses the problem takes us to the heart of the debate. To La Torre's argument (Chapter 1) that a rule authorizing

---

13   D. Luban, 'Unthinking the Ticking Bomb', *Georgetown Law Faculty Working Papers* (July 2008), available at: <http://lsr.nellco.org/georgetown/fwps/papers/68/> (accessed 21 August 2008), p. 25. La Torre, Ch.1 below, gives examples of this dialectic. Steinhoff's argument in Ch. 2, however, is deontological rather than consequentialist.

14   Moore, 'Torture and the Balance of Evils', pp. 327-32.

15   Ibid., p. 332. For an argument that this unspecifiability renders Moore's position untenable, see L. Alexander, 'Deontology at the Threshold', *San Diego Law Review* 37 (2000): 893-912.

16   Moore, 'Torture and the Balance of Evils', p. 337. The phrase is from M. Dan-Cohen, 'Decision Rules and Conduct Rules: On Acoustic Separation in Criminal Law', *Harvard Law Review* 97 (1984): 625-77.

17   There is clearly a problem in reconciling the idea of 'guilty' torture victims with the presumption of innocence – see Marina Lalatta Costerbosa, Chapter 8 below – though advocates of defensive torture could argue that it no more infringes the presumption than does self-defensive killing.

18   Dan-Cohen, 'Decision Rules', p. 673.

torture is not universalizable, because no-one can accept being subjected to treatment the very nature which is to be unacceptable, an ally of Moore can respond that there may be cases in which the consequences of refraining from torture are unacceptable. But one riposte to this – see La Torre – is that even to discuss such examples is immoral because it erodes the sense of the moral unacceptability of torture in order to establish an exception that has virtually no application in real life.[19]

The question of the morality of discussing torture is a particularly troubling one for us, since by the very act of editing and publishing the book we are engaging in a debate which, Slavoj Žižek has argued, 'every authentic liberal should see...as a sign that the terrorists are winning'.[20] The trouble with the 'Pandora's box' argument, as Henry Shue told us thirty years ago, is that Pandora's box is already open.[21] Torture has become a matter not merely of debate, but of actual practice not just by U.S.-backed and trained regimes as in the 1970s, but by the U.S. itself and its core allies, including some British forces in Iraq.[22] If Žižek was right in what he wrote in 2002, the terrorists have already won that round. And in that very essay, Žižek himself joined the discussion of what to do in exceptional cases:

> I can well imagine that, in a particular situation, confronted with the proverbial 'prisoner who knows', whose words can save thousands, I might decide in favour of torture; however, even (or, rather, precisely) in a case such as this, it is absolutely crucial that one does not elevate this desperate choice into a universal principle: given the unavoidable and brutal urgency of the moment, one should simply do it.[23]

'One should simply do it' looks suspiciously like a universal principle, the scope of which cannot (and must not) be precisely specified. This is not far from Moore's 'threshold deontology', and closer still to Brunkhorst's 'tragic choice'.

The question now is not whether, but how, to debate torture. There is a case for discussing real or hypothetical exceptional cases, if only to show how different they are from virtually all real cases in which torture is practiced. But it is important to contextualize this discussion by pointing out how difficult, if not impossible, it is to find *any* real, documented case where torture has clearly averted some terrible threat.[24]

19   Moore acknowledges the virtual absence of real cases, at least so far as 'innocent' torture victims are concerned: 'Torture and the Balance of Evils', p. 333.
20   S. Žižek, 'Are we in a War? Do we have an Enemy?' *London Review of Books* 23 May 2002 (accessed in the online archive, <http://www.lrb.co.uk> [subscription required]).
21   Shue, 'Torture', p. 124. On the global politics of torture at this time see N. Chomsky and E. Herman, *The Political Economy of Human Rights* (Nottingham, Spokesman, 1979).
22   Joint Committee on Human Rights, *UN Convention Against Torture: Discrepancies in Evidence Given to the Committee About the Use of Prohibited Interrogation Techniques in Iraq* (HL157/HC527, London, TSO, 2008).
23   Žižek, 'Are we in a War?'
24   For careful scrutiny of several alleged instances see P. N. S. Rumney, 'Is Coercive Interrogation of Terrorist Suspects Effective? A Response to Bagaric and Clarke', *University of San Francisco Law Review* 40 (2006): 479-513; D. Rejali, *Torture and Democracy* (Princeton and Oxford, Princeton University Press, 2007).

Once again, the Daschner case is instructive. The threat of torture failed to save the boy; the court was not satisfied that torture had truly been a last resort; and, significantly in view of the way the whole torture debate is framed by the twin towers, the case had nothing to do with terrorism. The threat of torture 'worked', but on a man who had no cause to serve, no comrades no protect, and thus little incentive to hold out or to feed his interrogators false information.[25]

Although no case we know of provides incontrovertible evidence of the benefits of torture, we can discuss a real 'ticking bomb' case:

> In the late 1950s, Paul Teitgen, the prefect of Algiers, caught Fernand Yveton, a Communist placing a bomb in the gasworks. Teitgen knew Yveton had a second bomb, and if Yveton had planted and exploded it, it would set off gasometers, killing thousands. Teitgen could not persuade Yveton to tell him where the other bomb was. Nevertheless, said Teitgen, 'I refused to have him tortured. I trembled the whole afternoon. Finally the bomb did not go off. Thank God I was right.'[26]

According to a former senior French intelligence officer (and unrepentant torturer), Yveton was in fact tortured despite Teitgen's orders.[27] Teitgen's reasons for refusing to torture (and later resigning his position) appear to have included the fact that he was himself a torture survivor[28] – an illustration, perhaps, of La Torre's point that one cannot impose on others what one cannot accept oneself – and his fear, all too well founded as it turned out, that once permitted, torture would escalate: 'if you once get into this torture business, you're lost.'[29] In Henry Shue's view, for a ticking bomb case to justify torture, this likelihood of escalation would have to be absent, and in reality there are no such cases.[30] (Perhaps the Daschner case, being an isolated incident, comes closer than the Algerian situation.) Rejali suggests that the reason Teitgen 'trembled' was not simply fear of an explosion but the knowledge that if the explosion occurred he would be blamed for not using every possible means to prevent it. When officials do resort to torture as a response to terrorism, he suggests, they are not simply 'responding rationally to ineffectiveness' but 'purging the wounded community's furious emotions with human sacrifices.'[31]

---

25 Ibid., p. 478.
26 Ibid., pp. 533-4. Rejali spells the prefect's name 'Teitgin' but it is spelt 'Teitgen' in other accounts.
27 P. Aussaresses, *The Battle of the Casbah,* quoted in A. Bellamy 'No Pain, No Gain: Torture and Ethics in the War on Terror' *International Affairs* 82 (2006): 121-48, p. 141, n. 86. On Aussaresses' career and the furore surrounding his book see F. Kaltenbeck, 'On Torture and State Crime', *Cardozo Law Review* 24 (2002): 2381-92.
28 T. Todorov, 'Torture in the Algerian War' *South Central Review* 24, no. 1 (2007): 18-26.
29 Quoted by Bellamy, 'No Pain', p. 141.
30 H. Shue, 'Torture in Dreamland: Defusing the Ticking Bomb', *Case Western Reserve Journal of International Law* 37 (2005): 231-9.
31 Rejali, *Torture and Democracy,* p. 835.

Shue and Rejali's analyses suggest that rare, non-institutionalized torture, of the kind envisaged by Steinhoff and Belvisi, is an impossible abstraction – like, as Shue puts it, the alcoholic who has only one drink.[32] The difficulty with this argument is that precisely because of the extreme rarity of actual known cases, we have no data on which to base empirical generalizations about their consequences. We can only speculate on what might have happened in, for example, the Daschner case, if torture had actually been used. We may assume that prior to this case, torture was not part of the martial arts trainer's job description. But if he had tortured, and had been legally exonerated, he and everyone else in the German police would know he was the person to call in next time there was an urgent need to torture someone. Would he not feel the need to prepare for such an eventuality – and to prepare a few trainees, in case he was not available when the time came? To step back from institutionalizing torture in such a situation would not be easy. But 'hard-nosed consequentialists' may think that is a risk worth taking, if the evil to be averted is great enough,[33] and some deontologists might argue that it does not defeat the moral right to defensive torture.

B. Alternative approaches

It is not clear to us that the debate over exceptional cases can ever be resolved. It involves a 'tragic choice', as Brunkhorst puts it, between incommensurable evils, exacerbated in any conceivable real life case by lack of certainty over the factors that will determine the outcome of either course of action. And in any real crisis, it is a safe prediction that the choice between evils will not be made on the basis of philosophical argument, but will reflect a range of factors such as political calculation, peer pressure, the gendered self-image of the potential torturer, and racialized perceptions of the potential victim.[34] It is also clear that the decision to torture is rarely an agonized choice between evils: more often it is a routine tool of governance, or a means to degrade and subdue political opponents.[35] The discussion of exceptional cases may be unavoidable, but it should not be the dominant theme of the torture debate.

In fact it is only the first group of chapters that follow – those by La Torre, Steinhoff, Belvisi and (in part) Brunkhorst, that address the ethical issue posed by excep-

---

32   Ibid., p. 234

33   Luban, 'Unthinking the Ticking Bomb', p. 29.

34   See for example Todorov, 'Torture in the Algerian War'; M. K. Huggins, M. Haritos-Fatouros, and P. G. Zimbardo, *Violence Workers: Police Torturers and Murderers Reconstruct Brazilian Atrocities* (Berkeley, University of California Press, 2002); D. Rejali, 'Torture Makes the Man', *South Central Review* 24, no. 1 (2007): 151-69; J. Butler, 'Sexual Politics, Torture and Secular Time', *British Journal of Sociology* 59, no. 1 (2008): 1-23

35   P. Green and T. Ward, *State Crime: Governments, Violence and Corruption* (London, Pluto, 2004), Ch. 7.

tional cases. The other chapters more or less explicitly *assume* that torture is (always or virtually always) wrong and discuss the issue on other levels.

The chapters by Tsvetana Kamenova, Patrick Birkinshaw and Agustín Menendez deal with legal doctrines regarding torture. Kamenova examines the jurisprudence of the UN's *ad hoc* tribunals, and Birkinshaw looks at the implications of the House of Lords' decision on the inadmissibility of evidence obtained by torture, and points out some of the limitations of that decision, and of judicial decisions in general as a means of opposing torture. Menendez takes a more theoretical approach in criticizing the interpretation of US constitutional law by the Bush government and its advisers – an approach which, like La Torre's, implies that torture is incompatible with the nature of law as a form of practical discourse.

Marina Lalatta Costerbosa and Alison O'Donnell's chapters, as well as a large part of Hauke Brunkhorst's, approach the issue from a historical perspective. Brunkhorst relates the history of torture to the changing nature of European legal systems since the 12th century. Lalatta looks back to renaissance and enlightenment debates about torture as a means of interrogation, and finds disturbing parallels between those debates and today's political situation. She finds particularly instructive the argument of Christian Thomasius (1655-1728) about the political character of torture: it is not simply a means of interrogation, but a tool for the powerful against their enemies. O'Donnell et al. do not discuss interrogational torture at all, but the involvement of nurses in the genocidal practices of the Nazi regime, of which torture, in the form of medical experiments for example, was a subordinate part. The chapter serves as a reminder that interrogational torture, isolated from other forms of state terror, is the exception rather than the norm.

Penny Green and Tony Ward also discuss torture as part of wider patterns of state terror, and argue that once torture is accepted as a permissible institutional practice it is most unlikely to be confined within the bounds of 'lesser evil' justifications. Finally, Bev Clucas examines the portrayal – and implicit endorsement – of torture in the highly successful TV series *24,* bringing us back again to the issue of the morality of discussing torture at all.

It seems clear to us that the morality of discussing torture depends on whether the goal is to prevent it. Whether the goal is the absolute elimination of the practice, or its elimination in all but the handful of Daschner-type cases, is perhaps of secondary importance. There is a lot more work to be done on the issue of preventive strategy[36] – and the issue is a very difficult one, not least because of the difficulty of knowing

---

36 Important works in this area include: M. D. Evans and R. Morgan, *Preventing Torture : a study of the European Convention for the Prevention of Torture and Inhuman or Degrading Treatment or Punishment* (Oxford, Clarendon, 1998); T. Risse, S .C. Ropp, and K. Sikkink, (eds.) *The Power of Human Rights: International Norms and Domestic Change* (Cambridge, Cambridge University Press, 1999); R. D. Crelinstein, 'The World of Torture: A Constructed Reality', *Theoretical Criminology* 7 (2003): 293-318.

whether preventive measures are really preventing the practice or simply making it less visible.[37] What we can be clear about is what does *not* help: the sort of irresponsible legal discussion criticized by La Torre and Mendendez, and the sort of irresponsible media portrayal exemplified by *24*.

---

37   Rejali, *Torture and Democracy.*

1. 'Jurists, Bad Christians': Torture and the Rule of Law*

Massimo La Torre

Detainee began to cry. Visibly shaken. Very emotional. Detainee cried. Disturbed. Detainee began to cry. Detainee bit the IV tube completely in two. Started moaning. Uncomfortable. Moaning. Began crying hard spontaneously. Crying and praying. Very agitated. Yelled. Agitated and violent. Detainee spat. Detainee proclaimed his innocence. Whining. Dizzy. Forgetting things. Angry. Upset. Yelled for Allah. [...] Urinated on himself. Began to cry. Asked God for forgiveness. Cried. Cried. Became violent. Began to cry. Broke down and cried. Began to pray and openly cried. Cried out to Allah several times. Trembled uncontrollably.[1]

I.

The September 11 attacks of 2001 marked a watershed in political and legal philosophy: What developed in the wake of these attacks has shifted the basic premises of discussion onto entirely different grounds, in what can be described in certain important respects as a reversal of the earlier paradigm, or even as a throwback, depending on how one chooses to look at the change.[2] In fact it used to be, in the 1990s, that philosophers of law could work on the idea of a cosmopolitan order, could work on ways to extend constitutional principles to the sphere of international relations, could even conceive (not ingenuously) of institutionalizing the Kantian project for a perpetual peace.[3] But that has quickly vanished, the discussion now fo-

*   Earlier versions of this paper have been presented at the School of Law of the 'Robert Schuman' University of Strasbourg, on 15 May 2007; at the School of Political Science of the Università Statale in Milan, on 26 February 2007; at the Centro de Estudios Políticos y Constitucionales in Madrid, for a researchers' seminar held on 19 February 2007; at an international conference on the rights of man held on 18–20 October 2006 and organized by the Instituto Universitario de Historia Simancas of the University of Valladolid; and at the University of Kiel for a seminar in legal philosophy held on 28 July 2006. I am grateful to the Alexander von Humboldt Foundation for making it possible for me to research this paper at the University of Kiel in the summer of 2006.
1   Internal log detailing the interrogation at Guantanamo of a man identified as Detainee 063, quoted by P. Sands in his article 'The Green Light', *Vanity Fair*, May 2008.
2   See the bleak and dreary assessment presented in E. Denninger, 'Recht, Gewalt und Moral – ihr Verhältnis in nachwestfälischer Zeit: Ein Bericht', *Kritische Justiz* 38 (2005): 359ff.
3   Significant in this regard, because emblematic of a certain outlook or *Stimmung* that had a noticeable hold on the community until a few years ago, is Jürgen Habermas's fine essay 'Kants Idee des ewigen Friedens – Aus dem historischen Abstand von 200 Jahren', now in J.

cussing on the merits of preventive war, on the eclipse of international law in the mould of Westphalia, and on 'benevolent hegemony' – and the idea has even been floated of empire and imperialism, literally so stated.[4] We thus have, among others, essayists and scholars like Michael Ignatieff and Michael Walzer, once styled as 'liberal,' who are making the case for a 'light' form of 'Empire,'[5] and Thomas Nagel reminds us that if we are to achieve justice on a global scale we will have to take a Hobbesian path, by going through the (equally global) injustice of rule by the strongest, with a de facto monopoly of force exercised on an international stage.[6]

The paradigm reversal goes even deeper, however. Before 9/11, we were still working from within a conception of law that minimized law's coercive side and to a certain extent extruded force and violence from the archetypal context in which law is experienced. When confronted with a choice between 'facts' and 'norms,' between 'facticity' and 'validity,' jurists and theorists generally seemed to favour norms and validity, embedding these in the language of rights, principles, reasons, and arguments. Law was thus conceptualized as being fundamentally grounded in argumentation, discourse, and persuasion rather than in coercion: Essential to law was its laying a claim to justice, not its being a fait accompli. In a word, a 'milder,' kinder law was being forged.[7]

But in a dramatic turn now, the idea of force and violence as essential, foundational elements of law has swung back into action.[8] This resurgence can primarily be observed in international law – with John Bolton, for example, former U.S. ambassador to the United Nations, arguing that this law does not 'really'[9] exist – and the

---

Habermas, *Die Einbeziehung des Anderen* (Frankfurt, Suhrkamp, 1996), 192ff. Similar, too, is G. Teubner, 'Globale Zivilverfassungen: Alternativen zur staatszentrierten Verfassungstheorien', *Zeitschrift für ausländisches öffentliches Recht und Völkerrecht* 63 (2003): 1ff. Evidence that the upbeat 'mood' was not to last, however, came as early as in J. Habermas, 'Hat die Konstitutionalisierung des Völkerrechts noch eine Chance?', in *Der gespaltene Westen* (Frankfurt, Suhrkamp, 2004) 113ff.

4   For a discussion, see M. La Torre, 'Global Citizenship? Political Rights under Imperial Conditions', *Ratio Juris* 18 (2005): 236ff.

5   Compare the words of the British historian and essayist Tony Judt: 'In today's America, neo-conservatives generate brutish policies for which liberals provide the ethical fig-leaf' (T. Judt, 'Bush's Useful Idiots', *London Review of Books*, vol. 28, no. 18, 21 September 2006, <http://www.lrb.co.uk/v28/n18/judt01_.html>)

6   T. Nagel, 'The Problem of Global Justice', *Philosophy and Public Affairs* 33 (2005): 113ff.

7   The appropriate reference here can only be G. Zagrebelsky, *Il diritto mite* (Turin, Einaudi, 1992). Cf. M. La Torre, *Constitutionalism and Legal Reasoning* (Dordrecht, Springer, 2007).

8   Perhaps the pithiest *policy* encapsulation of this new embrace should be credited to Cofer Black, the head of the CIA Counterterrorist Center who in testimony to Congress in late 2002 made the now-famous remark, 'There was a before-9/11, and there was an after-9/11: After 9/11 the gloves came off'.

9   See J. R. Bolton, 'Is There Really Law in International Affairs?', *Transnational Law & Contemporary Problems* 10 (Spring 2000). More or less in the same vein, though more sophisticated and 'law and economics' re-styled, is the argument presented by J. L. Goldsmith and E. A. Posner, *The Limits of International Law* (Oxford, Oxford University Press, 2005).

same is happening in the sphere of international relations, now being depicted as Mars contra Venus, as a Hobbesian world in which the Kantian (and European) ideal of peace cannot flourish except under the shield of American might and power.[10] This new paradigm has crept into domestic law too, however: Here the Bush administration and its *Kronjuristen* have pushed onto a nation the idea of an unbridled executive power, legitimized to eschew the general laws, and even the constitution in certain respects, not to mention international treatises, their force being regarded as mostly symbolic: 'I'm the decider,' says President Bush, 'and I decide what is best,'[11] which in political theory and jurisprudence translates to the proposition that protection of the law is the president's business. This formula, worthy of Carl Schmitt, captures the new doctrine of executive exceptionalism as set out by the administration's top theorist, John Yoo. It is doubtless significant, and an indication of the new zeitgeist, that this young constitutional theorist now teaches law where the great Hans Kelsen once taught, at the University of California, Berkeley.

Kelsen emphatically and rigorously upheld the primacy of international law over national law and spoke of peace through law; Yoo, in stark contrast, is saying there is no obvious reason why the United States should make it a policy objective to curb violence and contain war around the world, and the same goes for the U.S. constitution: 'It is no longer clear that the constitutional system ought to be fixed so as to make it difficult to use force.'[12]

Change the language slightly, and there reemerges the old doctrine of the president (chief executive) as *Hüter der Verfassung* – as keeper of the constitution. The underlying argument here is once more of a 'realist' cast and roughly Schmittian in origin: Legal reasoning is in large part political or policy-oriented, and therefore, says the argument, it cannot be entrusted exclusively to 'nonpolitical,' and hence 'politically unaccountable,' bodies such as courts of law: 'When courts resolve genuine ambiguities, they cannot appeal to any 'brooding omnipresence in the sky'; often they must rely on policy judgments of their own. Those judgments should be made by the executive, not the judiciary.'[13] This turns on its head the basic principle of constitutional justice as expressed by the U.S. Supreme Court in its finding that it

---

10   It is Robert Kagan who has famously described Americans and Europeans as coming from two different planets: Mars and Venus, the one Hobbesian (and powerful) and the other Kantian (and weak). This power equation is seen as essential to the transatlantic relationship, and its solution – i.e., peace through power – is outlined in his very much quoted 'Power and Weakness', *Policy Review,* June/July 2002.

11   From a speech delivered 18 April 2006. Cf. R. Cohen, '"The Decider" Has Rules, All of Them Are Big, "Yo"', *Herald Tribune,* 22–23 July 2006.

12   J. Yoo, *The Powers of War and Peace* (Chicago, University of Chicago Press, 2005), ix. See also J. Yoo, *War by Other Means* (New York, Atlantic Press, 2006).

13   C. R. Sunstein, 'Beyond Marbury: The Executive's Power to Say What the Law Is', *Yale Law Journal* 115 (2006): 2580 ff.

is 'emphatically the province and the duty of the judicial department to say what the law is,'[14] which is the main holding in *Marbury* v. *Madison*, the foundation on which rests the federal system of judicial review in the United Sates.

They say that if you want peace you should be prepared for war. This adage has been newly conceptualized as a primary government function, and as a justification for government action, by bringing war into analogy with law and arguing that just as a lawless state could not ordinarily exist, so a warless one could not, either: 'War, like law, sustains the State by giving it the means to carry out its purposes of protection, preservation, and defense.'[15] The notion of a just war sets international law into motion – it does so as the reaction consequent upon a violation of such law. But reaction (a response) morphs into aggression (an initiative), and so comes to also embrace the preventive use of force, which comes into play even in situations in which there is no imminent threat to national security (a point made by the White House in its annual *National Security Strategy* report of 2002). In fact the concept of collective security is effaced from international law, displaced by the concept of national interest, which becomes paramount and whose interpretation is brought under the exclusive control of the U.S. president in his capacity as commander in chief. The sovereign thus reclaims an unqualified *jus ad bellum*, a privilege no longer subject to any of the rules the international community lives by.

So viewed against this background, law essentially becomes force and violence – as it does in Carl Schmitt's conception – and sovereignty once more projects itself as decision-making power under an *Ausnahmezustand*, the dreaded state of emergency in which the tenuous fibre and connections by which the law is held together wear away under the ultimately overriding standard of friend and enemy. In fact, in this fibre, which is thinning out by attrition under the force of this revived framework, we find some old foundations of law, first among which habeas corpus: It is now a presidential prerogative to decide who has the right to petition for this writ; the president may qualify anyone as an 'unlawful enemy combatant,' a category hitherto unknown, and anyone so qualified is thereby denied any right or guarantee under any system of law, whether domestic, international, or humanitarian, and so becomes fair game (*Freiwild*), and can therefore be taken away to a secret black-site location, can be locked up in a prison camp off-limits to judicial oversight, can be detained indefinitely and without charges.

This doctrine has in large part been formalized in the Military Commissions Act of 2006, signed into law by President Bush on 17 October 2006, which also acts to undercut the significance of the U.S. Supreme Court's holding in *Hamdan v.. Rumsfeld* [126 S. Ct. 2749 (2006)], where it is argued that a state of war does not amount to a 'blank cheque' for the executive, and that the exercise of exceptional executive powers requires the approval of Congress. Yet the Military Commissions Act [under

---

14   *Marbury* v. *Madison* 5 U.S. (1 Cranch) 137 (1802), p. 177.
15   P. Bobbit, *The Shield of Achilles: War, Peace, and the Course of History* (New York, Anchor Books, 2003), p. 780.

Section 6(a)(3)] vests in the chief executive (in the U.S. president) the authority to interpret Common Article 3 of the Third Geneva Convention, relative to the treatment of prisoners of war, thereby authorizing the president to determine the article's purview. And under Section 948(d)(c) of the same act, the president is further authorized, along with the secretary of defense, to designate any non-U.S. citizen as an unlawful enemy combatant, a status that strips the person so designated of the right to petition for habeas corpus[16]. A 'state of exception' has thus been set up under the war on terror, a state in which force suspends the rule of law, and which produces its own brand of exceptional subjects, the unlawful enemy combatants—exceptional precisely because what applies to them is not law but force. In this sense the *jus ad bellum*, so reinstated without let or hindrance, ends up gutting the *jus in bello* and taking away all its force.[17]

II.

If we look through the *National Defense Strategy of the United States of America*, a report issued in March 2005 by the U.S. Defense Department and the Pentagon, we will find under the heading 'Our Vulnerabilities' the revealing proposition that 'our strength as a nation state will continue to be challenged by those who employ a strategy of the weak using international fora, judicial processes, and terrorism.'[18] What is revealing here is the underlying assumption that international institutions and judicial processes stand on the same level with terrorism: All three are tools that 'the weak' use to thwart and derail 'the strong.' There is a definite Nietzschean and capitalistic theme lodged in this idea: Law and rules can fall into the hands of 'the weak,' who can aptly use them to thwart the progress, triumph, and vitality of those on the 'winning' side.

Words are deeds, and their consequences are not long in coming. So it seems that among several other moral and legal aberrations of our time, there is one in particular which has been every legal system's bête noire since the Enlightenment and yet is creeping back upon us, this being the legalization of torture. Thus, even though in the first half of what has been called the 'dumb' century (the 18th century), Ales-

---

16 Such denial of habeas corpus has now been struck down by the Supreme Court in its *Boumediene* v. *Bush* decision (128 S. Ct. 2229, issued on June 12, 2008), whereby aliens detained in Guantanamo Delta Camp now have an acknowledged right to challenge their detention in U.S. Courts: see R. Dworkin, 'Why It Was A Great Victory', *The New York Review of Books*, August 14, 2008, pp. 18 ff.

17 Cf. D. Luban, "Liberalism, Torture, and the Ticking Bomb," in *The Torture Debate in America*, ed. K. J. Greenberg (Cambridge: Cambridge University Press, 2005), 64–65.

18 D. H. Rumsfeld, *The National Defense Strategy of the United States of America*, (Washington DC, U.S. Department of Defense, 2005), p. 5.

sandro Manzoni could confidently proclaim that torture is 'dead and gone, a thing of the past,'[19] the tide seems to be turning now, with a growing number of jurists and policymakers enthusiastically looking to convince us otherwise. And indeed torture, as an anticipatory and hence inevitably disproportionate use of force, reproduces to some extent the phenomenological mechanics of the preemptive war advocated in President Bush's newfangled national-security doctrine. It can be argued, by analogy, that torture is to criminal law as preemptive war is to international law, in that both make useless and ineffectual any criterion of predictability or proportionality in the lawful use of force. And both find their basis in the idea of an imminent yet uncertain threat, and in the overriding and exclusionary value of national security. The breakup of international law by way of preemptive war thus paves the way for the equivalent breakup of domestic law by way of 'the torment.'

It should not come as a surprise, then, that when White House Counsel Alberto Gonzales (later serving as U.S. attorney general) requested an opinion on the legality of torture under international law, the response, laid out in a leaked August 1, 2002, U.S. Defense Department memo of the Office of Legal Counsel, involved none other than John Yoo – the *Kronjurist* (then acting as deputy assistant attorney general) who has been responsible for theorizing for the United States the legality of preemptive war. The memo, coauthored by Yoo along with Assistant Attorney General Jay S. Bybee,[20] points out in the first place that while the United States does have international obligations under the 1987 'United Nations Convention Against Torture and Other Cruel, Inhuman or Degrading Treatment or Punishment' (or CAT), these obligations are restricted by an instrument of ratification the United States deposited upon signing the convention in 1988, an instrument exercising which the first Bush administration submitted its own, apparently narrower understanding of torture, which would later become law (with passage of the 1994 Federal Anti-Torture Statute: 18 USC § 2340), and under which nothing counts as torture unless it inflicts 'prolonged mental harm caused by [...] the threat of imminent death.'[21] In the second place, the Bybee memorandum further restricts this definition by finding it to mean that 'physical pain amounting to torture must be equivalent in

19   A. Manzoni, *Storia della colonna infame*, ed. by G. Lesca (Florence, Barbera, 1923), pp. 39-40 (my translation).

20   The full version of the document was signed by Bybee alone, for which reason it has come to be known as the 'Bybee memorandum.'

21   'Memorandum for Alberto R. Gonzales, Counsel to the President, August 1, 2002', now in M. Danner, *Torture and Truth: America, Abu Ghraib, and the War on Terror* (New York, New York Review Books, 2004), p. 115. The re-legalization of torture practices pursued through this first memorandum is later supported in detail and made more explicit by John Yoo in his 'Memorandum for William J. Haynes II, General Counsel of the Department of Defense', dealing with military interrogation of 'alien unlawful combatants held outside the United States, March 14, 2003. See also – to have a concrete image of what is at stake – Donald H. Rumsfeld, in his capacity as US Secretary of Defense, 'Memorandum for the Commander, US Southern Command', having as its subject 'counter-resistance techniques in the war on terrorism', April 16, 2003.

intensity to the pain accompanying serious physical injury, such as organ failure, or impairment of bodily function, or even death.'[22] Anything below this threshold – including repeated physical violence – does not, according to Yoo and Bybee, qualify as torture.[23]

Through a broad reading of the understanding the United States entered with its accession to CAT, Yoo seems also to be introducing a doctrine of double effect whereby nothing counts as torture unless there is a 'specific intent' to torture. Under this specific-intent standard, in other words, it is legitimate to inflict serious pain and suffering (there is no finding of torture) so long as such suffering is not the immediate and direct intent behind the conduct in question, that is, so long as the suffering is a side effect and not the primary purpose of the infliction.[24] Now, let us assume that the specific aim of any act of duress is to obtain information (rather than to inflict pain): If we couple this assumption with the doctrine of the double effect as found in the memorandum, we get a specific-intent standard under which *any* infliction of pain aimed primarily at extracting information is simply that, plain interrogation, even if it clearly *is* torture by any other account.

Indeed, the only meaning of torture Yoo accepts as valid for the United States is that referred to in 18 USC § 2340A (part of the 1994 Federal Anti-Torture Statute).[25] Yet even under this restriction, the final outcome is that *anything* will pass muster, regardless of whether it counts as torture or not, for in the Bybee memorandum, Yoo's doctrine on presidential powers is brought to bear in such a way that section 2340A of the U.S. Code would prove unconstitutional if it were to be constructed as a limitation on such powers: 'Even if an interrogation method arguably were to violate Section 2340A, the statute would be unconstitutional if it impermissibly encroached on the President's constitutional power to conduct a military campaign. As Commander-in-Chief, the President has the constitutional authority to order interrogations of enemy combatants to gain intelligence information concerning the military plans of the enemy.'[26] Terrorists, it is further commented, are not regular combatants, and this makes the Geneva Conventions obsolete and amenable to exception with respect to this class of subjects.

22 'Memorandum', in Danner, *Torture and Truth*, p. 115.
23 Under Bybee's (and of course Yoo's) standard, then, many cruel practices now widely regarded as torture no longer count as such, on which point see H. H. Koh, 'Can the President Be Torturer in Chief?', *Indiana Law Journal* 81 (2006): 1150.
24 'Memorandum', in Danner, *Torture and Truth*, p. 142.
25 The actual definition is stated in 18 USC § 2340, which quotes almost verbatim the understanding the first Bush administration submitted as a reservation to CAT. As defined in Section 2340, torture is 'an act [...] specifically intended to inflict severe physical or mental pain or suffering', which in turn 'means [among other things] the prolonged mental harm caused by [...] the threat of imminent death.'
26 'Memorandum', in Danner, *Torture and Truth*, p. 142.

16

When asked whether the president could, for example, be prohibited from torturing a child, John Yoo responded with an unqualified no – there is no binding treaty in this regard. The question was asked by Doug Cassel: 'If the president deems that he's got to torture somebody, including by crushing the testicles of the person's child, is there no law that can stop him?' Yoo's response: 'No treaty.' Moreover, according to the now Professor of Law at Berkeley University 'customary international law, whatever its source and content, does not bind the President.'[27] Further, even an act of Congress could not limit the president's exceptional powers in time of war. And the war on terror is a war proper (however unprecedented it may be, precisely on account of its being waged on an enemy whose methods are those of terrorism). This balance of public powers must, according to Yoo, be resolved by tipping the scales in favour of executive power: 'Congress cannot tell the president how to exercise his judgment as commander in chief.'[28]

Any provision of law that might interfere with the president's power to declare a situation extraordinary – such as to warrant the use of interrogation methods prohibited by law – must be held unconstitutional: 'If the president really made this decision, that there are these extraordinary circumstances where the president needs to order interrogation that's in conflict with the congressional regulation, that regulation will be unconstitutional, too.'[29] Bybee then adds to this that officials who may be involved in torture can still avoid criminal or civil liability by claiming that 'they were carrying out the President's Commander-in-Chief powers.'[30] The president's immunity from domestic, constitutional, and international law thus extends to all those who have acted under an order ultimately traceable to the president's authority.

In short, Article 2 of the U.S. Constitution (which makes the president commander in chief of the armed forces) is constructed as meaning that the president may at discretion declare a state of exception as a matter of final decision and may in this case use full executive powers, such as are deemed necessary to handle the emergency so declared: 'The Commander in Chief Clause is a substantive grant of authority to the President conferring all those powers not expressly delegated by the Constitution to the Congress.'[31] This does nothing short of taking the Ninth Amendment constitutional principle of the citizens' unenumerated *rights* and transmogrifying into a doctrine of the 'president's unenumerated *powers*'; that is, by a

---

27 J. Yoo, 'Memorandum for William J. Haines II, General Counsel, Department of Defense', January 9, 2002, now in K. J. Greenberg and J. L. Dratel (eds.) *The Torture Papers – The Road to Abu Ghraib*, (Cambridge, Cambridge University Press, 2005), p. 39.
28 'The Torture Question', interview with John Yoo, PBS, Frontline series, <http://www.pbs.org/wgbh/pages/frontline/torture/interviews/yoo.html> (posted 18 October 2005). See also Yoo's comments reported by J. Mayer, 'Outsourcing Torture: The Secret History of America's "Extraordinary Rendition" Program', *New Yorker*, 14 February 2005.
29 'The Torture Question', interview with John Yoo.
30 'Memorandum', in Danner, *Torture and Truth*, p. 146.
31 J. Yoo, 'Transferring Terrorists', *Notre Dame Law Review* 79 (2004): 1198.

dramatic analogy, just as the *citizens* retain any rights not expressly set forth (enumerated) in the Constitution, so the *president* acquires any and all powers the Constitution does not expressly reserve to the nonexecutive branches and agencies of government (in plain contradiction to the basic idea of the United States government as a government of enumerated powers and limited jurisdiction).

III.

Now, the passing events just briefly outlined serve as background, and I will take them as my occasion to broach the broader question of whether torture is consistent with the rule of law. Which connects, too, with another question, that of whether there is any *moral* justification for torture. But before I proceed, I should say something about the kind of perspective I am bringing to the subject of torture. This is, to begin with, something we should never have been compelled to write about in the first place. As Seth F. Kreimer has expressed the idea, 'there are some articles I never thought I would have to write; this one.'[32]

Alan Dershowitz – an advocate of torture, his preferred method at least since 1989 being that of driving needles under the terror suspect's fingernails[33] – submits that professors, such as he is, are there to bring up any subject of discussion and to question our deepest, most settled, and long-established convictions. As he puts it, 'professors have yet a different responsibility: to provoke debate about issues before they occur and to challenge absolutes.'[34] This may have some logic going for it as a general platitude about the role of academia; less so when we bring the idea to bear on the issues themselves, and torture is one such issue: it cannot be approached as a mere philosophical exercise, just as it is senseless to take a theoretical perspective on, say, violence committed against women and children.[35] So I must express my deepest disagreement with this learned fellow professor, finding instead common ground with Jeremy Waldron, whose words (at the other end of the spectrum) cap-

---

32 S. F. Kreimer, 'Too Close to the Rack and the Screw: Constitutional Constraints on Torture in the War on Terror', *University of Pennsylvania Journal of Constitutional Law* 6 (2003): 278.

33 The method, in his own words, is that of 'a sterilized needle inserted under the fingernails to produce unbearable pain without any threat to health or life': A. Dershowitz, *Why Terrorism Works: Understanding the Threat, Responding to the Challenge* (New Haven, CT, Yale University Press, 2002), p. 144.

34 A. Dershowitz, 'Tortured Reasoning', in *Torture: A Collection*, ed. by S. Levinson (Oxford, Oxford University Press, 2004), p. 266.

35 Cf. J. Gardner and H. Shute, 'The Wrongness of Rape', in *Oxford Essays in Jurisprudence*, 4th series, ed. by J. Horder (Oxford, Oxford University Press, 2000), p. 194.

ture precisely my attitude to torture: 'It is dispiriting as well as shameful to have to turn our attention to this issue.'[36]

Moral and legal philosophy – understood as reflection on what is right and wrong, on what we should and shouldn't do – lives in a sphere apart from that of theoretical philosophy, such as ontology, epistemology, or the theory of meaning. Theoretical philosophy is fundamentally concerned with what the world *is* and what can be known about the world. This is a sphere in which any question may legitimately be asked, in contrast to moral philosophy, wherein *not* every question can seriously and responsibly be put forward as a subject of discussion. To be sure, there are some frivolous questions that can conceivably be asked even in theoretical philosophy, questions such as what would happen if grass were pink instead of green, but these questions are precisely that: trivial and inconsequential. Not so in moral philosophy, for we are working here within the practical realm, where everything we do, speak, or think carries a consequence. And just as we all know there are certain things we cannot and should not say, so there are things we shouldn't even *think:* We have to be thoughtful about our own thoughts and be able to rein them in accordingly, before they become reality. Contemplating someone's death or suffering and *using* and practicing such power of imagination – even on someone we understand to be our worst enemy – is certain to morally taint and debase us, and to undermine our ability to exercise sound moral judgment and act on it.

In the realm of practical reason and reflection there are questions of legitimate conduct the very *discussion* of which can be consequential in unhelpful ways. True, discussion is in itself valuable, but it can cause us to have second thoughts about our deepest moral convictions (and this is not *always* useful) and it can equally become ambiguous and offensive (which is *never* useful). Thus, we could enter on a philosophical discussion to test the legitimacy of certain items of conduct under hypothetical exceptional situations: Is it okay to rape our own child if we are stranded on a desert island and know we are the only human survivors of a nuclear war? Would it be okay to sell our mother's organs if we were living under reduced circumstances and would otherwise go hungry? Would it be okay to kill our father and thus save ourselves? Would it be okay to round up all the criminals and undesirables of the inner city, deport them to concentration camps, and perhaps implement on them the Final Solution? Of course, we *could* engage in such discussions, but whether we should is an entirely different matter: we could bring subtle philosophical argument to bear on the discussion, but no matter how sophisticated, articulate, or eloquent we might sound, we would surely be judged morally blighted (or even downright evil) and undeserving of any public audience.

There is a relevant connection here with utilitarianism as a moral theory, since one of the biggest faults found with this theory is precisely that everything in it is up for discussion: no topic is off the table; any topic, no matter how offensive to moral

---

36   J. Waldron, 'Torture and Positive Law: Jurisprudence for the White House', *Columbia Law Review* 105 (2005): 1683.

sensibility or how trivial or counterproductive, can plausibly be taken up and discussed in full earnest.[37] But then, descanting on what is more appropriate – 'enhanced interrogation' by electric shock or by waterboarding (i.e., strapping the victim to a board and simulating drowning, a practice enthusiastically supported by the vice president of the United States, Dick Cheney) – will prove repugnant to anyone except to someone who has vowed a strict allegiance to utilitarianism.

So then, I believe that engaging in any discussion on torture comes close to the scenarios just briefly described: Torture is morally objectionable not only in itself but also as a subject of discussion (a discussion about its pros and cons, even a mock discussion staged for purely academic interest). This is the sort of discussion that Bernard Williams would likely call a 'moral unthinkable,'[38] and that Robert Alexy would describe as 'discursively impossible.' It behooves us, I think, to bring our best judgment to bear on what we decide to say – to use our sense of the morally unthinkable, so as to exercise control on what we say, and to some extent even on what we think. Debating whether torture is morally or legally admissible strikes me as plain despicable, and the reason I am doing it, in seeming contradiction, is that this is a sentiment that needs a public voice. In April of 1811 at the Cádiz Cortes, Lord of Villanueva requested that 'this point not be discussed,' and that, 'without further ado, a vote be taken to abolish the judicial practice of the torment.'[39] And this is precisely the appeal and example that needs to be made public: Any different attitude is cause for suspicion as either inhuman or as likely lead to inhumanity.

So if I am taking up the matter it is because other people more impolitic than I – whether it be politicians, lawmakers, judges, jurists, or philosophers – have unabashedly set themselves at work to open this Pandora's Box. Torture is being not only discussed but also practiced; the imperialist-minded political changes referred to at the outset have put it on the agenda, and it is by this unfortunate historical contingency that discussion about torture has now become a must: This is unbelievably not a what-if discussion about hypotheticals but a necessary and real one with respect to which there is no choice but to be engaged.

IV

If we look at the debate that has unfolded in recent years, and at the different schemes that have been evolved to bring torture back as a legitimate practice under

---

37 The point is stated in B. Williams, 'A Critique of Utilitarianism', in J. J. C. Smart and B. Williams (eds.) *Utilitarianism: For and Against* (Cambridge, Cambridge University Press, 1973), p. 93.

38 'One might have the idea that the unthinkable was itself a moral category' (ibid., p. 92).

39 Tomás y Valiente, *La tortura en España*, p. 7.

the laws of our states, we can make out in this landscape five main argumentative strategies that have been deployed to this end. In what follows, I briefly illustrate each of these strategies in turn and offer the arguments that I think make each of them invalid.

(i) The first strategy is that which John Yoo and Jay S. Bybee adopted at the U.S. Justice Department under White House Counsel (and later Attorney General) Alberto Gonzales. This is a strategy that has been instrumental in bringing about, among other horrors, the Abu Ghraib prison-abuse scandal and the extensive extraordinary-rendition program, i.e., taking suspects into U.S. custody, by abduction or other method, and delivering them to third-party countries where they can be more easily tortured at secret locations outside the reach of U.S. jurisdiction. The strategy, as was pointed out earlier, consists in asserting the exceptional executive powers of the U.S. president as commander in chief of the armed forces, a capacity in which (as the argument goes) the president has free rein and cannot be held accountable under any national or international law.

This assertion of powers comes into conflict with established constitutional doctrine in the United States,[40] with the doctrine of *jus cogens* in international law[41] (a doctrine upheld in a House of Lords ruling of 17 December 2005), and especially with the basic principles of democratic constitutional government, in which executive power forms the main focus of constitutional limitations. Unbridled executive power not subject to any control, whether in ordinary or extraordinary circumstances, has no place in a government established under the rule of law, much less in a constitutional government, in which the fundamental rights set a limitation on the scope and depth of political action, and in which human dignity delimits an area outside the reach of legislative power, and all the more so of executive power. Thus, there is no doubt as to what the Founding Fathers intended when, in framing the U.S. Constitution in 1787, they vested in Congress the power to declare war: Entry into war – far from being a privilege of the executive, as Yoo would have it – is a matter of such consequence for the nation as a whole and for its future that any decision to that effect must be entrusted to the wisdom and judgment of all of the nation's representatives. So says explicitly the Constitution, and so read the *Federalist Papers:* 'The President is to be the commander-in-chief of the army and navy of the United States. [...] In this respect his authority would be nominally the same with that of the king of Great Britain, but in substance much inferior to it. It would

---

40 For an authoritative statement of this doctrine, see J. H. Ely, *War and Responsibility: Constitutional Lessons of Vietnam and Its Aftermath* (Princeton, Princeton University Press, 1993) – and it is no coincidence that Yoo takes critical aim at this book throughout his theoretical construction.

41 See M. Jahn, 'Gute Folter – schlechte Folter? Straf-, verfassungs- und völkerrechtliche Anmerkungen zum Begriff "Folter" im Spannungsfeld von Prävention und Repression', *Kritische Vierteljahresschrift für Gesetzgebung und Rechtswissenschaft* 87 (2004): 33-34, where international law prohibiting torture is argued to enjoy *jus cogens* status.

amount to nothing more than the supreme command and direction of the military and naval forces, as first General and admiral of the Confederacy; while that of the British king extends to the *declaring* of war and to the *raising* and *regulating* of fleets and armies – all which, by the Constitution under consideration, would appertain to the legislature' (*The Federalist*, no. 69).[42] For James Madison and his fellow Federalists, one of the great advantages of republicanism over the monarchy, and of federalism over sovereign states, was that of making it so that a decision to make war does not fall into the hands of a single person or of a few but is rather entrusted to many, who will have to persuade one another and will thus have to exercise good reason and be thoughtful: The single person or the few are more likely to act in the heat of passion, whereas the many will be able to ponder the decision and put a check on one another through collective decision-making in legislative bodies. Monarchy was felt to be pernicious by the Federalists precisely because it grants the executive branch those powers that Yoo is now claiming for the chief executive.

If the president is not master of war and peace, but is bound in this very delicate matter by the Constitution and by Congress, then his role as supreme commander of the armed forces (under Article 2 of the U.S. Constitution) cannot be refashioned into a role designed for rule by diktat, beyond good and evil, above national and international law, and without regard to basic rights. Hence, not every means will be justified in view of military victory. The president as envisaged by Yoo – a president subject to no judgment other than his or her own, with regard to such fundamental matters as peace and war and the freedom and dignity of citizens and foreigners alike – would bring about a government of men (of a *single* man) rather than one of laws. It is *despotism* that this vision sadly prefigures.

(ii) The second strategy in the effort to ground torture on a moral and legal basis is to cast the practice in a presumptively descriptive light. Torture, in other words, is presented as a matter of fact, a manifold phenomenon that may come in any shape, from a terrorist strike to a serious threat to national security, and it is here to stay, which leaves us with only two alternatives: We can take the hypocritical stance of formally rejecting torture while allowing it go unchecked underground in the secret chambers of executive power, or we can come to terms with its presence in society as a necessary evil, thus legalizing its use as a practice subject to oversight, making it, therefore, a transparent, responsible practice. 'I pose the issue as follows,' writes Alan Dershowitz: 'If torture is in fact being used and/or would in fact be used in an actual ticking-bomb mass terrorism case, would it be normatively better or worse to

---

42   J. Madison, A. Hamilton, and J. Jay, *The Federalist Papers*, ed. by I. Kramnick (Harmondsworth, Penguin, 1987), p. 398 (italics in original).

have such torture regulated by some kind of warrant, with accountability, record-keeping, standards, and limitations?'[43]

The objection here seems quite obvious. The argument proceeds on the assumption that torture is a de facto practice in fairly wide use – an established government practice. But that is arguably not an assumption that can safely be made universally with respect to every country. Thus, for example, it is doubtful that torture ever became a serious option among Spanish law-enforcement officials in the wake of the Madrid train bombings of 11 March 2004, or among British law enforcement following the London subway bombings of 7 July 2005.

Despite Dershowitz's view of torture as an inevitable social fact, there can still be found countries in the world where government is based on the rule of law and where society is decent. But at any rate, this second justificatory strategy proceeds on an additional and important assumption; that is, in addition to assuming that terror suspects get tortured as a matter of course – i.e., the practice is part and parcel of the business of running a government: it 'comes with the territory' – we also have to assume that this phenomenon, precisely by virtue of its being a 'social' fact, cannot morally be judged inherently loathsome, and so does not draw onto itself such contempt as to rule out the idea of legalizing it. Legalizing a practice entails that the practice itself be judged all in all 'okay'; that is, the practice may not have all it takes to qualify as moral, and may even be immoral to a certain extent, but not intolerably so, and not so much as to unsettle and shock the conscience of those who are called upon to judge it, for if it did reach such an extreme point, it could not even begin to make a case for itself as legitimate enough to be legalized.[44] Yet these are precisely the extremes that torture reaches. We have before us a type of conduct so plainly wrong and intolerable to common moral sentiment that even its possible or likely uptake in society would still not offer a good reason why it should be legalized. In fact, legalization implies a value judgment that does not cast the practice in a completely negative light but rather views it in certain respects positively. If, by contrast, we are *morally* convinced that torture cannot be engaged in, and that this tenet carries the highest moral force, then there is no way that torture can *legally* be found legitimate.

---

43   A. Dershowitz, 'The Torture Warrant', *New York Law School Review* 48 (2004): 277.

44   It should be pointed out, too, that legalized practices appearing on their face to violate the Constitution (as torture would seem to do if it were to be legalized) come under what the Supreme Court has called a 'more searching judicial inquiry' (*US* v. *Carolene Products Co.* 304 U.S. 144 (1938), 152 n. 4), which has come to be known as 'strict scrutiny' and which forms part of the court's understanding of the due-process principle. Strict scrutiny clearly requires more than just loose acceptance of something as not immoral, and in fact one cannot help but notice its close resemblance to Radbruch's formula, from German legal theory, whereby a law or provision is found invalid (unconstitutional) if it oversteps the threshold of 'extreme injustice.'

(iii) The most powerful and widely used strategy for reintroducing torture in law consists in laying out the loosely utilitarian ticking-bomb scenario of a device that could go off any minute now – a hypothetical scenario, true, but which vividly seizes the imagination.

The case is that in which someone is arrested who is known or suspected to have somewhere planted an explosive device that will soon detonate, killing many innocent people. In a dramatic situation such as this one, the only way to prevent the bomb from exploding, thus saving the lives of many, is to resort to torture, coercing from the person in custody information about where the bomb has been placed.

A hypothetical case like this one was presented by Niklas Luhmann at a conference held in Heidelberg in December 1992,[45] and it has also been used by Winfried Brügger, a German professor of public law who has been defending for over a decade now what he terms a *Rettungsfolter*, or 'lifesaver torture,' with a view to legalizing the practice.[46] Similar, too, is the case Dershowitz invokes in his proposal to make torture subject to a court warrant.[47] The proposal had already been laid out along similar lines by Luhmann, who envisages a scheme under which international judges authorize torture and supervise its execution by way of video cameras that record the entire procedure live, thus enabling the judges to instruct the torturers in real time on how to appropriately gauge the infliction of pain (as by increasing or decreasing the intensity of it or otherwise interrupting the treatment altogether): 'Zulassung von Folter durch international beaufsichtigte Gerichte, Fernsehüberwachung der Szene in Genf oder Luxemburg, telekommunikative Fernsteuerung.'[48] It will be up to the 'torturee,' Luhmann comments, to decide whether to hold out and be a hero or give in and be a traitor. Certainly, he concludes, this falls far short of being a satisfactory solution, but it nonetheless does much better than the alternative, which is to let innocent people die at the hands of terrorists. Dershowitz seems unaware of Luhmann's conference paper, yet proceeds very much à la Luhmann in his oblique defence of torture, by laying insistent emphasis on there being no moral absolutes: Right and wrong is not an all-or-nothing affair but a matter of degree.

---

45   See N. Luhmann, 'Gibt es in unserer Gesellschaft noch unverzichtbare Normen?', (Heidelberg, C. F. Müller, 1993), p. 1: 'In Ihrem Lande – und das könnte in nich zu ferner Zukunft auch Deutschland sein – gäbe es viele linke und rechte Terroristen, jeden Tag Morde, Brandanschläge, Tötung und Schäden für zahlreiche Unbeteiligte. Sie hätten den Führer einer solchen Gruppe gefangen. Sie könnten, wenn Sie ihn folterten, vermutlich das Leben vieler Menschen retten – zehn, hundert, tausend, wir können den Fall variieren. Würden Sie es tun?'

46   See W. Brügger, 'Würde gegen Würde', in *Verwaltungsblätter* (Baden-Württemberg, 1995), 414ff.; W. Brügger, 'Vom unbedingten Verbot der Folter zum bedingten Recht auf Folter?' *Juristen-Zeitung* 55 (2000): 165–173; and W. Brügger, 'Das andere Auge: Folter als zweitschlechteste Lösung', now in *Rettungsfolter im moderneen Rechtsstaat: Eine Verortung* (Bochum, Kamp, 2005) 107-17.

47   Dershowitz presents the same proposal in Ch. 4 of *Why Terrorism Works*, pp. 131ff.

48   Luhmann, 'Gibt es in unserer Gesellscahft noch unverzichtbare Normen?' p. 27.

The reply here is that just as there is no absolute right and wrong, because these concepts are relative, so there can be no absolute relativity, either; that is, relativity is itself a relative concept subject to restraints: If all moral criteria were subject to infinite gradation, then they could all be thinned out until they became meaningless by attrition and exception, and we would eventually come to a world in which nothing would make sense. No longer would the Latin maxim say *Fiat justitia et pereat mundus* (Let justice be done, though the world perish), but '*Fiat justitia*, and let the world perish in consequence,' since it would no longer be the moral criterion that holds its ground against the exception, but the exception that trumps the criterion in the name of justice or (much to the same effect) in the name of utility. Indeed, this is the same sort of abrasive relativism the utilitarian theory is apt to usher in. The point can be illustrated in narrative by way of Agamemnon, who resolves to sacrifice his daughter in order to bring favourable winds and make it possible for the Achaeans to make sail toward Troy. He does so to please the vast majority of his people, and his behaviour on this occasion is that of a good utilitarian. But, as the story goes, the girl's mother, Clytemnestra, never forgives Agamemnon for that gesture. In fact, if the rationale behind Agamemnon's pliant behaviour were carried to its logical conclusion (i.e., all criteria are always and without exception relative), we could probably, and imperceptibly, bring ourselves to justify anything and everything, or something close to it. Thus, for example, it was this logic that came to bear in justifying the Jewish councils when for some time the Germans, in an unsurpassed cynical test of human behaviour in distress, made these councils responsible for drawing up the lists of people from the ghetto to be deported to extermination camp. Similarly, Carl Schmitt and Karl Larenz, two insightful legal theorists, appealed to the logic of the lesser of two evils to justify ex post facto their adherence to the Nazi movement. Yet we know at least since Auschwitz that evil is bottomless, and so we should likewise know that the lesser of two evils can descend ever so close to unfathomable depths.

Stated otherwise, once we relativize the absolute, rock-solid prohibition against doing what we regard and experience as an outright, intolerable evil, and start making concessions to such evil – balancing different evils against one another to see which is the lesser one, the one toward which we could bend our behaviour – we will soon find that we have made a practice out of such tradeoffs (allowing in a measure of evil as a condition for what seems like a great gain in practicability), and by a natural progression we will thus become inured to the blatant evil that had initially elicited our dismay and outrage: No longer will we be morally inhibited from acquiescing in any evil of any kind, for once we accept torture in one case, there will be no compelling reason not to do so in other cases, too. This is perhaps best known as the slippery-slope thesis, which Steven Lukes succinctly captures in this observation that 'removing the general prohibition would soon dissolve inhibitions.'[49]

To see this thesis borne out, we can look at the dynamics involved in the torture argument presented by Richard Posner, the U.S. federal judge widely known as a

49   S. Lukes, 'Liberal Democratic Torture', *British Journal of Political Science* 36 (2005): 15.

legal theorist and pragmatist, and as a prominent exponent of the law-and-economics school, and recently an advocate of torture on 'moral' grounds. What is significant here is that he starts out by accepting torture in 'exceptional' cases, only to accept it later on in 'less exceptional' ones. His main argument is pragmatic and consequentialist; that is, torture is the lesser evil, with the only other alternative being a far worse evil that torture is *effective* at preventing: 'Many consciences will not be shocked at the use of torture when it will ward off a great evil and no other method would work quickly enough to be effective.'[50] Which means, too, that if we should actually come face to face with a terrifying ticking-bomb scenario, it would be so much as irresponsible on our part to foreclose recourse to a tool so useful as torture: 'In so extreme a case, it seems to me, torture must be allowed,' Posner reflects. But he shortly thereafter softens this statement: 'And perhaps in less extreme cases,'[51] too, it should be allowed.

Another place where we can see the slippery-slope thesis borne out – despite all the attempts made at demonstrating its logical ineptness – is in Dershowitz's extensive rhetorical appeal. The Harvard professor first presents a hypothetical situation in the extreme (the ticking-bomb scenario) and then concedes that the very concept of extreme circumstances is subject to interpretation and can therefore be stretched indefinitely.[52] He therefore concludes that the judge must have full discretion in deciding whether to issue a torture warrant – the judge mustn't be hamstrung by rigidly framed statutory constraints. Indeed, the difference between the ad hoc discretion of law-enforcement and intelligence officials and the judge's discretion under the torture-warrant scheme, Dershowitz argues, lies not in any exceptional-circumstances standard the judge is held to (in fact, no such standard is envisioned under the scheme) but in the judge's accountability: The determination must be made 'openly and with accountability.'[53]

But now the question bears asking: If we are in fact willing to accept a lesser evil (here, torturing another soul) as a way to avert a greater evil (allowing many innocent others to die), why should we not also be willing to take the blame that comes

---

50   R. A. Posner, *Not a Suicide Pact: The Constitution in a Time of National Emergency* (Oxford, Oxford University Press, 2006), p. 85.

51   R. A. Posner, 'Torture, Terrorism, and Interrogation', in Levinson (ed.) *Torture: A Collection*, 293. Cf. Posner, *Not a Suicide Pact*, Ch. 4. Despite defending an exceptional use of torture on *moral* grounds, Posner rejects the idea of formally legalizing the practice, choosing instead to refashion the torturer's activity as a case of 'civil disobedience', to be judicially assessed on its merits with lenience and perhaps even justified by criminal exemption. This view is interestingly made to rest on the slippery-slope argument: If torture were legal, 'officials would be tempted to test the outer bounds of so extraordinary a grant of authority' (ibid. p. 86); law enforcers, in other words, might be apt to stretch the rule beyond its intended meaning and purpose.

52   See Dershowitz, 'The Torture Warrant', p. 283.

53   Ibid. p. 290.

with that evil (however much it may be a 'lesser' evil)? If we are willing to sacrifice *another*'s integrity and dignity – and reduce that person to a pulp, both physically and emotionally – why should we not also be willing to sacrifice our *own* dignity, and positively assert that what we are doing (if we *are* in fact doing it) is hateful and inexcusable?[54] If what we are doing is evil (albeit 'less' evil), why, then, should we need the community, the state, and the law to support us and lift us from responsibility for the exceptional violence and pain we have inflicted? If the circumstances are so exceptional and terrifying – and no less terrifying is our response (as both Brügger and Dershowitz own up to, albeit in not so many words) – then let those deeds recoil upon ourselves, upon the doers, the torturers: Let the consequences visit us with equal ghastliness; let the law be our judge us and let it punish us accordingly, with all its harshness.[55]

This is a proposition we are unlikely to accept. In fact, as Hannah Arendt points out, 'the weakness of the argument has always been that those who chose the lesser evil forget very quickly that they chose evil.'[56] And as it happens – precisely because we are so prone to forget – what only a moment ago we were claiming as an exceptional circumstance under which our bad behaviour might be justified, we are now claiming as a matter of *right*. This much can be observed in the dynamics of the argumentative strategy by which the German professor Brügger advocates the use of torture as a 'life-saving device': He first introduces an exceptional circumstance justifying torture so understood (as a means by which to save the lives of innocent people) and then converts this circumstance into a foundation for the *right to torture*, a right the state claims for itself under its duty to protect its citizens.[57]

(iv) One argument deployed in Brügger's writings, and especially in the Bybee memorandum, is that of legitimate self-defence: 'If an attack appears increasingly likely, but our intelligence services and armed forces cannot prevent it without the information from the interrogation of a specific individual, then the more likely it will appear that the conduct in question will be seen as necessary.'[58] Bybee concedes that this case does not make a fit with the traditional understanding of self-defence, which becomes available to us only when confronted with an immediate frontal threat that is certain to materialize: 'Self-defence as usually discussed involves using

---

54   This point has been made with insight and sensitivity by Elaine Scarry, 'Five Errors in the Reasoning of Alan Dershowitz', in Levinson, *Torture*, pp. 281ff. See also E. Scarry, *The Body in Pain: The Making and Unmaking of the World* (Oxford, Oxford University Press, 1987), esp. her discussion of torture, pp. 27ff.

55   Cf. H. Brunkhorst, 'Folter vor Recht: Das Elend des repressiven Liberalismus', *Blätter für deutsche und internationale Politik* (2005): 80-81.

56   H. Arendt, 'Personal Responsibility under Dictatorship', in H. Arendt, *Responsibility and Judgment*, ed. by J. Kohn (New York, Schocken Books, 2003), 36.

57   See Brügger, 'Vom unbedingten Verbot der Folter zum bedingten Recht auf Folter?' pp. 165ff.

58   'Memorandum', in Danner, *Torture and Truth*, p. 153.

force against an individual who is about to conduct the attack. In the current circumstances, however, an enemy combatant in detention does not himself present a threat of harm. He is not actually carrying out the attack.'[59] Still, this is someone who, by hypothesis, has had a part in *planning* the attack, and if he or she can disclose relevant information about such an attack, then we do (on Bybee's doctrine) have a case for self-defence. In support of this thesis, Bybee invokes an article by Michael S. Moore, who in the 1980s discussed the Israeli practice of torturing detained Palestinians suspected of terrorism. According to Moore a terrorist can be said to have 'culpably caused the situation where someone might get hurt. If hurting [the terrorist] is the only means to prevent the death or injury of others put at risk by his actions, such torture should be permissible, and on the same basis that self-defense is permissible.'[60] So the terrorist, having been a party to the planning, can be regarded as part of the threat itself, as an accomplice and author – a circumstance that may justify acting in self-defence. The same principle, Bybee further comments, applies equally to *individuals* under threat and to the *nation* as a whole if it should come under the threat of terror.

So the gist of the argument is that we can torture someone in self-defence. But surely there is something deeply amiss here – just speaking these words should be enough to alert us to the discordant note within. Indeed, the person on whom torture is inflicted (the 'torture recipient') is by definition *defenceless*, unable to do anything that may inhibit the torturer's ability to do anything at will: 'In an interrogation torture case, the person being tortured is attacking no one. He has already been physically subdued and imprisoned [...]. In traditional self-defense, the person against whom one uses defensive violence is dangerous; in the torture case, he is helpless.'[61] A person in these incapacitating conditions – having no power of mind or body – cannot plausibly be described as a source of danger, except in a sophism designed to justify the unjustifiable.

Further, there needs to be a direct causal connection between self-defence and the threat it is intended to drive back, and the connection must be such that this will be the likely result. Yet we cannot say as much about torture, in which it is uncertain whether the information being sought will be obtained, or whether any information coercively obtained will be useful, or whether any useful information so obtained will causally and decisively contribute to extinguishing the threat. In addition, self-defensive action needs to be proportional to the threat posed; torture, in contrast, is overkill, by definition disproportionate and abusive: A deep, structural imbalance is built into the torture situation, with the inflicted harm far outweighing the danger

---

59   Ibid.
60   M. S. Moore, 'Torture and the Balance of Evils', *Israel Law Review* 23 (1989): 323.
61   Luban, 'Liberalism, Torture, and the Ticking Bomb', p. 63; cf. Koh, 'Can the President Be Torturer in Chief?', p. 1163.

against which it is defending. If there does not seem to be an inherently one-sided situation, that is because the danger being repelled is understood as having in it the potential to bring destruction on a great scale – but in torture, *any* harm inflicted is *real* harm, and it meets up against a counter-harm that comes to nothing: It is either inexistent, since the torturee cannot counteract, or it is merely presumptive, based on an *assumption* of baneful things to come, not on any knowledge of them (for, otherwise, there would be no need for the torturous act in the first place). So there is a definite hypocrisy involved in styling torture as self-defence: It is doublespeak whose real purpose is to overlay with a veneer of legitimacy what is actually an aggression, a behaviour that is always offensive and never defensive.

(v.) The last argumentative strategy appeals once more to the ticking-time-bomb scenario: This is an exceptional situation that, precisely on that account, engages in the politician an ethic of responsibility. The focus thus shifts to the politician, in a role much like that which Max Weber describes: that of a decision-maker who takes responsibility for any decisions made. Hence, when an extraordinary circumstance comes up that calls for swift action, the politician rises to the occasion and sets a policy for which he or she will ultimately be held accountable.

In reply to this accountability argument comes the caveat about equality under the law. In other words, accountability as such is all well and good, but not when it amounts to exceptionalism, for in this avatar it must come to grips with the principle that no one is above the law: Even the politician, despite the connections and back-room dealing that bind him (or her) to the occult demons of power, cannot skirt the rules of civilization that hold for everybody without exception. The politician's responsibility as Weber understands it does not exempt the politician from the consequences that come by operation of law within an institutional setting of general rule-making. Responsibility in this sense is none other than the politician's responsibility before the law – a moral commitment to follow the rules that everyone else lives by. There is no apparent reason why the politician should subscribe to a separate standard and responsibility, one that is ultimately lower or laxer than that which the ordinary citizen is held to.

Then, too, it is unclear what is meant by *politician*, what kind of role this word refers to. The responsible politician is generally understood to be a statesman (or stateswoman) in the elitist and Weberian tradition of thought, designating a person of exceptional skill and leadership, someone on whom weighs responsibility for attending to the *res publica*, the public good, but who can equally interpret and satisfy the needs arising under the reason of state. We have here before us what might be described as a process of parallel hypostatization: There is an underlying substance, a preexisting 'stateness' or 'reason'; then out of this essence a constitution and a polity are formed as its concrete expression; and then *in* comes a subject who connects with this 'political essence' and grasps its meaning through a privileged relationship, a bond so special and strong as to lift this person from ordinary moral obligation. There is a quality about this conceit which is at once romantic and authoritarian, for it casts the politician in a heroic light: 'Whoever enters on such an enterprise must

29

have the makings of a leader,' says Weber. 'But that will not suffice: This leader will also have to emerge as a hero, however much in a subdued, almost muted way.'[62] On this conception, what ultimately drives political activity, the fulcrum around which this activity revolves, is the use of force: 'Those who seek wellness for their own soul and blessing for that others will not do so by going through politics, for the tasks undertaken here fall into an altogether different category, and are such as can only be accomplished through violence.'[63] It seems to flow naturally that a heroic and exceptional figure so conceived – not bound by common morality, a sort of Nietzschean overman for all seasons – should take a relaxed attitude toward torture and not scruple too much about resorting to it: 'Those who get involved in politics, that is, who make use of power and violence, make a pact with diabolical powers,'[64] and if that is the case, then it wouldn't be so much out of character for these persons to also draw the hangman and the torturer into their coterie.

But it is worth asking now: Is this truly and invariably what politics is about? Is this breed of 'heroic' politician, unhindered by scruple with respect to his own soul or that of others, the person to whom we would entrust our future? Is this the kind of figure a democratic polity should rely on in its management of public affairs? The politician's role in democracy should tend to closely resemble that of the *citizen*, and have very little to do with the aristocrat, the Hyperborean statesman conceived in a Weberian mould. Politics in democracy should tend toward a *taming* of force, and anywhere force plays a role in driving the course of the *res publica*, it will signify a failure in the effort to reach mutual understanding and agreement – the mainstay of a democratic order. How could citizens deliberate and make decisions together all the while knowing and accepting that any one of them could turn around and, should the occasion arise, declare a willingness to torture others in the group, reducing them to inert matter, extinguishing these persons as autonomous bearers of rights, and hence as beings endowed with an inalienable dignity?

After all, a constitutional democracy does not have its basis in any preexisting 'stateness' or political essence from which spring forth basic constitutional rights and principles. The *salus populi* and the reason of state – so often adduced as grounds for a constitutional democracy's use of force and violence, even a brutal use – still answer to the content of constitutional rights and principles. There is no dark, inner quintessence concealed within a constitutional democracy, no latent 'state of exception,' no unattended crucible of radical forces brewing beneath the surface, ever ready to break out into violence at the next prepolitical situation of existential danger. The only existence at stake in a democracy is that of the constitution and its

---

62 M. Weber, 'Politik als Beruf', in *Gesammelte Politische Schriften*, ed. by J. Winckelmann (3rd ed., Tübingen, Mohr, 1973), p. 560 (my translation).
63 Ibid. p. 557 (my translation).
64 Ibid. p. 554 (my translation).

rights.[65] For in a constitutional order, and under the rule of law generally, the state never exists as a pliant argument waiting to be filled in.[66] Here torture – far from being a sort of *arcanum constitutionis*, as some would have us believe – is the final seal attesting to the existential crisis of a political community willing to forsake its own principles and hence its own welfare and survival.[67] The point has been well expressed by Michael Ignatieff: 'For torture, when committed by a state, expresses the state's ultimate view that human beings are expendable. This view is antithetical to the spirit of any constitutional society whose raison d'être is the control of violence and coercion in the name of human dignity and freedom.'[68]

V..

In this concluding section I will defend the thesis that a necessary, conceptual connection holds between torture and illegality. The thesis found an early defender with Christian Thomasius, in his daring essay on torture, 'Dissertatio de tortura ex foris Christianorum proscribenda':[69] Torture victims perceive themselves as victims of *abuse*, and are so perceived by others.

This much seems intuitive. But it is not just that: The immediate evidence and accompanying sense of revulsion can be explained by a discursive reason, too, which is that torture resists universality. Torture defeats any attempt at bringing it under a principle of universal material application: No one who accepts infliction of torture on others will accept it on oneself; this is not a standard that anyone would advocate and at the same time choose to *live by*. And it stands to reason that no one should do so, because torture is experienced by those on the receiving end of it as an act of extreme, *intolerable* violence, as an abuse and an excess – and it *must* be so experienced if it is to qualify as torture, as an *unbearable* torment, as a method for effectively obliterating another's will. Torture could never pass the test of universal acceptability that acts more or less as a final criterion of morality, for it is defined as an excess and an abuse even by those who use and apply it. Nor should it be other-

---

65   Compare Hauke Brunkhorst on the constitutional order set up under the Federal Republic of Germany: 'A state existing *prior* to the constitution, and capable of obliging its citizens to ensure its own survival should the constitutional order cease to exist, is unknown to the *Grundgesetz* (or basic law of the republic) and is foreign as well to the emergency laws established under its framework' (Brunkhorst, 'Folter vor Recht', p. 78 (my translation, italics in the original)).

66   Cf. C. Möllers, *Staat als Argument* (Munich, Beck, 2001).

67   Cf. H. Brunkhorst, 'Folter, Würde und repressiver Liberalismus', in *Rückkehr der Folter*, ed. by G. Beestermöller and H. Brunkhorst, 88ff.

68   M. Ignatieff, *The Lesser Evil: Political Ethics in an Age of Terror* (Princeton, Princeton University Press, 2004), p. 143.

69   For a modern edition of this essay, see C. Thomasius, *Über die Folter*, ed. by R. Liebewirth (Weimar, Hermann Böhlaus Nachfolger, 1960).

wise, since the act is *designed* that way: Its deliberate aim is precisely to be intolerable and excessive; in the words of one expert, Professor Dershowitz, it must consist in the infliction of 'unbearable pain,' and for this reason it is graduated to the occasion – it is made to depend on the varying degree to which the victim can bear pain (the idea being to *break* that limit).

But at the same time, this very characteristic of torture – its being perceived as an intolerable abuse even by those who resort to it – also offers an argument *against* the practice. Indeed, while torture may fail the test of universality as a *standard*, it does not fail in its ability to cross that line and be universal in its *consequences*. In other words, it is not only the torturee's dignity that is being assailed in and through torture, but also that of the torturer (however much in a different and less painful way), who likewise gets transformed into an instrument, an instrument of evil and horror. It is for this reason that torture must not be allowed, because it would transform the whole of society into a 'body torturous,' a body of torturers and torturees. Who among us would ever like to live next to a torturer? But by the same token, who among us would like to live *as* a torturer, with a finger pointed at us, not only by others but also by our own consciences? As Hannah Arendt has put it,[70] what self, what individuality – in the permanent dialogue we each by ourselves carry on with the other, with that interlocutor who at the same time is our own conscience – would bear the company of a torturer within? And that is, too, the main argument used by Michael Ignatieff: 'The problem with torture is not just that it gets out of control, not just that it becomes lawless. What is wrong with torture is that it inflicts irremediable harm on both the torturer and the prisoner. It violates basic commitments to human dignity.'[71]

'In principle,' Michael Davis points out, 'torture is limited only by the tortured's endurance,'[72] which makes this an unreliable and shaky method – a point with a long history on its side, going back at least to Roman jurisprudence. Thus, Ulpian described torture as fragile and dangerous, and by no means a guaranteed way to arrive at the truth: a 'res fragilis et periculosa et quae veritatem fallat.' In effect, torture is overdependent on the degree to which the pain being inflicted can be tolerated: 'Nam plerique patientia sive duritia tormentorum ita tormenta contemnunt; alii fit, ut etiam vario modo fateantur, ut non tantum se, verum etiam alios criminentur' (*De officio proconsulis*, 48, 18, 1, 23). The same point was made by Cesare Beccaria, who in his celebrated book *On Crimes and Punishments* (Chapter 16, 'On Torture')

---

70   Arendt, 'Personal Responsibility under Dictatorship', pp. 97ff.
71   Ignatieff, *The Lesser Evil*, p. 140.
72   M. Davis, 'The Moral Justifiability of Torture and other Cruel, Inhuman, or Degrading Treatment', *International Journal of Applied Philosophy* 19 (2005): 165.

observed how 'it is confounding all relations to expect that [...] pain should be the test of truth, as if truth resided in the muscles and fibres of a wretch in torture.[73]

Torture therefore *is* abuse and excess – necessarily so, by its own phenomenology. Which goes to show that, unless law is itself conceived as abuse and excess, we cannot at one and the same time be subject to the rule of law and be acting as torturers. As evidence for this proposition, consider how paradoxical it would be to conceptualize and set forth in the law an offence called 'abusive torture,' 'excessive use of torture,' or 'cruel and unusual torture.' It rings odd for a reason, which is that torture carries these attributes by definition: It is *inherently* excessive and abusive; it cannot conceivably make for a use of the public powers congruent with the rules of law, a congruence that Fuller lists as one of the requisites essential to the very concept of law.[74] This holds true quite apart from the obvious fact about torture, namely, that it consists in a punishment inflicted *before* ascertaining whether a crime has been committed, and indeed regardless of whether such a crime is even on the books.

This failure of correspondence had been noted in the early 18th century by Thomasius, who discussed the possibility of the judge overseeing and 'controlling' the torturer at work. Yet this activity frustrates any attempt at objective regulation, for it is governed through and through by a criterion of rational instrumentality. The 'object' of torture – invariably a human being – has to be treated precisely as such, as an object, that is, as a means to something else. Torture can thus be framed in such a way as to make it functional to its *own* end, but it can never be brought under any *different* standard, a normative standard conceived from without. Indeed, the efficacy of torture turns precisely on its ability to drive its own action to excess. As Pietro Verri would write later on in the century, in his *Osservazioni sulla tortura*, in which he took up the work of the Italian jurist and magistrate Giulio Gallo, 'there being no certain norms that can be established in regard to the evidence justifying the use torture, the entire matter is remitted to the judge's discretion.'[75]

Discretion, understood as freedom to judge on one's own, is thus connatural with torture, and woven into its deep fabric. This made plain sense to Alessandro Manzoni, too, who noted certain inconsistencies in Verri's discussion, to be sure, but then observed that the point in question – about discretion falling into the judge's hands when no clear rule is available – had been a long-running theme among jurists. In fact, 'Bartolus himself introduced it as a matter of established opinion: *Doc-*

---

73   In the original: 'Ma io aggiungo di più, ch'egli è un voler confondere tutti i rapporti, l'esigere [...] che il dolore divenga il crociuolo della verità, quasi che il criterio di essa risieda nei muscoli e nelle fibre di un miserabile' (C. Beccaria, *Dei delitti e delle pene*, ed. by G. D. Pisapia (Milan, Giuffrè, 1973), p. 40).

74   See L. L. Fuller, *The Morality of Law* (New Haven, Yale University Press, 1969 (rev ed.)), pp. 81ff.

75   In the original: 'in materia di tortura e di indizj, non potendosi prescrivere una norma certa, tutto si rimette all'arbitrio del giudice' (P. Verri, *Osservazioni sulla tortura* (Milan, Feltrinelli),p. 83).

tores communiter dicunt quod in hoc non potest dari certa doctrina, sed relinquitur arbitrio judicis [Jurists commonly say that in the matter at hand (whether any evidence is deemed sufficient grounds for torture) there can be no certain doctrine, and that discretion is therefore relinquished to the judge]. And with this they were not meaning to offer any sort of principle, but were rather stating a plain fact, namely, that the law, having no criteria for determining when evidence is grounds for torture, leaves it to the judge to make this determination at discretion.'[76]

The effort in jurisprudence is nonetheless to *contain* the judge's discretion, using to this end various arguments and artifices – yet, as Manzoni concludes, these amount to nothing more than 'ineffectual patches for something that fundamentally could not be cast in any good shape.'[77]

No deontological criteria are at hand that could possibly help us work out in advance the measure or the means of violence to be used in torture. As Klaus Günther has underscored,[78] this indeterminacy begins with the very choice of instruments for the infliction of pain. And then the pain must always be carried to a level *beyond* the threshold of bearability: 'Until the tortured dies,' Michael Davis observes, 'the point at which the torture should stop is a matter of the torturer's judgment (or that of a superior).'[79] We could attempt to set out, as Brügger does,[80] types of cases in which government bodies might be allowed to use torture. But still, in doing so we could not, and should not, make provision for the degree of violence to be used, a measure that we would not be able to control. And as Thomasius observes, the executioner, the torturer, can always use his terrible instruments in such a way as to fool the onlooker, the judge acting as controller: 'Carnifex hic iudici in applicandis instrumentis fucum facere potest.'[81]

If these findings are all accurate, and everything suggests that they are, the rule of law – a rule by which to preestablish the boundaries of admissible behaviour in this or that circumstance, thus precluding abuse and excess in the behaviour so regulated – presents itself as phenomenologically incompatible with the way torturous action is structured. This crucial point is given a compelling statement by Klaus Günther,

---

76   In the original: 'Bartolo la ripeteva anche lui come sentenza comune: *Doctores communiter dicunt quod in hoc* (quali che siano gl'indizi sufficienti alla tortura) *non potest dari certa doctrina, sed relinquitur arbitrio judicis*. E con questo non intendevan già di proporre un principio, di stabilire una teoria, ma d'enunciar semplicemente un fatto; cioè che la legge, non avendo determinato gl'indizi, gli aveva per ciò stesso lasciati all'arbitrio del giudice' (Manzoni, *Storia della colonna infame*, pp. 56–57).

77   Ibid. p. 62.

78   See K. Günther, 'Darf der Staat foltern, um Menschenleben zu retten?' in *Rückkehr der Folter: Der Rechtsstaat im Zwielicht?* ed. by G. Beestermöller and H. Brunkhorst (Munich, Beck, 2006), 107.

79   Davis, 'The Moral Justifiability of Torture', p. 165.

80   Brügger, 'Das andere Auge', p. 115.

81   Thomasius, *Über die Folter*, title. 2, sec. 5.

among others, who argues that there is no such thing as 'clean' torture: This is an activity that cannot be made consistent with any scheme of law, on account of the increasing aggressiveness and violence this activity is inherently designed to exert.[82] In particular, there is no way to conceptualize a 'proportionate' and 'predictable' form of torture, which must invariably manifest itself as disproportionate and unpredictable: 'Assuming that torture is at all effective, it can be such only insofar and as long as the person under torture cannot anticipate how much it can still be escalated or be made to last.'[83]

Our conclusion, then, can only come down to this: There is no room for torture under the rule of law. In fact, torture would come as a setback in the process of civilization set in motion during the Enlightenment period and the modern age, a process aspiring to carry on in ways that will bring down the rate of violence in social relations and in the law itself. The cruelty of torture makes this an activity squarely antithetical to the *mildness* distinctive to the law as a principle and technique by which to tame and pacify social and interhuman relations. But more significantly perhaps, there is a structural reason why torture has no place under the rule of law. This form of rule acts as a criterion whereby any action, and all the more so the violent action of a government body, must be framed in ways that make it predictable and proportional. And there is no way that a criterion so conceived can accommodate torture, structurally designed as it is to repel any hint of predictability, proportionateness, or restraint.

And there is yet a third reason for the permanent illegality of torture, a reason showing this activity to be illegal in an even more fundamental way. A legal system is based on the assumption of its members being free and equal subjects under the law, and along with this subjectivity comes a dignity recognized for each such member as a person endowed with a free will, or a capacity for autonomous action. Now, torture is so conceived as to deny and violate this dignity and capacity in the most flagrant way possible. As Günther explains, torture must act on the tortured in such a way that their will be broken ('Sein Wille soll gebrochen werden').[84] And as another German scholar has emphasized, 'torture is incompatible with the rule of law precisely because the activity attacks individuals in their capacity to be subjects under the law – in fact the activity inclines toward crossing a *further* limit, beyond which one is broken and destroyed as an autonomous person.'[85] In this respect, torture stands on an equal plane with enslavement, for in either case a subject is transformed by law into *chattel*, into something to be disposed of at will, ad libitum. Tor-

---

82 Günther, 'Darf der Staat foltern', p. 107. Cf. also K. Günther, 'Folter kennt keine Grenze', *Die Zeit*, 13 March 2008.
83 Günther, 'Darf der Staat foltern', p. 107 (my translation).
84 Ibid. p. 106.
85 J. Ph. Reemtsma, *Folter im Rechtstaat?* (Hamburg, Hamburger Edition, 2005), 125 (my translation, italics added).

ture thus means despotism, slavery, *tyranny*. As Thomasius cautions us, 'quaestio omnibus tyrannis praebet occasione, sub specie iustitiae in subditos saeviendi.'[86]

VI.

I should like now to close my statement against torture with this addendum: 'Juristen, böse Christen!' (Jurists, bad Christians!). It was Martin Luther who gave forth with these words,[87] for it seemed to him that positive law – the justice of men – is inevitably tied up with violence, blood, coercion, even torture: 'Recht ist Gewalt' (Law is violence).[88] To a Christian, law paradigmatically presents itself in the shape of the cross, a tool of affliction and torture, and also a symbol of treatment that is degrading in the extreme and suppressive of dignity: It meant to slaves, but not to freemen, deep torment and punishment by death. Furthermore, the jurists had taken it upon themselves to judge their own kind, thus claiming a power that can rightfully be exercised only by God: 'Judge not, that ye be not judged,' 'He that is without sin among you, let him first cast a stone at her,' Jesus said. The jurists have paid no heed to these words, for they have taken the supreme moment of judgment into their own hands, wasting no time to cast the first stone.

There is also third reason why Luther denounced jurists as bad Christians. This can be described as a conceptual (or 'logical') reason, which is that the law they handle perpetrates its own injustice; it does so by its inability to overcome the *form* of justice, this being the form of *law*: 'Jeder Richter ist ein Feind Christi, weil er die Gerechtigkeit der Werke treibt.'[89] Stated otherwise, a form of justice that cannot be bent toward kindness and charity will convert into patent injustice. Jurists are in this sense bad Christians, an immoral lot, because they confine themselves to judging conduct by the classificatory and systematizing criterion of the formal rule.

Nor were these learned experts of the law much inclined toward the golden rule of reciprocity, 'Do not do to others what you would not have them do to you': This principle the jurists were unwilling to make into a universal law of torture, to take one example. In fact, the *jus commune* they all shared would not allow the hangman to ply on them the terrible trade he plies on others; the Medieval jurists, in other words, took care to exempt themselves from torture, an exemption that also took in (besides doctors of laws) judges, lawyers, physicians, and the nobility and clergy –

---

86 Thomasius, *Über die Folter*, title 2, sec. 4.
87 M. Luther, *Tischreden*, ed. K. Aland, Reclam (Stuttgart, 1981), 205.
88 Ibid. p. 207.
89 Ibid. p. 205.

all were granted immunity from 'the question' (though, in fairness, immunity was also extended to pregnant women and children).[90]

Now, the jurists who are urging today a return to torture – however much within its restricted use as a 'life-saving' device, or *Rettungsfolter* – must equally reckon themselves as bad Christians by Luther's standards, in the first place because they no longer have any notion of the sufferings endured carrying the cross, but even more so because there is a definite callousness about them, predisposing them to show what appears to be no compassion at all for the soul of a battered body. As we have learned, John Yoo's hand will not shake even at the sight of a tortured child,[91] though it should be mentioned here to Yoo's credit that he seems to endorse, appropriately enough, a universal extension of the criteria he adopts with respect to torture: This much can be gleaned from his comment that it would be legitimate for Al Qaeda militants to torture Donald Rumsfeld should they capture him.[92]

But Yoo, Bybee, Dershowitz, and Brügger, and many others following their lead, also show themselves to be 'bad jurists.' They do so in the first place by failing to honour certain basic duties under their code of professional ethics, such as the duty not to cater to the whims and wishes of those who pay them, even if it is the sovereign pro tempore they are working for. Yoo and Bybee should not make it their calling to devise ways by which to answer any request whatsoever their client may possibly express, regardless of how all-powerful this person may be.[93] More importantly, however, what makes them 'bad jurists' is their denying the law its quality as *form* – their willingness to bypass the rule of law, the sworn enemy of abuse and cruelty. Like the High Priest, they rehearse the motto of expediency whereby one man should die lest an entire people should perish (cf. John 18:14). Legality as we understand it brooks no abuse, but they say this kind of law can be broken when special circumstances arise that justify doing so. And one might think that these circumstances, justifying our rising above the law, should be used to exercise mercy – but no, they are used instead to indulge in lawless cruelty and excess.

And yet, as Blackstone observed in his *Commentaries on the Laws of England*, it is mercy that we can see being invoked as a justification for torture: 'It seems astonishing that this usage, of administering the torture, should be said to arise from a

---

90   See P. Fiorelli, *La tortura giudiziaria nel diritto comune*, vol. 1 (Milan, Giuffrè, 1953), pp. 276ff., and J. H. Langbein, *Torture and the Law of Proof: Europe and England in the Ancien Régime* (2nd ed., Chicago, University of Chicago Press, 2006), p. 13.

91   The allusion here is to the PBS interview with John Yoo: see note 26 above. Compare the hypothetical case used by M. Strauss to criticize the ticking-bomb scenario, in 'Torture', *New York Law School Law Review* 48 (2004): 275–276.

92   See Yoo, *War by Other Means,* p. 166. The comment was set down the context of Rumsfeld's former position as U.S. defense secretary and gets its full meaning within that context, but the point comes across clearly regardless.

93   On this point, and on the charge levelled at Yoo and Bybee for breaking the deontological code of lawyers and jurists, see the lucid considerations offered in R. B. Bilder and D. V.. Vagts, 'Speaking Law to Power: Lawyers and Torture', in *The Torture Debate in America*, ed. by K. J. Greenberg (Cambridge, Cambridge University Press, 2006), 151ff.

tenderness to the lives of men: and yet this is the reason given for its introduction in the civil law, and its subsequent adoption by the French and other foreign nation' (*Commentaries*, bk. 4, chap. 25). To be sure, mercy and torture do share a trait in this bizarre comparison, for they both break the formal constraints of justice – both debouch into the concrete – but they do so in dramatically different ways: Only torture does it *contra legem*, effecting abuse and assault in the process. So we have mercy, the highest *justice* in the concrete case, against torture, the highest *injustice* in the concrete case: Both break the rule of law, but one engages in cruelty, and outrageously claims a spurious equivalence with the other under the pretext of a parallelism it craftily uses as a shield by which to conceal what is actually a deep antithesis.

2. Justifying Defensive Torture

Uwe Steinhoff

In this paper I will argue that there is something like self-defensive torture (which can include the defence of others), and that such torture is morally justified if certain general requirements for the justifiability of self-defensive violence/force are met. These requirements come under the headings of imminence, necessity and proportionality. In the first part of the paper I will briefly discuss the English, US and in particular German legal regulations regarding self-defence. I will argue that the same moral reasoning that underlies these laws is also applicable to torture cases, and that the necessity and the imminence requirements can be met in some torture cases. In the second part of the paper I will turn to the proportionality requirement and in that context discuss arguments that attempt to show that torture is worse than killing. I will argue that these arguments cannot hold water. Many forms of torture are definitely not worse than killing. In fact, I will show that there are cases where self-defensive torture is the morally preferable and more humane alternative to self-defensive killing. I conclude that if self-defensive killing is justified in some cases – and it is – then self-defensive torture is also justified in some cases. Finally, I will deal with the charge that justifying torture in some perhaps legitimate cases nevertheless somehow contributes to the spread of the illegitimate use of torture, and that therefore publishing justificatory articles like the present one is itself immoral. I will argue that such rather cheap charges have no rational basis whatsoever.

A. What is torture?

For the purposes of this article I shall define torture as follows:

> *Torture is the intentional (as opposed to merely foreseen or accepted) and continuous or repeated infliction of extreme physical suffering on a non-consenting victim.*

Some claim that torture has to involve the intent to break the will of the victim.[1] This might be true for interrogative torture, where the torturer seeks to get some in-

---

1   S. Miller, 'Is Torture Ever Morally Justified?' *International Journal of Applied Philosophy* 19 (2005): 179, p. 191, n. 2. Miller accepts, though, 'that, notionally at least, there might be some cases in which extreme physical suffering is inflicted but in which the torturer does not have as a purpose the breaking of the victim's will. However, I do not regard these as the central cases when it comes to torturing human beings, as opposed to other sentient beings that lack a will in anything other than an attenuated sense.' As I say in the main text, punitive torture was widespread in the Middle Ages and is still practiced today. There is no reason to ex-

39

formation out of the tortured person. I say 'might' because it is not entirely clear what 'breaking the will' actually means, nor is it clear that the interrogative torturer must intend more than that the victim give the desired information. If the victim decides with an intact will: 'I do not want to be tortured anyany more, therefore I will give the information', this, it seems, should be fine with the torturer. Be that as it may, interrogative torture is not the only kind of torture; there is also punitive torture, which was widely practiced in the Middle Ages (and is, incidentally, still practiced today). Punitive torture, however, does not normally involve the intention to break the will of the victim. Whether his or her will is broken is completely incidental to the aims of this form of torture. The aim is simply to punish the victim by inflicting extreme physical suffering.

Some also claim that the victim has to be defenceless.[2] I agree that in most cases (perhaps even in all real cases) he or she will be defenceless, but this in itself is no reason to make this a definitional requirement. Consider this case: theThe robber breaks into the house of the jeweller, who has a safe with a lot of money in his house. The robber points a gun at the jeweller and says: 'Give me the combination, or I'll kill you.' The jeweller says: 'Well, if you kill me you won't get the combination.' 'Right', thinks the robber and draws something else, namely his pain-inflicting device, which when activated causes extreme pain (almost like drilling on the unprotected nerve of a tooth) to any person in the radius of ten metres, excepting the person holding the device. He activates it. The jeweller writhes with pain on the ground, the robber says: 'Give me the combination', but the jeweller manages to reach for her own revolver. For all the pain she cannot take real aim and can hardly hold the gun; yet she manages to shoot in the general direction of the robber, who dives behind a couch. 'Let go of the gun!' the robber shouts, but the jeweller, still in extreme pain since the device is still activated, shoots in the direction of the couch, which offers no real protection, and the bullets go right through. The jeweller is obviously not defenceless. However, it seems that she was tortured nevertheless. Someone was intentionally inflicting pain on her nearly as intense as the pain inflicted by drilling the unprotected nerve of a tooth, and doing so in order to get some information or in order to have the person do something (let go of the gun) – how could this not be torture? The mere fact that the victim still has means of defence seems not to satisfactorily answer this question.

At this point someone might object that this is a silly constructed example, nothing that could happen in the real world. Well, first, of course it could. Second, one might well see a taser as an equivalent of such a pain-infliction device. Thus there may already have been equivalent cases. Third, even if there has never been a real such case and never will be, that is not a counterargument against the definitional point. There is not, nor will there ever be, a tyrannosaurus rex walking through the

clude it from a definition of torture, which as a definition, after all, should include the 'notional' cases – the more so if those cases are also very real.

2   Ibid., p. 179; M. Davis, 'The Moral Justification of Torture and other Cruel, Inhuman, or Degrading Treatment,' *International Journal of Applied Philosophy* 19 (2005): 161, p. 164.

Black Forest in the years 2008-10. However, that does not mean that by definition a tyrannosaurus rex cannot do so. Whether one of them does is an empirical question, not a definitional one. A definition that simply stipulated that they cannot walk through the Black Forest in these years would be a *wrong* definition even if the tyrannosaurus rex actually is extinct once and for all. Thus, if we would say about the case of the jeweller that it is (or would be) a case of torture, the alleged fact that such cases are not real is no counterargument to the claim that it indeed is (or would be) a case of torture.

The international conventions concerning torture seem to consider torture, for the purposes of those conventions, as something that can only be done by state agents. However, the legal usage of certain terms does not always coincide with the ordinary one. In any ordinary use of the term, torture can be practiced by private agents (for example the Mafia or a sadist).

A note on the expression 'continuous or repeated': this is only meant to exclude isolated and single 'shocks' of intense pain. I find it hard to consider such 'shocks' as torture (which is not the same as saying that they are quite all right).

Finally, what is 'extreme'? That is contentious, but one kind of physical suffering that clearly is extreme is the above-mentioned pain produced by drilling on an unprotected nerve of a tooth. I will use this as a reference point throughout the paper. This in no way implies that I think that lesser pains or certain other forms of pain and suffering are not also extreme.

B. What is self-defence?

People have a right to defend themselves or others against wrongful aggression, in particular if the aggression is life-threatening. Let us take a look at how German law (which I know best) treats self-defence. In the course of doing so I will also make some comparisons with British law and US statutes before coming to a moral assessment.

§ 32 of the German Penal Code states (my translation):

(1) Whosoever commits an act that is required (*geboten*) in self-defence does not act against the law.

(2) Self-defence is the defence necessary to avert a present (*gegenwärtig*) unlawful attack on oneself or others.

A few comments are in order. First, while the *necessity* requirement is supposed to *prevent excessive violence* (i.e. violence that clearly goes beyond the amount of violence of equally promising alternative means that have not yet been tried), it is not intended to *guarantee minimal force*. In other words, its actual judicial interpretation prefers to err on the safe side – that is, it favours the defender, not the attacker. While the general idea is that the defender should select *among the equally effective means* the one that harms the attacker the least, German courts have made it abundantly clear that the defender is not obliged to use less dangerous means of defence if the effectiveness of those means is doubtful. In addition, a person defending with milder means may escalate his or her defence if these milder means have proven unsuccessful. And, of course, if no effective means are available, the defender is allowed to take his or her chances. A rape victim is not required to abstain from slapping the rapist merely because it is highly unlikely that this will have any effect. And although air rifles will hardly stop an aggressor (although it might slightly hurt him), I am completely within my rights to use them. Indeed, police would not prosecute a person according to the following logic: 'Well, Herr Fritze, blasting the aggressor away with your shotgun was of course an effective means of self-defence, but you should not have first used the air rifle. There was practically no probability of success. So you are off the hook for the shotgun, but we are afraid that for using the air rifle we have to prosecute you for battery.'

It is also important for the interpretation of the 'necessity' requirement that German law does not require one to retreat from the aggressor if one could safely do so. A basic German principle of law is *Das Recht muß dem Unrecht nicht weichen* (roughly: *law/justice does not have to give way to the unlawful/unjust*).[3] This principle does not exist in US law. However, it seems that there is no duty in US law to retreat from an aggressor threatening deadly force before defending with deadly force. As regards the UK, common law once contained a duty to retreat. This, however, is not the case any more.[4]

Thus, the 'necessity' requirement is in fact very lenient, in the USA and the UK as well. And rightly so. Although the self-defence paragraph gives *some* protection (namely against *excessive* violence) to the aggressor, its main task is to protect the defender. There is no moral symmetry between innocent defenders and culpable aggressors.

German law takes this asymmetry very far (which is a direct consequence of the principle that law/justice does not have to give way to the unlawful/unjust). *There is no proportionality requirement in the German self-defence law. The NECESSITY requirement is NOT the same as a PROPORTIONALITY requirement!* I put this statement in italics and use capitalization because necessity and proportionality are regularly confused by many people. This confusion is facilitated by the fact that we can say in *some* sense that the necessity requirement *is* a proportionality requirement. However, it is important to be clear in which sense it is and in which it is not. The 'necessity' requirement prohibits excessive violence or force when using defensive measures against unlawful actions. It does *not*, however, weigh the value of the defended good against the harm inflicted upon the aggressor. In other words, it says that you are not supposed to kill a thief if you can also stop him by knocking him out. It does not, however, say that you shouldn't use lethal force at all in defending

3   Kindhäuser provides a succinct overview of German self-defence law. U. Kindhäuser, 'Skript zur Vorlesung Strafrecht AT, § 16: Notwehr', <http://www.jura.uni-bonn.de/fileadmin/Fachbereich_Rechtswissenschaft/Einrichtungen/Lehrstuehle/Strafrecht3/Strafrecht_AT/s-at-16.pdf> (visited 25 March 2008).

4   E. Baskind, 'The Law Relating to Self Defence', <http://www.bsdgb.co.uk/index.php?Information:The_Law_Relating_to_Self_Defence> (visited 25 March 2008).

yourself against theft. It does *not* argue that human life is more valuable than property, and that therefore defending property with lethal force is disproportionate. This latter argument would be a proportionality argument, which exists, for example, in English law. In Great Britain you are not allowed to use deadly force if this is the only way you can keep a thief from stealing your car. In Germany, you *are* allowed to do so. Some *extreme* disproportionalities are now forbidden under German law (you are not supposed to shoot a thief in order to prevent him from escaping with an apple), but the fact remains that a principle that rules out *extreme dis*proportionalities is not yet one that demands proportionality.[5]

An attack is *present* according to German law if it is imminent, has started or is ongoing.

An *attack*, in German law, is every threat of a violation or actual violation of an interest that is protected by law insofar as this threat stems from human action. Thus, the German law makes use of the term 'attack' here in a way that does not necessarily follow ordinary usage, which associates 'attack' with fists and knives and guns – with 'action'. If someone has been kidnapped and is now alone in a room, we might, therefore, want to say that he is not *currently* under attack any more, but only was so when the gangster grabbed him and threw him into the car. For German law, however, the kidnapped person, stripped of his freedom, is still under attack.

In light of this brief exposition of German self-defence law, let us look at what I call a Dirty Harry Case (there are real-life examples of Dirty Harry cases, the most recent one being the famous German Daschner case):[6] A criminal kidnaps a child and puts her in a place where she will suffocate if not rescued in time. There is not much time left, according to the very claims of the kidnapper, who has been captured by the police. They ask him again and again where the child is. He refuses to tell. The police decide to torture the kidnapper in order to get the information they need to save the child. (In the Daschner case the kidnapper was only *threatened* with torture. Facing this threat, he gave up the location of the child. Tragically, the child was already dead.)

This case falls under the German self-defence law. The kidnapped child is still under 'attack', in the sense in which German law uses this expression. And the necessity requirement – whether in the German, British or American interpretation – in itself does not rule out the use of torture. The police had already tried normal interrogation, without success. In other words, the milder means did not work. So they were entitled to use harsher means.

At this point the usual objection will probably be heard, repeated like a mantra by many torture opponents: 'Torture does not work to gain information.' Actually, it sometimes does. In the real life Daschner case the threat of torture sufficed to make the kidnapper spill the required information. The child was already dead, but that

---

5   To be sure, from a moral standpoint it is actually not evident that defending an innocent person's property against a culpable aggressor by using deadly force if necessary really *is* disproportionate. But this is not a question we have to go into here.

6   See Introduction, pp. 1-2 above (eds.).

was not some kind of metaphysical necessity. If he had still been alive, he would have been saved thanks to the use of torture. Incidentally another case surfaced in the judicial proceedings of the Daschner case: In 1988 police had beaten up a kidnapper, who then gave up the information as to where he had hidden the child. The police were able to rescue the child alive from a wooden box.[7] I suppose that there are many more cases like these, but for obvious reasons police officers have an interest in denying that they used torture.

Moreover, even if torture were highly unreliable, this does not even matter. As already explained above, the so-called 'necessity' requirement, which actually is a No Excessive Force Requirement, allows you to use even 'improbable' means to defend yourself if your (or another innocent person's) life is threatened by a culpable aggressor. And that is exactly how it should be. Even if it were an empirically well-proven and commonly well-known fact that stopping a serial murderer and rapist by ramming a sharp pencil deep into his ear only works one out of 10,000 times, a victim of a rapist would still be well within her rights to ram a sharp pencil deep into the rapist's ear if that is the only option remaining that at least could have success.

But, so it is often said by torture opponents, couldn't the police have talked to the kidnapper longer? Maybe then he would have finally given up the information. Yes, maybe, but as already stated, if milder means – like talking – do not work in a self-defence situation, the defender is allowed to try harsher means. Besides, there are in fact cases where a rapist has been verbally persuaded by his victim to stop. However, hardly anyone would say to a rape victim: 'Why did you ram the pencil into his ear after only 30 minutes of rape? Why didn't you endure some more rape, maybe half an hour more? Maybe your begging would finally have worked.' Similarly, it should not be forgotten that the situation faced by the police is not one where the child is happily playing in a garden and would then, if the kidnapper does not give the required information, suddenly and peacefully die. While the kidnapper is not being tortured by the police, the child *is* being tortured, namely by the kidnapper. It is suffocating in a box the kidnapper put it in.

Thus, in Dirty Harry cases torture is not excluded by the 'necessity' requirement, that is, the requirement that among equally promising methods of defence that have not yet been tried in that particular case the one that inflicts the smallest harm upon the aggressor has to be used. (Whoever wants to object at this point that torture is somehow 'intrinsically excessive' only confuses necessity and proportionality again. I will come to proportionality shortly.)

From the perspective of German law the child is clearly in a situation that could justify self-defence. Is this also the case from the perspective of British and American law? The self-defence laws in these jurisdictions allow self-defence against the unlawful use of force only if the *imminence requirement* is fulfilled, that is, if the unlawful use of force is ongoing or imminent. Clearly, this requirement is fulfilled in the Dirty Harry case (as it is in ticking bomb cases, incidentally). *The child is al-*

7   V.. Erb, 'Folterverbot und Notwehrrecht', in W. Lenzen (ed.), *Ist Folter erlaubt? Juristische und philosophische Aspekte* (Paderborn, Mentis, 2006), p. 19.

ready victim of unlawful force, and not only at the moment when it dies. It is also already victim of *deadly* force. Deadly force is not only force that has already killed you, but force that is typically capable of doing so. Someone who has been poisoned with something that will kill her in a month has suffered deadly force already at the moment she was poisoned, and not first at the end of the month. Thus, under British law and US statutes as well, the Dirty Harry case is one where the child is in a situation that can justify self-defence.

However, for the sake of argument, let us take a look anyway at whether it does morally make a difference – as it is sometimes claimed – that in ticking bomb cases or Dirty Harry cases *death* is not always imminent (the deadly *force* is, of course). Some think it does. The underlying idea seems to be that if the expected harm (here in the form of death) is not imminent, there remains enough time to try all kinds of milder means to avert the danger. However, that is simply not always true. The fact that the ultimate harm might befall me much later, does not mean that I have much time to react. The incubation time of rabies can be up to 10 years, but after having been bitten one only has a couple of hours to get a vaccination. After that everything is too late. Now consider this situation. Jeanette is in a jungle camp with Bob. A black mamba bites her. The poison will kill her in few minutes if she does not immediately get the antidote from the refrigerator. Bob wants Jeanette dead and blocks the refrigerator. She draws her gun and threatens to shoot him if he does not go out of the way. He does not, and so she shoots him in the leg. If for some reason it were necessary to kill him in order to get him out of the way, she would even be allowed to do that. It is a clear case of self-defence. Now imagine that she has not been bitten by a black mamba but by a dog with superrabies. It will kill her in five years, but she needs the antidote as quickly as she needed the one against the mamba poison. Again Bob blocks the way to the refrigerator. Is she now not allowed to shoot him in the leg or to kill him if necessary to reach the antidote? Of course she is. The difference in the time frame of the ultimate *harm* is normatively irrelevant. What is decisive is the time frame wherein *defensive action* to avert the danger is still possible. This is, incidentally, reflected by a large part of US case law, by the Model Penal Code and by the statutes of some US states.[8]

Thus it seems that torturing an aggressor in order to save an innocent life from the aggressor's claws can be justified with the law of self-defence. To be sure, one might object that torture is still prohibited by international anti-torture conventions, which are also binding for the national jurisdictions of the UK, the USA and Germany. However, it seems that the anti-torture conventions define torture as something undertaken by *state* agents. Thus, they might not be applicable to private defensive torture (for example, a Dirty Harry case where not a police officer but the father of the kidnapped child tortures the kidnapper). Second, for the German case, Volker Erb argues that a law or an international convention that protects the kidnapper from being tortured even where torture would be the last available means to save

---

8   See V. F. Nourse, 'Self-Defense and Subjectivity', *University of Chicago Law Review* 68 (2001): 1235-1308.

the innocent child violates the human dignity of the child.[9] The highest article of the German constitution, however, states that human dignity must not be violated. International conventions that violate that article would therefore be null and void under the German constitution.

Be that as it may, here I can set aside the question as to whether torture is *actually* legal in the three jurisdictions. I am dealing with the *moral* question. Why am I then discussing self-defence *laws* in the first place? Because the self-defence law and its application in case law reflects intuitions many people have about self-defence. It also reflects the moral reasoning behind it. My moral argument is that if injuring or killing a person can be morally justified in self-defence as long as the defence abides by the so-called necessity, imminence and proportionality or no-gross-disproportionality requirements, the same is true for torture. To be sure, a legislator or an international convention could simply stipulate: 'Never mind the self-defence law. We just want to rule out torture, even if it occurs in self-defence.' (Or: 'Never mind the self-defence law. We just want to rule out stabbing, even if it occurs in self-defence.') However, such a stipulation would not follow the previous legal reasoning nor in particular the moral reasoning supporting the self-defence laws. It would be something externally imposed on the self-defence law and the moral reasoning behind it, something *contradicting* it. And since self-defence law is extremely plausible and the moral reasoning behind it very convincing, the contradiction would not show that self-defence law and the moral reasoning behind it are mistaken if they allow torture. Rather, it would show that the absolute prohibition of torture is wrong.

The only way out for the absolutist opponent of torture or the opponent of self-defensive torture would be to show that there is a normatively relevant difference between killing a person in self-defence and torturing him in self-defence that rules out the permissibility of the latter act. As I have already argued, appeals to the necessity and to the imminence requirements do not work. Yet, apart from the proportionality requirement (or the no-extreme disproportionality requirement, respectively), *there are no other requirements*.

This fact is often ignored. For example, sometimes it is considered to be a good argument against torture that you can never know *for certain* that the person tortured in the Dirty Harry case (or a ticking bomb case) really is guilty. However, there is no certainty requirement in self-defence cases. In fact, in German law there is not even the requirement that the defender reasonably believes him- or herself to be under attack. If the defender *is* under attack, then necessary and not grossly disproportionate counter-measures are justified, whether the belief of the defender to be under attack is itself reasonable or not. As regards American and British self-defence law, there is certainly no requirement that there be no reasonable doubt for the defender that he or she is under attack. Thus, the fact is that there are many cases of legally and morally

<hr>

9   Erb, 'Folterverbot', pp. 28-33. In an earlier article, I mistakenly took the legal prohibition of torture for granted. U. Steinhoff, 'Torture – The Case for Dirty Harry and against Alan Dershowitz', *Journal of Applied Philosophy* 23 (2007): 337-353, p. 346.

justified killings in self-defence where the certainty that an actual attack was imminent was much lower than the certainty the policemen in the Daschner case had that they were dealing with a child kidnapper. The circumstance that the no-certainty argument gets repeated and repeated and repeated does not make it any better. If self-defensive killing without certainty is justified, self-defensive torture without certainty is justified, too.

Another rather bad argument I came upon is this: A Kantian maxim allowing torture in certain cases would be too complicated. I offer two replies. 1. complicated $\neq$ wrong. 2. A Kantian maxim allowing self-defensive torture is not more complicated then a Kantian maxim allowing self-defensive killing. As far as I know, Kant did allow self-defensive killing and injuring. So where is the problem?

A further strange argument one sometimes encounters is that torture is 'inherently limitless'. What is that supposed to mean? Carl von Clausewitz said that war is inherently limitless, that the logic of war is escalation. However, he admitted that in reality war can be restrained and often has been restrained successfully. The same holds true for torture (whether justified or not). In the Middle Ages punitive torture was often used in a restricted way – that is, the amount of torture previously prescribed as punishment was administered, not limitless amounts of torture. Interrogative torture also has been limited in many cases by certain regulations (for example in Israel). But must interrogative torturers, if they want to be successful, not be ready to use any means – so that as long as the tortured person does not give up the information, they will use harsher and harsher means? Well, *if* the painful interrogator is ready to use any means, she will use any available means unless somebody stops her. So she might become a very painful interrogator. But the same logic applies to *any* course of action which aims by any means at making another person do something. Thus, it not only applies to painful interrogation, but to *any* interrogation. *Any* interrogator who is ready to use any means will transform into a painful interrogator, if need be, and a very painful interrogator, if need be, etc. Thus, the argument 'proves' more than it can take. Besides, there actually *is* an inherent limit to interrogative torture: Killing the painfully interrogated person is not an available means to get the information. Dead people do not speak. Thus, killing is not a possible means for interrogative torture. Other forms of self-defence, however, do not acknowledge this limit. Killing *is* a means by which one can keep an aggressor from attacking with a knife. Thus, it seems that self-defensive interrogation is actually more limited than self-defensive non-interrogative beating, stabbing or shooting. Besides, why should the fact that a certain course of action *could* escalate into something excessive make the course of action wrong even if it does not so escalate? After all, *any* self-defensive course of action, for example in the form of hitting an opponent or stabbing him, *could* escalate – that, however, obviously does not make all self-defensive action wrong. In short, the argument that torture is 'inherently limitless' and therefore unjustified is confused.

Thus, the fact remains that the last hope for someone who does not deny the permissibility of self-defensive killing or harming but nevertheless wants to show that defensive torture in Dirty Harry cases is impermissible can only lie in the proportionality requirement or the no-extreme-disproportionality requirement. Here, however, the proponent of defensive torture has a certain advantage. For the torture opponent it would not be sufficient to show that torturing is somehow worse than killing in order to rule out its permissibility. That one means of defence is harsher than another means of defence does not yet in itself show that the harsher means is unjustified. After all, killing someone in self-defence is harsher than merely knocking him out; still, self-defensive killing is justified in certain circumstances. Thus, even if torture were harsher than killing, torture could still be justified in certain circumstances. On the other hand, if the proponent of torture in certain cases can show that *killing* is worse than many forms of torture, than the fact that killing is sometimes morally justified demonstrates that torture can sometimes be morally justified too. With this in mind, let us turn to the question as to how bad torture really is in comparison to killing.

C. Proportionality or: Many forms of torture aren't as bad as killing

Now, why should torture always be wrong? Of course, on the face of it,

(a) the intentional and continuous or repeated infliction of extreme physical suffering on a non-consenting victim

sounds like a pretty gruesome practice. But how gruesome? After all,

(b) the intentional blowing out of someone's brain with a .44 Colt,

or

(c) the intentional chopping off of someone's head

also sound like pretty gruesome practices. In fact, practices (b) and (c) sound *much more gruesome* than practice (a). Yet, according to the principle of self-defence, most accounts of just war theory, and the overwhelming majority opinion of people around the world, these practices are permissible in some circumstances (for example in circumstances where they are the only promising defence of an innocent person against a culpable and life-threatening aggressor). Why, then, should torture not also be permissible in some circumstances (for example where it is the only promising means to save an innocent person from a culpable aggressor)? If *you* could choose to be the victim of practice (a), (b) or (c) – which would you choose? It depends, of course. There are *some* forms of practice (a) that might be worse than any form of practices (b) and (c), but, for example, being subjected to a pain nearly as excruciating as that of an unprotected nerve maltreated by a drill for 15 minutes is not one of them. If this were the choice, most people would, no doubt, prefer being a victim of this form of practice (a) to being a victim of any form of the other two practices. The fact of the matter is that most people prefer extreme physical suffering to death. Death is *worse* than (most forms of) extreme physical suffering.

Once this is granted (and there is no *rational* way around granting it) the person who thinks that torture is never permissible is in a tight spot. So is the person who thinks that torture can only be allowed in certain extreme threshold cases, for example in ticking bomb cases where the live of hundreds, thousands or even millions of innocents are at stake. After all, killing is permissible in a good many less spectacular cases; and if being tortured is not worse than death, the obvious question arises as to why torturing should be worse than killing.

It should be noted, of course, that the mere fact that death is worse than many ways of being tortured does not logically imply that killing is worse than torturing. Losing most of your property in a poker game nobody compelled you to take part in is worse than many forms of being stolen from; this, however, does not show that winning most of another person's property in a poker game nobody forced the other person to take part in is worse than stealing a rather limited amount of money from him. Nevertheless, the mere fact that a particular answer to the obvious question posed regarding the comparative moral status of killing on the one hand and torture on the other is not logically impossible does not make the question go away. It still has to be answered. In the case of stealing and winning it is not too difficult to point out essential differences between the two cases and then to demonstrate that they are normatively relevant (such explanations, for example, would involve reference to the presence and absence, respectively, of consent to the poker game and to being stolen from).

In the case of torture, however, such explanations are much more difficult to provide. One of the most prominent attempts has been offered by Henry Shue. For him torture necessarily involves inflicting suffering on *defenceless* people (while killing does not); and he thinks, appealing to just war theory, that there is a moral constraint against assaults on the defenceless.[10] However, as I have argued elsewhere,[11] there simply is no such constraint in just war theory. While attacking defenceless people might conflict with some warrior's code of honour (I am sceptical about how strong that code actually is), it is not regarded as immoral in just war theory – nor in the laws of armed conflict, for that matter, nor should it be. I do not want to go into this debate again here, so let me illustrate my point with another example, which stems not from just war theory but from self-defence theory instead. In this theory talk about the fat innocent man falling from a cliff is ubiquitous. Let us say Jeanette is beneath the cliff, and for whatever reasons she is unable to move out of the way of the falling man. When he lands on her, she will be crushed (but he will survive due to the cushioning effect). She has a ray gun, though, with which she can vaporize the man (who himself is unarmed). This man, thus, is completely defenceless; in vaporising him Jeanette would attack a defenceless person. Yet, on the accounts of most

10   H. Shue, 'Torture', in S. Levinson (ed.) *Torture: A Collection* (Oxford, Oxford University Press, 2004): 49-60, pp. 48-51.
11   Steinhoff, 'Torture', pp. 337-338.

moral philosophers (Shue included, as far as I can see), vaporising the man would be justified.

One could attempt to amend Shue's position by saying that in this case the principle that you ought not to attack defenceless people is overridden by a principle that allows the attack on threats (even if they come in the form of innocent and defenceless persons). This move, however, does not help much. It only converts the previous obvious question ('Why should torturing be worse than killing?') it is supposed to answer into this obvious question: 'Why should torturing a *culpable aggressor* be worse than killing an *innocent threat*?' And this question cannot be answered in favour of the more or less absolutist opponent of torture any more easily than the previous one.

To see this more clearly, consider this amended example:

The fat man has been pushed off the cliff by an evil aggressor, who was simply in the mood to kill a person (he does not care much whether it is Jeanette or the fat man). Jeanette has not only a vaporizing gun, but also a pain-infliction gun (that inflicts pain nearly as extreme as the pain from drilling on the unprotected nerve of a tooth). The fat man does not fall directly; some strange rock formation is involved that works like a long and intertwined slide so that it will take some time until the fat man crushes her (however, he himself is completely unable to stop his fall or slide). The evil man above, on his part, accidentally stepped into one of his own devious traps so that he cannot move any more and can easily be shot at by Jeanette. He is unarmed. Jeanette is trapped in one of the evil man's traps (that is the reason why she cannot move). The man knows the combination of the locks, and Jeanette knows that he knows (he is, however, unable to free himself of the trap he is caught in, due to a malfunction of this trap). She also knows that unlocking her trap would simultaneously activate a mechanism that would save the falling man. Jeanette sees two options to save her life: Vaporize the falling innocent man (who, let's say, has a gun himself and would try to shoot Jeanette if she tries to vaporize him – thus, he is not defenceless) or torturing the evil aggressor with the pain-infliction gun until he gives her the combination of the lock so that she can save the lives of the only two innocent people involved in this situation. What should she do? It seems completely obvious that she should use her pain-infliction gun and try to get the combination. In fact, I consider this example to be an absolutely compelling refutation of the claim that torture could never be justified and of the claim that it could only be justified in ticking bomb cases involving high numbers of innocents instead of just one or two. What rational and moral way could there possibly be to get around this conclusion?

Thus, I think Shue's argument as well as the modified argument (that being a threat trumps being defenceless) does not work.

The above example shows that it is better to torture a culpable aggressor than to kill an innocent threat. However, most forms of torture are preferable not only in situations where the choice is between torturing an aggressor and killing an innocent person, but also in situations where the choice is between torturing or killing one and the same aggressor. Consider this longer example.

The case of the humane torturer and the bloodthirsty anti-torture fanatic:

Bill works for a company that has a lot of trolleys on its enormous property to transport different goods. He is in charge of the maintenance of the trolleys. There is some kind of animal in the region that often enters the trolleys from below and bites through the wires. Therefore, Bill planted several foot traps, which, however, can also trap humans. The traps have combination locks, and Bill knows the combination. In order to set in motion certain trolleys, one has to hold on to a lever well above one's head. Since Bill is very small, he has to jump to reach the lever. One day, Jeanette and Paolo, two completely innocent persons, cross the tracks and both accidentally step into a foot trap. Jeanette shouts to Bill: 'Help us!' 'You wish', he shouts back. 'I prefer to kill you.' And he jumps up to a lever and sets in motion a trolley, which is slowly but fatally moving in Jeanette's and Paolo's direction. If not stopped, it will crush them. Jeanette has with her both her explosive projectile gun (these projectiles can blow people into small pieces but do not much affect trolleys) and her pain-infliction ray gun. Bill, for whatever reasons, would rather die than let the two escape. Fearing that they might shoot at him with normal guns so that he lets go of the lever, which would stop the trolley, he handcuffs himself to the lever and throws away the keys, and shouts sneeringly: 'I know the combination of your traps – but I won't tell you. I will watch you die.' Even if they shoot him dead, that would not stop the trolley since Bill would still be hanging on to the lever by the handcuffs. Jeanette draws her pain-inflictor and shows it to Bill: 'If you do not tell me the combination of the traps, I will torture you! This gun inflicts pain like a dentist drilling on an un-protected nerve.' Bill remains silent. Jeanette sadly aims the pain inflictor gun at him. 'What are you doing', screams Paolo now. 'What am I doing? I am trying to save our lives!' 'No, no, but you can't torture him. Torture is brutal, it's – the horror, the horror!' 'So what am I supposed to do?' 'Well, non-torturing self-defence is permissible. Draw your projectile thrower and blow him into small pieces!' 'Are you crazy? That is not minimal force! Besides, maybe the guy is just having a psychotic break, or somebody's drugged him, and maybe he has family. If I get the combination by a few minutes of torture, maybe we can all still become friends. Why should I kill him?' 'You like to torture, you like to torture', Paolo shouts, his face red in righteous indignation.[12] Two police officers ap-

---

12 One comic at the Hull torture conference shouted in his talk: 'Dr. Steinhoff likes to torture, Dr. Steinhoff likes to torture.' What I do is to defend torture in certain extreme circumstances. To do that I do not have to like torture more than one has to like killing in order to argue for the right of self-defence. I am aware, though, that the subtle art of differentiation is well beyond the intellectual capabilities of some people.

proach from behind. They too step into traps and cannot interfere. They have overheard the loud argument. As Jeanette aims with the pain-inflictor, one police officer shouts: 'Don't do it! Torture is really bad. Blowing people into small pieces is much better.' Jeanette is for a moment paralysed by the sheer amount of idiocy and moral insanity she is confronted with. Paolo uses the opportunity and knocks her out, takes her explosive projectile gun, aims at Bill and blows him into small pieces. The trolley stops. 'Thanks', say the police officers. 'You did the right thing. So good that we prevented torture.' 'My pleasure', says Paolo, while he is picking bloody pieces of Bill's flesh and bones from his jacket. 'I'm always happy to uphold human rights and human dignity.'

This elaborate example shows quite clearly that the whole idea that torture necessarily violates human dignity while at the same time self-defensive killing does not is untenable. Don't get me wrong: Of course nearly all instances of torture in our actual world violate human rights and human dignity. But so do nearly all instances of killing (I use the term 'killing' exclusively for homicide in this paper). *Self-defensive* torture and *self-defensive* killing, however, as long as the general moral requirements of self-defence are met, do *not* violate human dignity or human rights. Therefore, the habit of some (by no means all) absolutist torture opponents of brandishing the concepts of human rights and human dignity as if they had a monopoly on them is quite inappropriate. The argument I am propounding here is a *rights-based* argument. It is not utilitarian or consequentialist at all. It is based on the *right* to self-defence.

While in my view the above examples already show conclusively in themselves the unfeasibility of any attempt to demonstrate that torture is more difficult to justify than killing, all else being equal, let us nevertheless have a look at another failed but instructive attempt. Heiner Bielefeldt argues as follows:

> The point of torture is not merely, as it is for example in coercive detention or in many other coercive measures of the state, to impose upon a person unpleasant consequences of his actions (or non-actions) that are supposed to *influence* his voluntary decisions [*Willensentscheidungen*] without directly [*unmittelbar*] breaking the will. Nor is the point to limit his external freedom of action ... through such police measures as for example tying him up, or to completely eliminate it in the extreme case – through a death shot. Rather, the intent of torture is precisely to strategically use the physical and psychological vulnerability of a person for *directly breaking his inner freedom of the will*. For this reason torture is the direct negation of the subject status of the human being and hence of his dignity.[13]

---

13   H. Bielefeldt, 'Menschenwürde und Folterverbot: Eine Auseinandersetzung mit den jüngsten Vorstößen zur Aufweichung des Folterverbotes', Deutsches Institut für Menschenrechte, Berlin 2007, <http://files.institut-fuer-menschenrechte.de/437/IUS028_E_Folter_ RZ_WWW _ES.pdf>, p. 13 (my translation). David Sussman argues similarly: 'What's Wrong with Torture?', *Philosophy and Public Affairs* 33 (2005): 1-33. For a critique of Sussman, see Steinhoff, 'Torture', pp. 338-340.

Really? I doubt it. First, I already noted at the beginning that I am quite sceptical about the notion of 'breaking the will'. What precisely does that mean? I took the liberty to google the expressions 'Wille gebrochen', 'gebrochener Wille', 'broken will', 'will was broken' in connection with different sports. Judging from this, it seems that in football, boxing and other sports the wills of persons are broken quite often. Is the person's status as human being negated in such cases? Do sports violate human dignity? One might indignantly object that in these contexts the expression 'his will was broken' is only used metaphorically. Indeed, it is. However, my contention is precisely that there is no non-metaphorical use of the expression. All one typically means by saying that someone's will is broken is that after having for a while determinedly endured in some undertaking he has finally given up in the light of obstacles or some kind of attrition or because all hope was gone or because he was finally too exhausted to go on. What 'breaking the inner freedom of the will' means, in contrast, is entirely unclear.

Besides, in criticising Rainer Trapp, Bielefeldt complains:

> Well-nigh cynical is the claim that the person [namely the kidnapper of a child who has put it in some hole to let it suffocate and is asked by the police for the location] subjected to the painful interrogation procedure would merely suffer the 'disadvantage of being confronted with the choice between the voluntary and the coerced exercise of his duties.' For the alleged freedom of choice in this situation can be nothing else but the freedom to collapse; and the collapse will sooner or later occur nearly inevitably either because of unbearable pain or because of the fear of unbearable pain.[14]

One might wonder, of course, whether Bielefeldt's suggestion that in the case of threats with death shots we still *are* dealing with freedom of choice is not also well-nigh cynical. Be that as it may, although I agree with Bielefeldt that Trapp's use of language is unduly euphemistic, I definitely do not agree that the kidnapper's only option is collapse. For example, in the face of the threat of torture (Trapp is in particular referring to the famous German Daschner case) the kidnapper could say: 'Hey boys, slow down, take it easy ... I had no idea that you guys take the life of that child so seriously. I certainly don't. So, what the heck: Here's the address.' Where is the collapse here?

More important, however, is that Bielefeldt says that even just the *fear* of unbearable pain can break a person's will. This undermines his position. Since, as argued above, nearly all people fear death more than some forms of torture,[15] it follows that fear of death can break the will of nearly all persons *more easily* than fear of some forms of torture. Then, however, the police shouting to a criminal who fears death more then some forms of torture (which is true of practically all criminals and of practically all other people) 'Don't move, or we'll shoot!' or 'Put down the gun, or we'll shoot!' would 'negate' the criminal's 'inner freedom of will' and his human

14 Bielefeldt, 'Menschenwürde' pp. 12 f. (my translation).
15 To be sure, if Bielefeldt understood 'unbearable' in such a way that pain would only be unbearable if people preferred death to this pain, my argument of this paragraph would not
work. His argument against torture as such, however, would not work either, for not all torture is unbearable in this sense.

dignity. In fact, however, such warnings and threats are completely legitimate, and it seems that Bielefeldt does not want to deny this. But then 'breaking' someone's will is not always illegitimate, and hence torture not always wrong.

One could try to avoid this conclusion by taking back the claim that even just the threat of torture is capable of 'breaking' a person's will and instead claim that only real torture can achieve this. Yet, there still remains the problem of what 'breaking the will' is supposed to mean. Why is the case of someone who after fifteen minutes of torture says 'Please stop it, please stop it, I'll tell you what you want to know' a case of broken will, while the case of someone who after fifteen months of coercive detention says 'Please let me out, please let me out, I'll tell you what you want to know' is not? Without providing some phenomenological account of what breaking the will means and empirical evidence that it is caused by all forms of torture but not by coercive detention or death threats, the whole talk that torture breaks the will while those other forms of coercion do not is nothing but empty rhetoric.

Besides, it should be noted that some people *hold out under torture*. They do not give up the information. Furthermore, as already said, punitive torture does not even *aim* at the will of the victim, hence it does not aim at breaking his will, either. Bielefeldt claims that Jörg Splett has proffered the 'most succinct' definition of torture by designating it as the 'abolition (by physical or psychological means) of the freedom of the will while maintaining consciousness'.[16] For the reasons already adduced, this definition is not so much succinct as confused, as is any critique of torture that relies on it.

Last, but not least: Even if there were anything to this whole talk about 'breaking the will', it by no means answers the question at all as to *why* torture is worse than killing. Bielefeldt has quite correctly identified a difference between killing and torture – the first one, if successful, necessarily eradicates the consciousness of the target person, whereas the latter does not. But *why* does that make killing worse? *Why* is torture 'the direct negation of the subject status of the human being and hence of his dignity', while killing is not? Could Paolo in our above example say: 'Well, true, I blew Bill against his consent into small pieces – but at least I did not negate his subject status as a human being'? Isn't this statement downright idiotic? And if it is not – could not Jeanette make the claim of being much more respectful of Bill's subject status, a status she, after all, does not want to destroy once and for all by killing him? The answer can only be yes. Thus, Bielefeldt has certainly not provided any *argument* that would demonstrate that torture is worse than killing. He has only made a dogmatic claim.

This dogmatism, for the record, can also be found in the statements of one of the most outspoken opponents of torture at the torture conference in Hull, Massimo La Torre. He claims:

> Torture defeats any attempt at bringing it under a principle of universal material application: No one who accepts infliction of torture on others will accept it on oneself; this is not a stan-

---

16   H. Bielefeldt, 'Menschenwürde', p. 13 (my translation). Bielefeld quotes Splett from an unpublished manuscript.

dard that anyone would advocate and at the same time choose to *live by*. And it stands to reason that no one should do so, because torture is experienced by those on the receiving end of it as an act of extreme, *intolerable* violence, as an abuse and an excess—and it *must* be so experienced if it is to qualify as torture, as an *unbearable* torment, as a method for effectively obliterating another's will. Torture could never pass the test of universal acceptability that acts more or less as a final criterion of morality, for it is defined as an excess and an abuse even by those who use and apply it.[17]

First, torture is *not* defined as an excess and an abuse even by those who use and apply it. If La Torre thinks it is, his knowledge of the history of torture is very limited indeed. Nor is there any reason, as should be clear from my above remarks on the definitional issues, to define it in such a way. There is, after all, also no reason to define self-defensive killing as an abuse even though most people would rather be tortured for a few minutes than killed for good. Second, as already said, not all torture is unbearable. Some people do bear it and do not break. Unsuccessful interrogative torture is still torture (why is that so difficult to understand?). Third, interrogative torture is indeed to some extent *aimed* at being 'unbearable', but so is coercive detention. 'Unbearable' coercive detention, however, can still be justified. So can 'unbearable' torture. Besides, for both interrogative torture and coercive detention limits can be accepted by those who use these methods. Fourth, the criterion of universal acceptability is not a final criterion of morality; rather, it is itself unacceptable – and perhaps universally so. The norms 'Do not abuse children for your sexual pleasure', 'Do not suppress free speech only to keep yourself in power', 'Do not torture for fun' are not universally acceptable, for they are not acceptable to dedicated rapists, child abusers and sadistic dictators. However, that obviously says nothing against their validity. Fifth, will anyone who accepts that others are killed in self-defence also accept that she be killed in self-defence? Perhaps not, in the act, but what does that say against the permissibility of self-defence? Nothing. Moreover, one might still (and most people do) accept a maxim that allows self-defensive killing, in the full knowledge that this maxim might lead to oneself being killed in self-defence. And again there is no difference here to the case of self-defensive torture. Many people, myself included, *do*, after all, support a moral maxim allowing self-defensive torture.

It does not help matters here, by the way, to claim that at least in principle one might accept *even in the act* being killed in self-defence (thinking, with the bullet entering the heart: 'I had it coming, I accept it'). I suppose that is indeed *possible*, but it is of course also possible in the case of torture. To be sure, my definition of torture rules out that a person is tortured with her consent, but one can still *accept* things one did not *consent* to. Since most people would prefer being tortured for a few minutes to being killed, the case in which someone accepts being tortured is, all else being equal, more likely than the case in which someone accepts being killed. Besides, I can define a special kind of self-defensive killing, namely 'unaccepted self-defensive killing', which by definition only takes place when the person killed

17   La Torre, p. 34 above.

in self-defence does not accept being killed in self-defence. Then obviously the same would be true of this form of self-defensive killing that La Torre thinks is true of torture: No one who accepts that others be killed in unaccepted self-defensive killing would accept being killed by unaccepted self-defensive killing herself (if she did, it would obviously not be unaccepted self-defensive killing any more). However, unaccepted self-defensive killing (practically all actual self-defensive killing is of this kind) is certainly justified in certain circumstances. So is unaccepted self-defensive torture.

To summarize: There just is no argument that could show that torturing is always worse than killing. Thus, if killing in self-defence or defence of others or in a justifying emergency is justified, torture in self-defence and defence of others is justified too.

D. Is justifying torture bad even if torture is sometimes justified?

Some people claim that our talk about torture should be accompanied by a certain 'shyness'. What that means is that rational argumentation should only be allowed to go so far. Bielefeldt, for example, claims:

> The uncircumventability [*Unhintergehbarkeit*] of human dignity has also an emotional side. It manifests itself, for instance, in a kind of *intuitive shyness* to argumentatively engage with fictional scenarios that are aimed at undermining the unconditional respect of human dignity.[18]

He experiences this shyness with regard to one of my examples, in which a dictator confronts a prisoner with the choice to either kill one of ten prisoners or to torture one of them for two hours (all these prisoners are innocent and have no special relation to the first prisoner). If the prisoner refuses to choose and to act on his choice, all ten prisoners will be killed. He is not permitted to ask them (if he did, all ten prisoners would be killed). Of course, I argue that the prisoner is justified under these conditions in torturing one of the other prisoners.[19] Bielefeldt declares:

> The intuitive shyness to argumentatively engage such a constructed scenario has nothing to do with ingenuousness or intellectual incompetence. One might even admit that the macabre situation constructed by Steinhoff could become reality. However, to positively develop in light of such a mere eventuality a normative criteriology that is supposed to make it possible to weigh violations of dignity against one another is a monstrous undertaking; it leads us legally and ethically astray.[20]

First of all, this scenario is not one of self-defensive torture. Most of my examples, however, are, and they are precisely supposed to show that torture does *not* always violate human dignity (after all, self-defensive killing does not violate human dignity either). To not even rationally consider such examples and to simply

---

18   Ibid, p. 22 (my translation).
19   Steinhoff, 'Torture', p. 339.
20   Bielefeldt, 'Menschenwürde', p. 22, (my translation). .

stipulate instead that all torture violates human dignity might not attest to shyness so much as arrogance.

Secondly, this talk about the 'normative criteriology' that 'leads us legally and ethically astray' is sheer phrase-mongering. As already said, the case of the ten prisoners is not a case of self-defence. It is a case of what the German law calls justifying emergency (*rechtfertigender Notstand*) and what other jurisdictions call *necessity*. The laws of necessity *were precisely made to cover extreme situations like this one.* In fact, since the international torture conventions are arguably not applicable to private torture, torturing a prisoner in my scenario probably *is* legal under German, British and American law. But whether legal or not: necessity clauses *require and allow* the weighing of health against health, injuries against injuries, lives against lives,[21] life against health, injuries against lives, pain against lives etc. – why should the weighing become more difficult or even 'monstrous' when torture is involved? I assume Bielefeldt is too 'shy' to ask this question, let alone to answer it.

Besides, examples like the Daschner case, my Jeanette/Paolo/Bill case and the case of the prisoners not only show that torture is justified in such circumstances, they *also* show that the shyness Bielefeldt and others recommend is quite inappropriate. If the police officers in the Daschner case said 'Oh, no, no, we are too shy to even consider the possibility of torture, when in doubt it's just better if the child suffocates'; if the prisoner who could save the life of one other prisoner said 'Oh, no, no, I am too shy to even consider the possibility of torture, when in doubt it's just better if one of you dies, whether you agree with me or not'; when Paolo says 'Oh, no, no, I am too shy to even consider the possibility of torture, when in doubt it's better if we just blow up somebody', then this is not only irrational but also *immoral*. I think the ten prisoners, Bill and the suffocating child would agree. They would have little sympathy for Bielefeldt's 'shyness'.

Sometimes some absolutist opponents of torture cannot resist the temptation of morally blaming a proponent of a limited permission of torture for somehow contributing to the spread of illegitimate torture. Of course, they think that all torture is illegitimate. I don't. If I somehow contribute to the spread of self-defensive torture that helps to save innocent children from culpable kidnappers, then that would be a good thing. If absolutist torture opponents with their arguments or pseudo-arguments contribute to more children suffocating in the hands of kidnappers, then that would be a bad thing.

However, I completely agree that *nearly all* torture currently being undertaken on our planet is *immoral*. There are very few cases of defensive torture or torture justified in light of a justifying emergency. (There are also very few cases of killing

---

21 Weighing of life against life is, according to majority opinion, not allowed under the German justifying emergency paragraph. It is allowed under the necessity statutes of some US states. See P. D. W. Heberling, 'Justification: The Impact of the Model Penal Code on Statutory Reform' *Columbia Law Review* 75 (1975): 914-962, n. 33.

that are justified by self-defence or in light of a justifying emergency.) Thus, one criticism I have heard (and several times) is this: 'Even if you were right about self-defensive torture, by publicly justifying torture in some cases you contribute to a slippery slope, you contribute to there being more cases of illegitimate torture too.' Can that criticism stick?

First of all, let us remember that absolutist torture opponents argue against torture by appealing to the notion of rights. When, for example, they argue against a nuclear ticking bomb case, they say: 'Even if millions of lives are at stake, the terrorist has a *right* not to be tortured. This right cannot be overridden by utilitarian considerations.' Well, perhaps my right to speak my opinion can also not be overridden by utilitarian considerations. In other words, even if by speaking my opinion I contributed somehow to the spread of torture, I would still have the right to do so. To be sure, one might object that liberty of speech is not absolute (the right not to be tortured isn't, either). So it could perhaps be overridden. But, of course, if it were to be overridden, this would have to happen on grounds of *credible and substantial evidence* that my speaking my opinion indeed does cause harm on a scale large enough to override my right to free expression.

Maybe, however, the criticism does not so much want to suggest that one does not have the *right* to present arguments that justify torture under certain circumstances, but that nevertheless one *ought not* to present such arguments. After all, one can have a right to do immoral things. Having a right only means that others are not at liberty to forcibly keep you from doing what you have a right to. For example, people have a right to claim that the Holocaust never happened; however, making such a claim is still immoral. Thus, if the claim is only that I ought not to justify some forms of torture, the opponents would perhaps bear weaker burdens of proof.

They do still bear a burden of proof, though. However, in fact there is not a shred of evidence for the claim that by justifying self-defensive torture one also contributes to the spread of torture that is not self-defensive. Indeed, the claim is rather silly. *How* is this contribution supposed to work? Is some spokesperson of the US State Department supposed to quote me in support of torturing in Guantanamo? That would be counterproductive, for anti-torture groups could immediately point out that I have argued that the torture in Guantanamo is not self-defensive nor an instance of a justifying emergency, and therefore not justified; and that I have argued that the *institutionalization* of torture is wrong.[22] They could thus blame the spokesperson for manipulating and distorting things. That would hardly help his case.

I suspect that behind the charge that by justifying torture in some circumstances you also contribute to the spread of illegitimate torture is nothing more than the vague suspicion that one contributes to some kind of 'general atmosphere' in which

---

22   Steinhoff, 'Torture', pp. 346-351.

torture can 'thrive'.[23] This charge is more or less as intelligent and substantiated, though, as the claim – and such claims *have* been made – that by arguing for the right to sexual self-determination one contributes to a general atmosphere of sexual permissiveness in which rape will thrive. The claim is also comparable to the one – interestingly, hardly ever made – that by arguing for the right to self-defensive killing one contributes to an atmosphere in which murder thrives. There is no way of either proving or disproving such claims. Making them anyway simply amounts to the manipulative and defamatory attempt to shut people up whose arguments one doesn't like and probably cannot refute.

Finally – there *is* some evidence that morality and moral behaviour profit more from rational discussion than from censorship, prejudice and thought-restraint.

E. Conclusions and some clarifications on the scope of my argument

I have argued here that self-defensive torture is morally justified. Thus, I have argued that torture is justified in very rare and extreme circumstances, for the cases in which self-defensive torture could be applied are extremely rare. Torturing so-called terrorists to find out more about their networks is not a case of self-defensive torture. The Daschner case, on the other hand, is a case in which self-defensive torture could have been applied.

I also think – although I have not further argued here for it – that it is not in itself contradictory to legally prohibit torture while admitting that it can in certain circumstances be morally justified.[24] Yet, I do not think that all torture should be legally prohibited (and perhaps it isn't either).[25] However, there is as little need to introduce a special paragraph allowing self-defensive torture into the penal codes as there is a need to introduce a special paragraph allowing self-defensive throat-cutting. Both forms of self-defence can be easily covered by the normal self-defence regulations.

---

23   In this context, one observation: If thought experiments like, for example, the ticking bomb case are so dangerous and might be 'abused', then one probably should not give them a platform. However, in most pamphlets and articles of torture opponents these and other examples are always described (if not always discussed) and presented to people who probably have never heard of them before. Those torture opponents who really think that these thought experiments are dangerous can then hardly exclude the possibility that they themselves are contributing to the spread of torture by acquainting their audience with these arguments. In other words: Why, then, don't *they* shut up?

24   For a contrary opinion see R. Trapp, *Folter oder selbstverschuldete Rettungsbefragung?* (Paderborn, Mentis, 2006), Ch. IV

25   I had not quite made up my mind on this question in Steinhoff, 'Torture': see p. 346.

Finally, I am adamantly against the institutionalization of torture – and thus against training torturers or introducing the infamous torture warrants. Doing so, as I have argued elsewhere,[26] would have disastrous consequences. As history has shown, the state is not to be trusted to use torture only in self-defence cases once it becomes institutionalized. This, however, in no way undermines the argument that self-defensive torture is morally permissible.[27]

26   Ibid., *pp.* 346-351.
27   Wolfendale thinks otherwise, if I interpret her correctly: J. Wolfendale, 'Training Torturers: A Critique of the 'Ticking Bomb' Argument' *Social Theory and Practice* 32 (2006): 269-277. While I mostly subscribe to her arguments as to why the institutionalization of torture would be bad, I do not see how from that finding one could possibly derive the moral impermissibility of torture in concrete cases. A basic assumption of her argument seems to be that in the ticking bomb case a torturer can only be justified in torturing the 'terrorist' if the torturer is some kind of super-torturer – that is, highly trained and extremely capable of getting results. Apart from the fact that even if one granted this assumption, it would not provide the conclusion Wolfendale is looking for, the assumption is also wrong. After all, no one is required to be a super-shooter or super-stabber or, more generally, a super-defender in order to be justified in defending herself against an aggressor by, for example, using a knife or a gun. As I have already argued, even in cases where the defender has not much of a chance to stop an attacker by using a certain form of violence, he is still permitted to try if there are no other means left that would promise more success. Thus, self-defensive torture, too, is justified in certain cases – and not only in hypothetical, but also in real ones.

3. The Ticking Bomb Scenario as a Moral Scandal[*]

Francesco Belvisi

I.

A *skandalon* is an insidious obstacle, a stumbling block. Here it is a *'ticking bomb'* known to have been triggered by a terrorist group in a densely populated area. Not just a tricky talking point, the obstacle becomes a hellish trap: tripping up on it stretches the safety wires of our moral *convictions* to the limit.

Considering the ticking bomb scenario means accepting a 'tragic choice' since there is no one inexorably right and just solution in terms of a consistent application of legal and moral values.

Let us, however, accept the challenge to lift the cover of the trap and examine the loaded question: 'What would you do? Would you resort to torture?' I shall consider the case as if I were the politician or a policeman, putting myself in their uncomfortable position, not maintaining the *lofty distance* of those who assert the inviolable nature of human rights, but assuming the viewpoint of the *politically responsible*. In so doing, I plunge into the abyss where, paradoxically, the very foundation of our moral order is to be found: not high moral principles but *Abgrund,* its murky depths, abomination, or that which is 'morally unthinkable'.[1]

What lies in the abyss is torture, a subject we would rather sidestep. 'It is dispiriting as well as shameful to have to turn our attention to this issue,' laments Jeremy Waldron.[2] But *torture*[3] has been put squarely on the agenda by the 9/11 attacks and

---

[*]   I would like to thank Stefano Bertea, Thomas Casadei, Marco Goldoni, Massimo La Torre and Gianfrancesco Zanetti for their important comments and suggestions on the first version of this contribution.

1   B. Williams, 'A Critique of Utilitarianism', in J. J. C. Smart and B. Williams, *Utilitarianism: For and Against* (Cambridge, Cambridge University Press, 1973) 77-150, pp. 92-93. Williams is wrong, however, to exclude this category from moral considerations since it can highlight an event that, although logically conceivable had not been entertained, and although highly improbable, has actually taken place. It is just this *contingency* that is the main feature of a complex society: see N. Luhmann, 'Kontingenz als Eigenwert der modernen Gesellschaft', in N. Luhmann, *Beobachtungen der Moderne* (Opladen, Westdeutscher Verlag, 1992) 93-128 [English trans. *Observations on Modernity,* Stanford, Stanford University Press, 1998]. Clearly, then, morals cannot duck the ungrateful task of debating these intriguing albeit unique cases. Otherwise we would have to capitulate and admit that Luhmann, is right to maintain that basing an argument on values becomes untenable in the very instances where values are at stake, in those *tragic choices*. Rather than withdraw scandalized and powerless before the unthinkable, philosophers – and especially Kantian philosophers – should reflect on the *conditions for the possibility* of an adequate solution. N. Luhmann, *Gibt es in unserer Gesellschaft noch unverzichtbare Normen?* (Heidelberg, Müller, 1993), p. 20.

2   J. Waldron, 'Torture and Positive Law: Jurisprudence for the White House' *Columbia Law Review* 105 (2005): 1681-1750, p. 1683.

consequently the war on terrorism. One aspect of the wider debate is the ticking-bomb scenario. This essentially is the case in which the police have apprehended a terrorist who knows the whereabouts of a deadly bomb or unconventional weapon set to go off soon and likely to cause hundreds, thousands or even more casualties. The only way to extract information about the bomb's whereabouts is to torture the prisoner who otherwise refuses to collaborate. The question is: 'What would you do? Would you resort to torture?'

The 'absolutists', those who maintain that the ban on torture is an absolute principle to be upheld in all circumstances without exception, do not understand – and therefore object[4] – that the example given can vary widely and be portrayed deliberately in extreme terms so as to make decision-taking dire. The decision, indeed, appears obligatory, part of the very order of things created by the hypothetical scenario.[5] Yet such a catastrophe-invoking move is made necessary by the intractability of those who will tolerate no waiver, either legal or moral, of the absolute prohibition on torture.[6]

The question was first posed by Niklas Luhmann, in 1992, in a conference entitled: 'Do unrenounceable norms still exist in our society?',[7] as an exclusively theoretical issue. Luhmann set out to demonstrate that in our complex and functionally differentiated society underpinned by positive and contingent law,[8] unassailable norms no longer exist since the social conditions that made them possible no longer exist either. The existence of unchangeable, over-arching rules presupposes principles serving as universal criteria according to which all questions are settled. But *our*

---

3   For his definition, see: R. Marx, 'Folter: eine zulässige polizeiliche Präventionsmaßnahme?' <http://www.proasyl. info/texte/mappe/2004/91/16.pdf> (visited 11-05-2006), 5-9; S. Miller, 'Torture', in The Stanford Encyclopedia of Philosophy, Spring 2006, <http://plato.stanford. edu/archives/spr2006/entries/torture/> (visited 11-05-2006), 2-5.

4   D. Luban, 'Liberalism, Torture, and the Ticking Bomb', in K. J. Greenberg (ed.), *The Torture Debate in America* (New York, Cambridge University Press, 2006) 35-83, pp. 36 and 51: 'The ticking time-bomb scenario is an intellectual fraud.'

5   This is the case of the provocation launched by Luhmann, *Gibt es unverzichtbare Normen?*, p. 2. For this reason some authors try to solve the question on the grounds of the highly improbable and artificial nature of the case: see H. Shue, 'Torture', in S. Levinson (ed.), *Torture. A Collection* (Oxford, Oxford University Press, 2004) 47-60, p. 57. In this way, perhaps sustaining that the *hard cases* that can be tackled by morals must be much less *hard*, Shue holds: 'There is a saying in jurisprudence that hard cases make bad law, and there might well be one in philosophy that artificial cases make bad ethics.' But the central issue here is that neither the cases are artificial or the ethics good, but the limits of deontological ethics. Trying to undermine the scenario by pointing out inconsistencies and improbable aspects creates a similar situation to when the sage points to the moon and the dunce looks at the pointing finger.

6   See Part I, Art. 2, para. 2 of the UN Convention against Torture and Other Cruel, Inhuman or Degrading Treatment or Punishment: 'No exceptional circumstances whatsoever, whether a state of war or a threat of war, internal political instability or any other public emergency, may be invoked as a justification of torture.'

7   Luhmann, *Gibt es unverzichtbare Normen?* pp. 1-2.

8   A situation that is not accepted by J. Waldron, 'Torture and Positive Law', pp. 1709-1713, who asks: 'Is nothing sacred?'

society has no centre from which similar principles emanate, nor are such principles embodied by a pre-eminent social class able to establish and impose rules and values congruous with its dominant position, and then ensure the constant validity of these rules whatever the consequences of their application.[9]

The same argument applies if the issue is shifted to the plane of what are claimed to be universal values (human dignity and human rights). At this level, the case of conflicting individual rights can lead to paradoxical situations[10] solvable only by balancing *objective* values and taking reasonable yet *arbitrary* decisions that then serve as precedents.[11] This paradox becomes acute in the case of (massive) human rights violation: 'norm-generating scandals'.[12] These are cases where the violation of human dignity is such that effective protection requires some violation of the dignity of the perpetrators.[13] The 'ticking bomb' scenario is a case in point.

Luhmann's challenge was theoretical in nature. His intention was to show that there are circumstances that, albeit hypothetical, though not completely absurd nor unlikely, can rock the raft of principles we take as unquestioned and unquestionable truths. Luhmann's example was meant to warn against the naive belief that the workings of a legal system, set up to judge right from wrong, can be founded and justified even when its claimed validity is grounded in values. But in *our* social reality the distinction between right and wrong has a much more flimsy basis, namely the contingency of legal decision-making that may be indifferent to moral judgement. If this is how our legal system works, then establishing a given value as the principle underpinning legal judgement is fraught with difficulties.[14]

Subsequently, however, the attacks in Madrid and London made Luhmann's provocation highly relevant to real-life situations at the beginning of the new millennium when the *ticking-bomb* scenario was no longer seen as implausible or unthinkable as its critics claimed.

---

9   Luhmann, *Gibt es unverzichtbare Normen?* pp. 8-16.
10   For an effective example, see Brugger's presentation in W. Brugger, D. Grimm, B. Schlink, 'Darf der Staat foltern?' – *Eine Podiumsdiskussion*. Humboldt Forum Recht, 4/2002, <http://www.humboldt-forum-recht.de/4-2002/Drucktext.html> (visited 10-03-2005), 17: the person who, in a situation of necessity defence, uses violence against the kidnapper of his daughter in order to find out where she is being held and risks death by suffocation, should desist on the arrival of the police since the police have the duty, as guardians of the kidnapper's dignity, to take action against the father of the victim. In fact Art. 1, para. 1, Grundgesetz reads: 'Human dignity is inviolable. Respecting and safeguarding human dignity is the duty of every power of the State.'
11   Luhmann, *Gibt es unverzichtbare Normen?* pp. 17-23.
12   Ibid. pp. 28, 30 and 31-32.
13   Ibid. pp. 27 and 30.
14   For a more in-depth reconstruction of the author's thought, see F. Belvisi, 'Niklas Luhmann e la teoria sistemica del diritto', in G. Zanetti (ed.), *Filosofi del diritto contemporanei* (Milan, Cortina, 1999) 221-245.

II.

Unlike Luhmann's challenge, the debate following the September 11th attacks focused on the practical issues at stake: Whether the action of security forces, soldiers and governments fighting against international terrorism, particularly Islamic terrorism, can be morally and/or legally justified or must be rejected as unlawful. Opinion is split by and large into three major positions:

1) the deontological position that upholds, without exception, the absolute moral and legal illegitimacy of torture,[15] often arguing this on the grounds of the principle of inviolable human dignity;[16]

2) the 'emergency' position of Alan Dershowitz who holds that torture should be legalized in exceptional circumstances and only after receiving authorization from a judge (the *torture warrant*), who would be the guarantor of the legitimacy of the request and act as an agent of control;[17]

3) the pragmatic position that recognizes the moral legitimacy of '*preventive interrogational torture*' practised in exceptional cases to save the lives of potential attack victims, but at the same time, advocates the need to maintain the ban on torture.[18]

1. The deontological postion

The first position is that of scholars who conceive morals as the rigorous application of principles irrespective of the consequences. Faced with the hypothetical ticking-bomb case, they consider neither the possibility of the bomb going off nor the political responsibility that encumbers such a decision.[19] Such scholars do not consider the scenario in which, following a terrorist outrage, a Minister of Internal Affairs or Chief of Police has to inform the public that despite the fact that a member of the terrorist group had been apprehended, no information had been obtained during questioning on the whereabouts of the bomb, and that before the terrorist's refusal to

---

15 See, for example, Ch. W. Tindale, 'Tragic Choices: Reaffirming Absolutes in the Torture Debate' *International Journal of Applied Philosophy* 19 (2005): 209-222.

16 Waldron provides an exemplary case: J. Waldron, 'Torture and Positive Law', pp. 1726-1728.

17 A. Dershowitz, *Why Terrorism Works* (New Haven, Yale University Press, 2002), chap. 4. See also A. Dershowitz, 'Tortured Reasoning', in S. Levinson (ed.), *Torture* 257-280. For similar critiques, see: O. Gross, 'Are Torture Warrants Warranted?' *Minnesota Law Review* 88 (2004): 1481-1555, pp. 1534-1553; R. A. Posner, 'Torture, Terrorism, and Interrogation'. in S. Levinson (ed.), *Torture* 291-298, pp. 295-298; R. A. Posner, *Not a Suicide Pact*. (Oxford, Oxford University Press, 2006) pp. 35-38; B. A. Ackerman, *Before the Next Attack* (New Haven , CT, Yale University Press, 2006), pp. 108-109; Miller, 'Torture', pp. 15-16.

18 See O. Gross, 'Torture Warrants', pp. 1490-1497 and 1500-1511; O. Gross, 'The Prohibition on Torture and the Limits of the Law' in Levinson, *Torture*, pp. 231-232; Miller, 'Torture', pp. 7-11; Posner, *Not a Suicide Pact*, pp. 12, 38, 77-87 and 152-158.

19 An aspect also underlined by Gross, 'Prohibition on Torture', p. 238.

collaborate, the police had declined to resort to torture because this would have been a grave affront to the prisoner's dignity as a human being. In the light of a similar situation, it is difficult to give meaning to the statement that 'we aspire to... a State that pursues its purposes (even its most urgent purposes) and secures its citizens (even its most endangered citizens) honorably and without recourse to brutality and terror'.[20] It might indeed imply that the State is in part responsible for the victims it did not protect.

The ruling of the Israeli Supreme Court stands out as an exception on this 'absolutist' scene. In 1999, examining a case of violent interrogations of alleged Palestinian terrorists by secret service agents, the Court while admitting that 'a democratic society... is prepared to accept that an interrogation may infringe upon the human dignity and liberty of a suspect,' nonetheless upheld the absolute ban on torture or any other violent means of interrogation.[21]

This seemingly 'absolutist' stance of the Israeli Court is not simply grounded in universal values and the Kantian obligation to respect moral law in compliance with the deontological conception of morals. In their concluding remarks the judges affirmed that 'deciding these petitions weighed heavily on this Court... the possibility that this decision will hamper the ability [of the State] to deal properly with terrorists and terrorism disturbs us. *We are, however, judges. We must decide according to the law...* [and] act according to our purest conscience'.[22]

Such *self restraint* sums up the specificity of a Constitutional Court's 'non-political' function,[23] in the sense that even when faced with the problem of the State having to guarantee public security, and thus with the issue of rights versus security, the judges' decisions must uphold rights in accordance with the principle of judicial review. In other words, Courts cannot be asked to put themselves in the place of the politician or public officer who, by his very function, has to consider the aims and consequences of his actions. This is something that may be asked of philosophers.[24] For philosophers, a deontological concept of morals may present as one of the possible options. For judges, however, respect for the law and the constitution is an obligation sanctioned by the principle of the division of powers.

---

20   J. Waldron, 'Torture and Positive Law', p. 1750. In this, hopefully rare instance, the politician and police chief could be – rightly – held responsible for the death and suffering of innocent victims. This is also the view of J. B. Elshtain, 'Reflection on the Problem of 'Dirty Hands'', in S. Levinson (ed.), *Torture* 77-89, p. 83.

21   *Public Committee against Torture in Israel v. The State of Israel* HCJ 5100/94. In Judgments of the Israel Supreme Court: Fighting Terrorism within the Law, <http://www.mfa.govil/MFA/Government/Law/Legal+Issues+and+Rulings/Fighting+Terrorism+within+the+Law+2-Jan-2005.htm> (visited 20-05-2006) 23-58, pp. 42-48.

22   HCJ 5100/94 (2005), 55 (italics added).

23   G. Zagrebelsky, *Principî e voti* (Turin, Einaudi, 2005), pp. 35-40.

24   For a sound example, see M. Walzer, 'Political Action: The Problem of Dirty Hands', *Philosophy and Public Affairs* 2 (1973): 60-80, partially reprinted in Levinson, *Torture*.

2. The 'emergency' position

Turning to the view of Dershowiz, this is admittedly consistent with the idea of *rule of law* whereby all State organs must function in compliance with the law. However, legalising torture, albeit in specific cases, can be opposed on at least three different counts.

a) The *ticking bomb* scenario is posited as an *exceptional* instance for which legitimate recourse to torture might be possible, on the condition that it remain within the realms of an exception. However, in no legal order can exception – which is literally '*extra ordinem*' – be foreseen in terms of a specific event and regulated accordingly.[25] An exception goes against the very nature of the law, which aims to provide rules governing recurrent situations, not rare occurrences. According to Posner, in the case of emergencies it is appropriate to maintain 'the distinction between authority and power'.[26] Exceptional situations must therefore be dealt with not following the criteria and procedures of legitimate authority, but according to the power. In these cases something must be done not because it is required by law, but simply through sheer power, because of someone's 'raw ability' to do it.[27]

Making rules for specific exceptions is an oxymoron and would inevitably undermine the coherence of the legal system and the guarantees this provides, with grave consequences for fundamental rights.

b) Some considerations in the theory of institutions and organizations also lead to the rejection of legalized torture on account of the real likelihood of its *escalation*.

Institutions and organizations trigger what I call adaptive behaviour,[28] i.e., behaviour that is not the result of truly autonomous individual decision, but action conditioned by the particular environment or organization in which the individual operates. Adaptive behaviour is not born simply out of a desire to avoid clashing with other members of the institution, rather it is induced by coercive influences or by what Emile Durkheim calls *contrainte sociale*.[29] Adaptive behaviour develops when, for example, the members of an organization pursue the same aims, carry out the same tasks, hold by the same rules and follow the same procedures – in a word –

---

25 The recent German law on flight security (*Luftsicherheitsgesetz*) of 11 January 2005 goes in this direction. In the wake of the public outcry caused by the September 11th attacks, Art. 14, para. 3 of the law provides for the use of military airplanes to shoot down hijacked passenger aircraft that have been aimed to crash against targets on land. With its ruling BvR 357/05 of 15 February 2006, the German Federal Constitutional Court declared the law illegal on the grounds that it violated the principle of human dignity and the right to life of the passengers and crew.

26 Posner, *Not a Suicide Pact*, p. 38.

27 *Ibid.* p. 14: This according to his 'law of necessity' (pp. 12 and 158).

28 The term derives from the concept of 'adaptive preference' coined by J. Elster, *Sour grapes: Studies in the Subversion of Rationality* (Cambridge, Cambridge University Press, 1983), pp. 109-124.

29 E. Durkheim, *The Rules of Sociological Method*, ed. by S. Lukes (New York, Free Press, 1982).

share the same institutional 'culture.' Opposing that culture, innovating or removing certain practices and behaviours becomes extremely difficult.[30]

If we transfer these general considerations to specific institutions and organizations like the military, security forces and police, it becomes clear how real the risk is of violence becoming widely practised and torture an interrogational option were it to be legalized, even if only for exceptional cases.[31] The logic is the same: *By its very nature* the organization tends to metabolize the exception, transform it into a practical possibility, *institutionalize* a practice, and consider it a *routinely* available resource. In this sense, one can truly speak – as Henry Shue does – of 'torture's metastatic tendency'.[32] Furthermore, even if the practice of torture did not directly involve all the members of a given organization, becoming a standardized, and thereby tolerated, practice, the adaptive behaviour mechanism means that the torture would become accepted out of a sense of solidarity by those who would not themselves be willing to practise torture or who would resort to torture only in cases sanctioned by law.[33]

From a normative point of view, these theoretical considerations could underpin a dual weakness: that of not being based on principles, but on generalizations that lead to the formulation of purely inductive argument; and, in consequence, that of being instrumental and purpose-driven (restricting a practice) rather than geared to upholding the intrinsic value of the principle to be preserved (the absolute prohibition of torture). On this last point, mine is certainly not a 'principled' defence of the absolute ban on torture. With regard to the first objection, I believe that the legal argument cannot be divorced from an understanding of the particular situation for which the solutions must be *adequate*.[34]

c) Even conceptual considerations of principle are against legalising torture on an exceptional-case basis.

Torture is the antithesis of everything a liberal-democratic regime stands for, since torture strikes at the very core of the citizen (as a person) and his capacity for independent decision-making,[35] a component of the Kantian concept of human dignity. Hence the absolute prohibition on torture is the strongest form of protection and 'the only realistic barrier against governmental abuse of powers in the context of interrogational torture'.[36] Furthermore, the torture prohibition is a powerful factor

---

30　See Miller, 'Torture' (2006), pp. 12-14.

31　See also Posner, 'Torture, Terrorism, and Interrogation', p. 296.

32　Shue, 'Torture', p. 58.

33　See also Miller, 'Torture', p. 13.

34　On this question, see F. Belvisi, 'Una riflessione normativa per la società multiculturale' *Diritto, immigrazione e cittadinanza* 5 (2003): 28-47, pp. 28-34. See also G. Zanetti, *Introduzione al pensiero normativo.*(Reggio Emilia, Diabasis, 2004), in particular Ch. 2.

35　M. Ignatieff, *The Lesser Evil. Political Ethics in an Age of Terror.* (Princeton, Princeton University Press, 2004), pp. 136 and 143; J. Ph. Reemtsma, *Folter im Rechtsstaat?* (Hamburg, Hamburger Edition, 2005), pp. 119-120 and 124-126.

36　Gross, 'Prohibition on Torture', p. 236.

contributing to the political legitimization of the democratic system and a corner-stone of the legal foundation on which our society rests.

These are important considerations amply dealt with by several authors and con-tributors to this volume, and do not require further explanation here. More pertinent to the argument is the *logic* underpinning banning torture on the grounds of an abso-lute principle. It is one thing to conceive the ban on torture as an absolute principle (a practical aspect); it is another to recognize the need to maintain the ban on torture expressed in absolute terms (a semantic aspect). In this case, a distinction must be made between the empirical validity of the principle (the practical aspect) and its formulation (the semantic aspect). As a principle – similar to what happens for other so called universal principles (e.g., human dignity that in Germany is considered an absolute principle by a large part of public law scholars as well as by the German Federal Constitutional Court),[37] the ban on torture must manifest the claim to abso-lute validity if it is not to fall into a sort of performative fallacy.[38] As a valid norm, however, it can be applicable only taking the circumstances into consideration and thus, envisaging possible exceptions. In criminal law this is the *ratio* for the mitigat-ing circumstances of self-defence and necessity.

The absolute, uncompromising wording of Art 2 of the 1984 UN Convention against Torture and Other Cruel, Inhuman or Degrading Treatment or Punishment flags its very weakness, demonstrating in a nutshell the very reason for its great fra-gility: the easy and obvious facility with which such prohibitions may be disre-garded. What indeed is more banally human than to inflict 'severe pain or suffering, whether physical or mental… on a person'?

As a *petition* of principle therefore, the ban on torture is a 'formula that contains its own disappointment'.[39] Just as freedom cannot be unconditional or equality abso-lute, nor can the torture ban. Compared to these principles, the real questions arise the moment the principles are disregarded for justified motives supported by sus-tainable arguments. It becomes evident that principles undergo a strange metamor-phosis as soon as they are applied. From a universal 'basic quality' they mutate into a mouldable 'scalar quality'.[40]

Circumstances do the job of showing up the weakness of the absolute principle. As Justice Ben-Porat ruled: 'There simply are cases in which those who are at the helm of the State and bear responsibility for its survival and security, regard certain

---

37 For a critique, see R. Alexy, *Theorie der Grundrechte*. (Frankfurt a. M., Suhrkamp, 1986), pp. 94-97.

38 I refer to the concept of R. Alexy, *Begriff und Geltung des Rechts* (Freiburg, Alber, 1992), pp. 64-70: To avoid an error in the construction of the concept, just as those who make the law must assert that such law is just (*richtig*), similarly, those who establish a principle must assert the absolute validity of such principle.

39 N. Luhmann, 'Gesellschaftstheorie und Normentheorie', in U. Fazis and J. C. Nett (eds.), *Gesellschaftstheorie und Normentheorie* (Basel, Karger Libri, 1993), pp. 15-29, at 21.

40 For the distinction between 'basic quality' and 'scalar quality' see G. Zanetti, 'Patrick Lee on Human Dignity and Equality'. Paper presented at the conference on *The Philosophical Foun-dations of Human Dignity* (Washington DC, 8/10-03-2007).

deviations from the law for the sake of protecting the security of the State, as an un-avoidable necessity'.[41] Moreover, this sense of duty not only exists among those ac-countable for a country's security, it is indeed demanded of them by their citizens.[42]

An absolute torture ban is something we all immediately understand and applaud as long as *we* are not directly concerned. It is easy to see things in terms of butchers on the one hand, and Jews and persecuted minorities on the other, or people fighting for independence, the victims of authoritarian regimes, prisoners of war etc. Yet the moment we are in the front line faced with defending ourselves from a looming threat, the torture taboo is quickly set aside and its practice suddenly becomes an available, and feasible, resource, calling into question a prohibition that up to that point had seemed obvious. The circumstance triggering this possibility today has been terrorism.

3. The pragmatic position

Finally, the third position – the pragmatic approach. This approach justifies the moral and political legitimacy of torture as a last resort, to be inflicted in exceptional cases in order to acquire information to prevent a terrorist attack, but opposes, how-ever, legitimising torture.

The argument is clear: While the legal ban on torture must be upheld, in excep-tional cases, persons with public security responsibilities will find themselves in situations requiring them to break the law, committing 'official disobedience'[43] by using force to oblige a terrorist suspect to reveal information. Although this illegal action may be considered morally appropriate, and the torture carried out to be in the officer's line of duty, it can only be justified in law *ex post*, by means of due proc-ess. Oren Gross and Richard Posner agree that this is the best way to deal with a grave national threat: realistically upholding the ban on torture and taking effective measures to censure against the risk of this odious practice spreading. In their words: 'Civil disobedience can be a duty of government in extreme circumstances to its citizens, even if not a right.'[44]

---

41 Referred to by O. Gross, 'Prohibition on Torture', p. 237.
42 Ibid. p. 236: Gross notes that the opinion whereby 'torture... may have to be resorted to in certain circumstances... is shared by many segments of the population. '
43 *Ibid.* pp. 239-248; Gross, 'Torture Warrants', pp. 1487-1488 and 1519-1534; Posner, *Not a Suicide Pact*, pp. 85-87. The original idea was voiced by Shue, 'Torture', p. 58.
44 Posner, *Not a Suicide Pact*, p. 14. See also Gross, 'The Prohibition on Torture', p. 249. Gross states: 'most of us believe that most, if not all, government agents, when faced with a genu-inely catastrophic case, are likely to resort to whatever means they can wield – including pre-ventive interrogational torture ... And most of us hope they will do so.'

III.

By and large I agree with this last position since it arrives at a nuanced solution of the questions posed by the ticking bomb scenario and deals appropriately with the relations existing between the parties involved. In fact the key relation is not that which sets victim against butcher in a torture scenario. Clearly, however, if the apprehended terrorist is seen as a defenceless victim at the mercy of cruel police officers, no act of torture can ever be morally justified. In the ticking bomb case, however, the terrorist is no longer a defenceless victim, but a criminal whose failure to collaborate is tantamount to aiding and abetting a murderous attack by other members of his terrorist group. On this basis, the prisoner has it in his power to avoid torture, or end it, by collaborating.[45]

When viewed from this perspective, a third party appears on the scene for the first time: the citizens targeted by the terrorist attack. This leads intuitively to the moral justification of torture.[46] It seems evident to me that the dignity and life of (many) innocent people are of greater value than the dignity of one guilty person.[47]

Supporting this, is a series of factors that have not been taken into account in the current debate, but come into play in a ticking-bomb scenario. Firstly, the preventive strategies with which our welfare State governs our complex 'risk society'.[48] The State's fundamental task is to ensure the *security* of its citizens and do so in a much less abstract manner than conceived by any modern 19th century State of law.[49] It is undoubtedly true – as Oliver Lepsius argues – that the transformation of the democratic constitutional State into a preventative State entails risks in terms of the safeguard of human rights[50] with the 'de-individualization of freedom,' whereby 'individual rights are replaced by collective interests' of security and 'subject to society's

---

45   R. Trapp, 'Wirklich 'Folter' oder nicht vielmehr selbstverschuldete Rettungsbefragung?' In W. Lenzen (ed.), *Ist Folter erlaubt?* (Paderborn, Mentis, 2006), pp. 106-108: he redefines the torture practised in the ticking bomb case as 'interrogation geared to safeguard attributable to the criminal' (selbstverschuldete finale Rettungsbefragung).

46   See: F. Allhoff, 'A Defense of Torture' *International Journal of Applied Philosophy* 19 (2005): 243-264; Miller, 'Torture', pp. 8-9; U. Steinhoff, 'Warum Foltern manchmal moralisch erlaub, ihre Institutionalisierung durch Folterbefehle aber moralisch unzulässig ist', in W. Lenzen (ed.), *Ist Folter erlaubt?*

47   This intuitive concept is not shared either by the case law of the German Federal Constitutional Court which holds that human dignity is an imponderable principle, or by those who uphold the doctrine of 'dignity as essential human feature': On this point, see H. Hofmann, 'Die versprochene Menschenwürde', Humboldt Forum Recht, 8, 1996, <http://www.rewi.hu-berlin.de/online/hfr/8-1996/Drucktext.html>, pp. 3-6.

48   See E. Denninger, *Diritti dell'uomo e Legge fondamentale*, ed. by C. Amirante (Turin, Giappichelli, 1998) Part 1 and Appendix. For a social and legal approach to this issue, see T. Pitch, *La società della prevenzione* (Rome, Carocci, 2006).

49   U. Volkmann, 'Sicherheit und Risiko als Probleme des Rechtsstaates' *Juristenzeitung* 59 (2004): 696-703.

50   E. Denninger, *Diritti dell'uomo e Legge fondamentale*, p. 86.

purposes'.[51] On the other hand, 'for some time now, citizens no longer expect the State just to safeguard their freedom; they also expect it to guarantee their security'.[52] In this way security 'becomes, in a very general sense, a fundamental right that can be jeopardized by the failure of a State to take action, a circumstance that could be brought by citizens before a court of law'.[53] It must be recognized therefore that the role of the State does not stop at respecting and guaranteeing human rights but includes (active) protection of its citizens. Guaranteeing the rights and ensuring security are mutually complementary and constitute a single, fundamental two-pronged task of the State.

This argument in no way intends to underestimate the concerns expressed regarding the risk of a democratic State taking a degenerate, authoritarian turn,[54] as testified by current US events. It does draw attention, however, to the important fact that the academic world and ordinary citizens may be at odds and have different perceptions of social phenomena. These perceptions cannot be preferred unilaterally by critical reflection, but must be considered together as elements of the same social reality. In this way, following the concept that 'the true meaning of social practices is their social meaning',[55] the sense of social phenomena is (also) given by their social perception, i.e., by public opinion's perception of such phenomena.

There is the risk that terrorism, considered as a 'danger brought on by an external enemy... from which the community... is obliged to defend itself against,' may be a figment of popular prejudice, the latest version of that 'summary political dialectic... already pointed out by Carl Schmitt in the reductive dichotomy between friend and enemy'.[56] However, the widespread and not just popular perception of the terrorist as a public enemy, cast in the *existentialist* mould described by Schmitt,[57] is also extremely relevant to sustaining a normative argument that attempts to tackle the issue in a *socially adequate* manner. For this perception, not only creates in the potential victims a sentiment of extreme injustice, but also introduces an important element to the debate: fear, or in other words, the need for security. This is a central component of the terrorism phenomenon that obviously cannot be dismissed by, for example, rational argument or even appeal to the population to show 'courage'.[58]

---

51 O. Lepsius, 'Liberty, Security, and Terrorism' *German Law Journal* 5 (2004): 435-460, pp. 454-459.

52 E. Denninger, *Diritti dell'uomo e Legge fondamentale*, p. 2.

53 U. Volkmann, 'Sicherheit und Risiko als Probleme des Rechtsstaates', p. 700.

54 Concerns these expressed by authors like: J. Waldron, 'Security and Liberty' *Journal of Political Philosophy* 11 (2003): 191-210; B. A. Ackerman, *Before the Next Attack*; R. Dworkin, *Is Democracy Possible Here?* (Princeton, Princeton University Press, 2006) Ch. 2.

55 J. Raz, *Ethics in the Public Domain.* (Oxford, Clarendon Press, 1995), p. 186.

56 F. Rimoli, 'Più sicuri o più liberi?' in A. Giannelli, and M. P. Paternò (eds.), *Tortura di Stato* (Rome, Carocci, 2004), p. 128.

57 C. Schmitt, *Le categorie del 'politico'* (Bologna, il Mulino, 1972), pp. 108-111 [English trans., *The Concept of the Political* (New Brunswick, NJ: Rutgers University Press, 1976).]

58 See: Waldron, 'Security and Liberty', p. 194; E. Scarry, 'Five Errors in the Reasoning of Alan Dershowitz', in Levinson, *Torture*, pp. 281-290 and 282-283; Dworkin, Is *Democracy Possible Here?* pp. 50-51.

It is in this real-life context that the State is expected by broad sections of society to produce effective measures that will safeguard its citizens. And it is just these real-life contexts and the social and psychological circumstances imposed by terrorism that have made lifting the torture taboo even thinkable.[59] In a situation where there can be no appeal to human solidarity for terrorists, where one's existence is at stake, the instinct for survival becomes paramount and the (quality of) life of the other person (the terrorist) is of little count. In fact the traditional consensus against torture crumbles swiftly before a scenario in which the human dignity of the terrorist/enemy is all there is preventing the safeguarding of innocent lives,[60] with whom moreover the ordinary citizen can immediately identify.

Faced with the fatal question: 'Would you torture him?' Jan Philipp Reemtsma has a clear answer: 'Yes, I would inflict suffering on this man until he reveals where the bomb has been placed. In any case, however, the limit of my actions would not be dictated by any compassion for this person but by the disgust that sooner or later I would have for my own behaviour. What I did, I would do without considering the criminal liability of my actions... In the end, however, the deciding factor will be not so much what suffering we inflict upon another person, but what we expect of ourselves,' because we are what we do and we are judged by our actions and in the light of the values by which we abide.[61]

This is all very true, but it is valid in a reflexive way. Indeed, we must bear in mind that as the circumstances in which the potential torturer finds him/herself demand that action be taken, they also concur to justifying whatever action is taken to acquire urgently needed information that would enable a bomb to be defused and human lives saved. In such circumstances, not only does our threshold of disgust for ourselves rize several notches but our very *reason for action*, our duty to save human lives turns an odious, immoral act like torture into a moral one.

---

59   See F. Rimoli, 'Più sicuri o più liberi?' pp. 122-125.
60   M. Herdegen, Art. 1, Abs. 1 GG, in Th. Maunz, G. Dürig et al., *Grundgesetz Kommentar* (Munich, Beck, 2003), rn. 45. For Trapp, 'Wirklich "Folter"?' p. 104, resolving the ticking bomb scenario by reiterating the absolute ban on torture would lead to 'ethically scandalous consequences.'
61   Reemtsma, *Folter im Rechtsstaat?* pp. 122-123.

4. Torture and Democracy

Hauke Brunkhorst

Torture and law were always already closely connected in the Western legal tradition. In the 13th Century, torture was put on a legal basis in the context of the inquisition trials. This juridification is a late part of a large-scale law reforms of the 12th and 13th Century, from which the church (according to Harold Berman's groundbreaking studies on the Papal Revolution)[1] emerged as the first modern state that was ruled by law. 'Inner' actions, attitudes, schemes, desires and intentions were no longer liable to prosecution – with the exception of the two strictly defined, if spectacular, offenses of *treason* and *heresy*.

Ordeals and torture during the hearing of evidence and adjudication were first prohibited within canon law and replaced with formal requirements of evidence so strict that a condemnation in criminal cases was often difficult, and in hard cases or cases of covert crime, nearly impossible.[2] Although the formal presumption of innocence did not exist yet, the burden of proof was put on the prosecution from then onwards. A professional lawyer was admitted to trials. Fact finding and sentencing became separate processes, and at least two independent eyewitnesses were required for a complete hearing of evidence. The confession became the silver bullet of criminal proceedings. Later, towards the end of the 13th Century, torture was reintroduced but subject to norms in accordance with the rule of law. Torture was approved in certain hard cases of capital crime, and especially in those that were related to criminal states of consciousness, such as heresy and treason.

Yet, the application of torture was strictly standardized and, thus, limited. It was to be applied only if at least one eyewitness and strong evidence indicated the defendant's guilt. Moreover, a confession extorted from someone under torture was only valid if it was repeated voluntarily in court.[3] If the defendant revoked it, he or

---

1   H. Berman, *Law and Revolution. The Formation of the Western Legal Tradition*, (Cambridge, Harvard University Press, 1983).

2   J. H. Langbein, *Torture and the Law of Proof. Europe and England in the Ancien Regime*, (Chicago, University of Chicago Press, 1977). One must add that there were not only moral and legal reasons for the abolishment and condemnation of ordeal and torture but also simple class interests of the noble and the higher clergy, and in particular of the new and highly increased powers of the mighty kings of Sicily, France and England, and the Pope who strived for the monopolization and centralization of all power in their own hands and to get control over the local communities. Therefore it was no longer in the interest of the new ruling class that ordeal and great parts of the jurisdiction laid in the hands of decentred local communities, and they now were persecuted as heresy and pagan praxis, see: R. I. Moore, *The First European Revolution, c. 970-1215* (Oxford, Blackwell, 2000).

3   Berman, *Law and Revolution II. The Impact of the Protestant Reformations on the Western Legal Tradition* (Cambridge, Harvard University Press, 2003), p. 133.

she was exposed to torture again, and if he/she repeated the confession, the 'voluntary' confession was obligatory for verification in the second 'round' as well. Why was torture reintroduced in canon law? The problem partly was a self-produced trap because the burden of proof in the 12th and 13th Century was simply too high. Therefore the new criminal law was too weak to fulfil the stabilizing function of law as an 'immunity system' of the society (Luhmann). But the *legal* revolution was not only oriented to the *stabilizing function* of law but law was also, and for the first time in history, designed as a *means of changing the world*, and to realize parts of the *civitas dei* within the *civitas terrana*.[4] Since that time modern law has the double function of stabilizing expectations (Luhmann) *and* emancipating us from informal power.[5] The jurists and legal philosophers of the 11th and 12th Centuries were aware of the repressive use of law and its stabilizing function but they also wanted to improve and correct the individual's behaviour, and they wanted a criminal law that worked not only as punishment but also as an expression of divine grace and as an embodiment of parts of the realm of God on earth. In strengthening the stabilizing function of law since the late 12th Century, torture (and in particular the persecution of heresy) became a means for those in power to reduce the tension between the two fundamental purposes of law and to get its emancipatory use (and with it the poor who were the subjects of their rule) under control, and this was due to the new economic and political class structure that was established after the revolution.[6]

This is the famous Habermasian Janus face of law: *'rechterfüllte Kriege'* – 'lawfull wars' (Carl Schmitt) and *'rechterfüllte'* or 'lawful' torture – in the name of God, and both at the same time fitting very well the 'material interests' (Weber) of the ruling classes. A case study in the dialectic of enlightenment: The end of ordeal and result enlightened Christian legal reforms during the so called Renaissance of the 12th Century empowered the individual human with the full responsibility for his or her deeds, and in particularly made the judges individually responsible for their judgments. The legal reforms indicated an emancipation of subjectivity and an increase of autonomy[7]. Therefore they increased the burdens of proof in cases of capital crime, and this *progress* then became the *reason* for the re-invention of torture in great measures, because this re-invention in the course of time (and in particular in times of crisis) became a useful instrument for the increased oppression and expropriation of peasants and the destruction of self organized rural communities.[8]

A book written by a German legal historian in 1940 (when he was serving as a soldier in the *Wehrmachtsgerichtsdienst* [Army legal service] in Berlin in a time of terribly increased use of torture) shows very well how this dialectic of enlightenment worked during the late 14th and 15th Century. At that time the interest of the emerg-

---

4   Ibid.; see also H. Brunkhorst, *Solidarity. From Civic Friendship to a Global Legal Community* (Cambridge, MIT Press, 2005), pp. 23-54.
5   C. Möllers, *Die drei Gewalten. Legitimation der Gewaltengliederung in Verfassungsstaat, Europäischer Integration und Internationalisierung* (Weilerswist, Velbrück 2008), p. 226.
6   Moore, *The First European Revolution.*
7   Langbein, *Torture and the Law of Proof.*
8   Moore, *The First European Revolution.*

ing territorial state in the social order of things increased. Torture then was used systematically to produce reliable knowledge about criminality, security of citizens, and better means of stabilization of power.[9] More and more facts became criminal facts, and new and extraordinary crimes were invented to justify the use of torture for the 'protection' of indigenous and economically well established good citizens against the poor people, homeless knights and (as usual since the 12th Century) the Jews. These groups became then the preferred subjects of torture, and if they had done their part to increase knowledge and discursive power of the state or the city, '*nit vil umbstand*' was made with them if they had come through the torture alive.[10] This anticipates already a distinction which emerged during the debate about the new security and anti-terror legislation in Germany. This distinction is that between two kinds of penalty law: *Bürger-* v.. *Feindstrafrecht*, or in English: 'penal law for citizens' v.. 'penal law for enemies' which denies enemies or illegal fighters the status of legal persons who belong to the race of beings that are born equal.[11]

Yet, in the late 13th Century there was also an *intrinsic* motivation to reintroduce torture then, and this was more ideological and religious. Even if it was related completely to the stabilizing function of law it corresponded even more to the 'ideal interests' (Weber) of the ruling (clerical and noble) elites than to their material interests, and I guess one should take this *ideal interest* as seriously as material interests. Torture, re-introduced simultaneously with enhanced prosecution and the death penalty for heresy, was designed as a means to make the world safe not (as in present day America) for democracy but for the true believers in the holy and only church of Rome, and to save the indestructible soul and eternal life of all Christians. For that spiritual purpose the fundamentalist opposition, the Antichrist and the inner and outer Axis of Evil should be excluded and exterminated. In Christianity the inner self mattered, and in particular this was so since the new discovery or construction of the *individual subject of consciousness* in legal theory, scholastic philosophy, theology and poetry during the Renaissance of the 12th Century.[12] The intrinsic purpose of torture now reveals another chapter of the negative dialectic of enlightenment, subjectivity and progress. Torture was supposed also to offer the defendant a chance to salvage his or her immortal soul from eternal condemnation by means of revocation and acknowledgment of Christianity's objective truth, and – as a true believer – accepting the physical penalty authentically.[13] Torture in the inquisition trials of the 13th and 14th Century was '*Rettungsfolter*', i.e. *salvation-oriented torture*, torture exerted as a legal instrument to save the eternal life of men. It was a regime

9   E. Schmidt, *Inquisitionsprozess und Rezeption* (Berlin, 1940), p. 24.
10   Ibid., pp. 17, 54, 84.
11   G. Jacobs, 'Bürgerstrafrecht und Feindstrafrecht', *HRRS* 3 (2004): 88-95, pp. 89ff, in particular p. 93. [Available at: <http://www.hrr-strafrecht.de/hrr/archiv/04-03/hrrs-3-04.pdf>]
12   R. M. Kiesow, 'Das Experiment mit der Wahrheit. Folter im Vorzimmer des Rechts', *Rechtsgeschichte* 3 (2003): 98-110. For the broader context of the development of individualization see: N. F. Cantor, *Medieval History. The Life and Death of a Civilization* (London, Macmillan, 1969).
13   Berman, *Law and Revolution*; Berman, *Law and Revolution II*.

of truth, the intertwinement of reason, belief and torture, a power discourse that once was opened by Jesus' word 'I am the truth' – a truth belonging to nobody, being completely egalitarian but had to be introduced by *torture* as well as by *grace* and *insight*.

II.

The German term '*Rettungsfolter*' or *salvation-oriented torture* originally was not invented by the old canonists but by a German legal scholar, Wilfried Brugger, who was the first German lawyer after World War II who suggested an argument for the legalization of torture in certain cares of terror suspects, hijackers etc.[14] Yet, Brugger's idea of juridified and lawfull ('*rechtserfüllte*') *Rettungsfolter* – law no longer expected to save eternal but mortal life of victims of crime and terror – fits nicely with the canon law of the late 13th Century, and so does the whole social and legal context. In the same way as 700 years ago, torture again is accompanied by enhanced prosecution, much extended punishment, death and life sentence for terrorism, heavy and notorious criminals etc.; by new forms of discoursive power, biopower etc.; by new disciplinary instruments to control and construct the inner self; by a strong preference for the stabilizing and repressive function of law and a growing suspicion against its emancipatory component;[15] by the ideal and – not to forget – the material interests of an emerging and again transnational but now global ruling class.[16]

Those who argue today in favour of legalized torture clearly argue from *within* the Western legal tradition. As we have seen, within the legal principles of this tradition *Rettungsfolter*, the salvation-oriented torture is completely compatible with *rule of law* or the *state of law* (*Rechtsstaat*). Yet, here the question arises if *Rettungsfolter* is also compatible with a *Rechtsstaat* that is *democratic*?

14 W. Brugger, 'Würde gegen Würde', *Verwaltungsblätter Baden-Württemberg* (1995): 414ff; Brugger, 'Darf der Staat ausnahmsweise foltern?', *Der Staat* (1996): 67 ff; Brugger, 'Vom unbedingten Verbot der Folter zum bedingten Recht auf Folter?', *Juristenzeitung* 55 (2000): 165-73.

15 N. Berman, 'Privileging Combat? Contemporary Conflict and the Legal Construction of War', *Columbia Journal of Transnational Law* 43 (2004): 1-72; O. Lepsius, 'Freiheit, Sicherheit und Terror: Die Rechtslage in Deutschland', *Leviathan* 1 (2004): 64-88; *Ehrhard Denninger*, 'Freiheit durch Sicherheit? Anmerkungen zum Terrorismusbekämpfungsgesetz', *StV* (2002): 96 ff.; T. Groß, 'Terrorbekämpfung und Grundrechte', *KJ* (2002): 1 ff.; S. Buckel and J. Kannankulam, 'Zur Kritik der Anti-Terror-Gesetze nach dem 11. September', *Das Argument* 44 (2002): 34 ff; G. Frankenberg, 'Kritik des Bekämpfungsrechts', G. Beestermöller and H. Brunkhorst (eds.), *Folter: Sicherheit zum Preis der Freiheit* (Munich, Beck, 2006).

16 On the emergence of this class: Brunkhorst, 'There Will Be Blood. Konstitutionalisierung ohne Demokratie?', in: Brunkhorst (ed.) *Demokratie in der Weltgesellschaft*, Special Issue of *Soziale Welt* (Baden-Baden, Nomos, 2008); Brunkhorst, 'Cosmopolitanism and Democratic Freedom,' in C. Thornhill and S. Ashenden, (eds.), *Normative and Sociological Approaches to Legality and Legitimacy* (forthcoming, 2008)

I think not. From the point of view of German law, European law and International Law torture is forbidden unconditionally: *'notstandsfestes' ius cogens* with *erga omnes* binding power.[17] As Mathias Hong rightly says: 'A new constitution is needed by those' German lawyers who want to alter the German laws against torture, and one should add: a new European and Intentional Law as well.

Yet, the more philosophical or theoretical debate of this question – so I argue – depends deeply on our understanding of *law, constitution* and *constitutionalism*. From its very beginning the Western legal tradition has been characterized, as I already mentioned, by the tension or even dialectical opposition between a *repressive* and an *emancipatory* understanding of law. Since Hobbes and from Austin, through Laband and Jellineck, to Carl Schmitt, including even Hans Kelsen and Niklas Luhmann, a onesided understanding of law as *peace-keeping repression* (the legal system as the *expectations stabilizing immunity system*) has prevailed on the one hand; but on the other hand a lot of philosophers of law have interpreted the very concept of law, not as repressive and peacekeeping, but *basically* and *primarily* as *emancipatory*. Law, in this reading that is inspired by the French Revolution, is deeply connected with the idea of realizing and implementing *equal freedom of all*, and not only of all *citizens*, but of all *people*. From Kant´s definition of law as *compartibilization of reciprocal spheres of freedom* that relies completely on the one and only human right to *equal freedom*, this track of argumentation runs via Savigny and Hegel's famous definition of law as the *existence of freedom* ('Dasein der Freiheit') to Rawls, Habermas or Ingeborg Maus today.

Since the German and English Protestant Revolutions of the 16th and 17th Centuries, and since the American and French Constitutional Revolutions of the 18th Century, both competing understandings of law have been reflected by different comprehensive ideas of a *constitution*, and during the 19th and 20th Centuries both ideas were implemented and tried out in different constitutional regimes. The first one historically stems from the German and English revolutions, and the early inventions of constitutional Monarchy are its paradigmatic cases. This kind of constitution, following Christoph Möllers, can be called a *power-limiting* constitution.[18] That means that the constitution is invented to limit the *already prevailing power* of a certain *non-democratic regime*. Granting its citizens a constitution, this regime binds itself

---

17   M. Hong, 'Das grundgesetzliche Folterverbot und der Menschenwürdegehalt der Grundrechte – eine verfassungsjuristische Betrachtung', in G. Beestermöller and H. Brunkhorst (eds.), *Rückkehr der Folter* (München, Beck, 2006), pp. 24-35; see further: A. Peters, 'Compensatory Constitutionalism: The Function and Potential of Fundamental International Norms and Structures', *Leiden Journal of International Law*, 19 (2006): 519-610, S. Oeter, '*Jus cogens* und der Schutz der Menschenrechte', in S. Breitenmoser, B. Ehrenzeller, M. Sassòli, W. Stoffel and B. W. Pfeiffer (eds.), *Menschenrechte, Demokratie und Rechtsstaat*, (Baden-Baden, Nomos, 2007), pp. 499-521; A. Emmerich-Fritsche, *Vom Weltrecht zum Völkerrecht* (Berlin, Duncker & Humblot, 2007), pp. 493ff, 706f.

18   On the distinction between *power limiting* and *power founding* constitutions: C. Möllers, 'Verfassungsgebende Gewalt—Verfassung—Konstitutionalisierung', in A. von Bogdandy (ed.), *Europäisches Verfassungsrecht* (Berlin, Springer, 2003), pp. 1ff. The distinction is prominently used by H. Arendt, *On Revolution* (Harmondsworth, Penguin 1973).

to the rule of law (Jellinek). Though it only grants (like a merciful and good prince: like the prince of the mythical tale of a 'Glorious Revolution') individual rights and legal remedies to its *subjects*. These *subjects* or in French or German: *sujets/Untertanen* are citizens only as long as the regime is pleased to treat them as citizens. The *consitutionalized asymmetry* between the ruler and his subjects never vanishes except in the case that the regime transforms itself into a full fledged democracy (as it was the case with English history during the late 19th and early 20th Century). The point here is that power limiting constitutionalism must not but can be reduced to a mere *repressive understanding of law*. The repressive understanding in any case has priority over the emancipatory or freedom-enabling understanding of law (which form the very beginning was much more alive in the English than in the German constitutional monarchies).

The philosophical background of power-limiting constitutionalism is clearly Hobbesian. *Freedom has to be relative with security*, and in case of emergency or exception the self preservation of the constituent power, of the monarchy or the 'state' (Jellinek) becomes an absolute and unconditioned norm even at the price of individual rights, legal remedies and democratic participation. Torture, in this case of a self-tamed, self-bound Leviathan can or even *must* become a legal and constitutional measure in the struggle against public enemies who oppose the constitutional regime fundamentally. Following Lord Tony Giddens: *Human rights could not be applied to enemies of the basic human rights.*[19]

The latter is an implication of a power-limiting understanding of constitutionalism for which the work of Georg Jellinek is paradigmatic. Power-limiting constitutionalism presupposes a 'law-free' state which is of the ready beyond law as an 'emergency resource of argument' (*'argumentative Notstandsreserve'*) in order to 'withdraw the legal standards it originally granted.'[20] Or in the affirmative words of Ernst Forsthoff (from the 1970s): 'Only where government and administration appear as an executive that is no longer bound to law, they are the 'state' and nothing else.'[21] One of the present advocates of legalized torture, who suggest the introduction of a specific criminal law for enemies (*'Feindschaftsrecht'*), the highly recommended legal scholar from Bonns Law School, Günther Jacobs brings that to the striking formulation: 'Those who win the war define the law.'[22] (This is nothing else than a reformulation of Carl Schmitt's infamous definition of sovereignty: *The one who determines the state of emergency is the sovereign.*)

19   Speech in the debate on the Terrorism Bill, H. L. Debs, 1 March 2005, cols. 148-51. [Lord Giddens did not use the phrase in the text, but it could be seen as implicit in his argument that we cannot 'sustain our traditional procedures' in the face of 'new style terrorism' – eds.]

20   C. Möllers, 'Skizzen zur Aktualität Georg Jellineks', in S. L. Paulsen and M Schulte (eds.), *Georg Jellinek – Beiträge zu Leben und Werk* (Tübingen, Mohr, 2000), pp. 164-5.

21   E. Forsthoff, *Der Staat der Industriegesellschaft – dargestellt am Beispiel der Bundesrepublik Deutschland* (München, Beck, 1971), pp. 46-7, 105.

22   Jacobs, 'Feindstrafrecht', p, 95.

III.

The other kind of constitutional regime, the power-binding kind, introduces a completely different perspective. The paradigm cases of power-*founding* constitutions stem from the French and American Revolutions. Not how to *limit* power was – according to Arendt – the problem of the American Revolution but how to *establish power*, and how to preserve, enlarge and improve the constituent power of the people?[23] The revolution (with Thomas Jefferson) should be transformed into a *permanent* revolution, and a German jurist and revolutionary from the year 1848 Justus Fröbel followed the Jeffersonian track and defined democracy as a 'permanent legal revolution'.[24] Contrary to power-limiting constitutions power-founding constitutions are from the very beginning democratic. Power founding constitutionalism is *democratic constitutionalism* because it is relying on the legal principal of *democratic inclusion*.[25]

A power founding constitution constitutes a *citizenship of free and equal citizens* who control the state and its branches of power. In this case of a power-founding constitution it is not an already existing power that grants rights to its subject but the *citizens themselves ascribe rights to each other reciprocally*.[26] Therefore, in a modern democracy exists no *legitimacy* ('*Legitimität*') of rulership or a ruler (like the *legitimate king*) but only procedures of the egalitarian *legitimation* ('*Legitimation*') of binding decisions (legal norms). Power-founding constitutionalism *necessarily* is committed to an *understanding of law that is emancipatory* because there are no longer any legal norms *allowed* which are not legitimated by the free and equal discourse and free and equal decisions of all legal subjects affected by the specific norm. Democratic legitimation does transfer the right to equal freedom into positive law that interprets and implements this right that does not exist before the self-corrective procedure of its legitimization.

Now, the basic idea of a democratic constitution is first that there exists no longer any sovereign subject that keeps outside or rules over the law because a free and equal citizenry is constituted by the always already legal procedure of implementing and concretizing this very constitutional procedure. Democracy allows 'only as much state as its constitution creates.'[27] There is no state outside the legal procedure of constitutional and normal legislation and concretization of law, hence there is no difference left between state and law (as in Kelsen's theory of law).[28] Yet, also the

23 Arendt, *On Revolution*.
24 Quoted from J. Habermas, 'Ist der Herzschlag der Revolution zum Stillstand gekommen?', in Habermas (ed.) *Die Ideen von 1789* (Frankfurt, Suhrkamp, 1989).
25 See: S. Marks, *The Riddle of all Constitutions*, (Oxford, Oxford University Press, 2000).
26 I. Maus, *Zur Aufklärung der Demokratietheorie* (Frankfurt, Suhrkamp, 1992); J.Habermas *Faktizität und Geltung* (Frankfurt, Suhrkamp, 1992; trans. W. Rehg as *Between Facts and Norms,* Cambridge, Polity, 1996).
27 A. Arndt, 'Umwelt und Recht', *Neue Juristische Wochenschrift* 25 (1963): 848 ff.
28 On Kelsen see now: H. Brunkhorst and R. Voigt, *Rechts-Staat. Staat, internationale Gemeinschaft und Völkerrecht bei hans Kelsen* (Baden-Baden, Nomos, 2008).

people are no longer a substantial *sovereign* before and over the law. The *pouvoir constituant* is (and must be if democracy is possible at all) always already mediated by the *pouvoir constitué* in a (hopefully) virtuous circular process. The difference between the two is not a fundamental *dualism*, as in Sieyes (natural v.. positive law) or in Carl Schmitt (state of exception v.. legal state) but a gradual difference within a *continuum*, and with the idea of transforming dualism into a continuum I try to combine John Dewey's pragmatism with in Hans Kelsen's legal theory.[29] Only then we can keep Kelsen's anti-sovereign inside but to get rid of Kelsen's Non-Kantian, yet already formal, Apriorism.

Second, modern democracy is *not* simply rulership of the majority over the minority (constrained by law or not) but 'rulership of the ruled' or self-rule, self-legislation. Democracy therefore formally and procedurally presupposes the *identity of rulers and ruled*. Self-rule or self-legislation is possible only, if *everybody* who *is affected* by *collectively binding decisions* has a say, has a voice and a vote, has equal access to the whole process of political discussion, creation and concretization of legal norms on all levels of Kelsen's 'Stufen des Rechts' (hierarchy of legal actions) which is on all levels at once is legislation *and* application/ implementation of norms and standards (against we have here a *continuum* of creation and implementation of legal actions). As individual human being everybody who is affected by a legally binding decision has to have sufficient and equal access to the discussion, creation and implementation of legal norms, on all levels of the legal hierarchy, in parliaments as well as in referenda, in international organization as well as in courts, in governments as well as in local administrations. Hence, *universal human rights* are the indispensable and necessary condition for any democratic will formation that is *self-legislative rulership by the ruled* ('*Herrschaft Beherrschter*').[30] Without these *rights* no *equal* access would be possible, and without *universal* rights no access for *all* affected would be possible. This is mirrored by constitutional history: All democratic power-founding constitution textbooks are based on the dialectical tension between universal human rights which *do not allow to exclude anybody* on the one hand, and concrete rights of citizenship, constitutional norms of check and balances etc. on the other hand, which never can avoid to *exclude* or silence *some* people or groups, minorities or even majorities etc.[31] Therefore we can argue with Susan

29   For more see: H. Brunkhorst, 'Kritik am Dualismus des internationalen Recht – Hans Kelsen und die Völkerrechtsrevolution des 20. Jahrhunderts', in R. Kreide and A. Niederberger (eds.) *Internationale Verrechtlichung. Nationale Demokratien im Zeitalter globaler Politik*, (Frankfurt am Main and New York, Campus, 2008); further the last section of Brunkhorst, 'Cosmopolitanism and Democratic Freedom'.

30   For this definition see C. Möllers, 'Der parlamentarische Bundesstaat – Das vergessene Spannungsverhältnis von Parlament, Demokratie und Bundesstaat', in *Föderalismus – Auflösung oder Zukunft der Staatlichkeit?* (München, Boorberg 1997), p. 97; Brunkhorst, *Solidarity*, 70ff.

31   This is Derrida's point: see J. Derrida, 'Force of Law: The "Mystical Foundation of Authority"' in D. Cornell, M. Rosenfeld and D. G. Carlson (eds.) *Deconstruction and the Possibility of Justice* (London, Routledge, 1992).

Marks, that the function of the legal principle of democratic inclusion in national and international law is to keep the *meaning of democracy open* for ever new voices, new definitions of citizenship, democratic participation beyond representative government, and new institutions of democratic legitimation beyond prevailing national borders etc.

IV.

Coming back to torture, there can be no doubt that the principle of democratic inclusion and the idea of *self-legislative rulership of all ruled individual human beings* (of all human being affected by collectively binding decisions) categorically *excludes torture*. A democratic constitution stipulates the *relativization of security with freedom* and prohibits in reverse the relativization of freedom with security. Security however fundamental for the exercise of rights, is limited by the basic right that is to protect. A democratic legal system that does not allow a loophole for 'salvation' torture, 'does not miss the opportunity to a state of emergency, it only refuses to offer the revocation of itself in that case', Gertrude Lübbe-Wolf wrote already in the 1980s, now judge at the Federal Constitutional Court of Germany.[32] This is so because legalized torture would destroy the possibility of individual self-determination of the one exposed to torture, hence, torture would destroy the possibility to say freely *yes* or *no*. Moreover, torture in particular would destroy the democratic self-determination because legalized, and *only legalized torture* oppresses the opportunity of subjects to the law of torture, to intervene *every time* into the public issue on this law once it is applied to her or him. Thus, the most elementary method of the individual affected by law to participate democratically in its making – namely to be able to interfere with an argument about its validity at every time, as the chain of democratic legitimacy demands it – would cease to exist. A law to which *both*, the torturer and the tortured could accept or reject, no longer would be possible. As opposed to legal torture, not even the otherwise barbarian death penalty destroys that option. The condemned individual can agree or disagree with it until the very last second in order to continue the egalitarian argument about its validity even beyond his own death.

V.

A brief additional remark on the ticking bomb: Legal and moral discourse are different matters. Besides other advances, the differentiation of legal and moral norms increases our individual freedom. The difference enables us to behave immorally

---

32 Quoted from Heribert Prantl, 'Rettungsfoltern', *Süddeutsche Zeitung* 19 November 2004, p. 13.

without fear of legal sanctions. The increase here is an increase of liberal freedom, the freedom of Kant's '*Volk von Teufeln*' – 'people of devils', or Hobbes' negative or legal freedom that allows the citizens to do everything they want to do unless it is not explicitly forbidden by law. Yet there is also an increase of moral (or practical-rational) freedom because acting in accordance with the moral law now depends *only* on the individual conscience, deliberation and decision of the actor; hence the difference of law and morality increases the (Kantian) personal autonomy of the individual human being who is no longer bound to the imperative of the concrete moral life or *Sittlichkeit* of the societal community, and its traditional overlap of morality and law.

The separation of morals and law therefore puts the full responsibility for decisions on the conscience on the individual. Someone who thinks for moral reasons that it is in a case of emergency necessary to torture and to violate the constitution fundamentally as a bearer of public authority, has to set the record straight with his or her own conscience, and with the public moral discourse which cannot *bind* him or her *externally*, and can not excuse him or her legally. For the sake of legal and moral freedom, law cannot resolve this tragic conflict. There may be cases where arguments both for and against torture can present morally sound arguments. Once the bomb has started ticking, the respective officials (and only they) may see it fit to violate the constitution, because they believe to have good moral reasons for torture.

As opposed to law, morality doesn't know any limits and does not allow for dogmatics. That in itself excludes an overlap of moral and legal discourses. Contradictions between morals and law can, contrary to Kant's beliefs, never be excluded. Therefore, it is true that an, in current law, irreparable *collision between morals and law* can occur in any single case, although positive law has to remain morally acceptable as a whole. This is the price to be paid for what is gained from differentiation. From the perspective of law, there is nothing 'outside the law code': 'Torture is either right or wrong – tertium non datur. Legal prohibitions of torture do not prohibit the political and moral discussion. But they do assign the competence to decide.'[33] The law would have to be executed on the German chancellor Merkel, or any other official who takes his or her competence to order torture to prevent Berlin from falling victim to a nuclear bomb, as Kant's in this case justified rigorism demands. Kant would have had her executed because of high treason. In the people's collective memory, however, that same chancellor would probably be worshiped as a moral hero – even if both the legal and the moral prize for this rescue would remain visible (like in classical tragedy).

---

33 Hong, *Folterverbot* 25.

5. Survey of the Crime of Torture in the Jurisprudence of the ICTY

Tsvetana Kamenova[1]

A. Introduction

The International Tribunal for the Prosecution of persons responsible for serious violations of international humanitarian law is governed by its Statute, adopted by the Security Council of the United Nations on 25 May 1993 and by the Rules of Procedure and Evidence of the International Tribunal, adopted by the Judges of the International Tribunal on 11 February 1994, as amended. Under the Statute, the International Tribunal has the power to prosecute persons responsible for serious violations of international humanitarian law committed in the territory of the former Yugoslavia since 1991. Articles 2 through 5 of the Statute further confer upon the International Tribunal jurisdiction over grave breaches of the Geneva Conventions of 12 August 1949 (Article 2); violations of the laws or customs of war (Article 3); genocide (Article 4); and crimes against humanity (Article 5).

The practice of torture has existed through all periods of history and is not confined to any single political system, regime, culture, religion or geographic location.[2] The offences of torture as they are set forth in the ICTY Statute are not defined, thus leaving the determination of the meaning of 'torture' to the jurisprudence of the Tribunal.

The prohibition of torture in international law derives from a number of instruments, notably Article 3 of the European Convention on Human Rights (ECHR), Article 7 of the International Covenant on Civil and Political Rights (ICCPR) and Article 5 of the Universal Declaration of Human Rights and from international *jus cogens*. It is generally understood to be without any exceptions whatsoever, but attempts have recently been made to reduce the prohibition, allowing torture in situations of grave emergency, for instance, in the notorious case of the ticking time bomb. It may therefore be said that the prohibition of torture is indeed absolute, regardless of recent attempts to reduce this prohibition.

The Appeals Chamber of ICTY determined that under customary International Law crimes against humanity could be committed in peacetime and that war crimes are punishable when committed in non-international armed conflict. As one renowned scholar states '[these findings are of direct relevance to the International criminalization of torture, which was already acknowledged to be a crime against

---

1   Dr. Kamenova is at present judge at ICTY and law professor at the Institute for Legal Studies, Bulgarian Academy of Sciences. The views expressed are those of the author.

2   D. Derby, 'Torture' in M. Cherif Bassiouni (ed.), *International Criminal Law* (2nd ed., New York, Transnational Publishers, 1999) vol. I, p. 705.

humanity as well as a war crime, but only in a narrow ambit.'[3] It had been contended that the crime of torture as a crime against humanity could only be committed in association with armed conflict. At least this is what article 5 of the ICTY statute seem to say:

> *Article5*
>
> *Crimes against humanity*
>
> The International Tribunal shall have the power to prosecute persons responsible for the following crimes when committed in armed conflict, whether international or internal in character, and directed against any civilian population:
>
> (a) murder;
>
> (b) extermination;
>
> (c) enslavement;
>
> (d)   deportation;
>
> (e) imprisonment;
>
> (f) torture;
>
> (g)   rape;
>
> (h) persecutions on political, racial and religious grounds;
>
> (i) other inhumane acts.

The traditional view that war crimes could only be committed in international armed conflicts would have excluded torture prosecutions with respect to internal conflict. The conclusions of the Appeals Chamber were of great importance for rejecting such restrictive interpretations. Note that these conclusions were made in 1995, before the adoption of the Rome Statute of the ICC[4]. The first indicted before the Tribunal, Tadic, was found responsible for acts of torture by the Trial Chamber of ICTY in May 1997.

B. Developments in the case law of the ICTY with regard to the definition of torture

I. Prosecutor v. Delalic et al.[5]

In one of the early cases before the ICTY, the so-called Celebici case, known by the name of the Celebici prison-camp, a detention facility, located in Central Bosnia and Herzegovina, the Trial Chamber accepted that the prohibition against torture is *jus*

---

3   See W. Schabas, 'The Crime of Torture in the International Criminal Tribunals'. *Case Western Reserve Journal of International Law* 37 (2006): 349.

4   The Rome Statute of the International Criminal Court accepted a far broader definition of torture.

5   Trial Chamber Judgment, 16 November 1998

cogens.[6] In this Judgment the Trial Chamber referred to various international instruments that prohibit torture starting with the Universal Declaration of Human Rights, including the Convention against torture and the Declaration on the prohibition of torture. The Trial Chamber said that these General Assembly declarations and the various treaty provisions established that the prohibition of torture was also a norm of customary International Law. Accepting that the prohibition of torture was a norm of jus cogens, the Trial Chamber cited as authority for the proposition the UN Special Rapporteur for torture.. 'The prohibition of torture contained in the International instruments is absolute and non-derogable in any circumstances, says the Judgment in Celebici case.

1. The Definition of Torture under Customary International Law

There are two international instruments that are solely concerned with the prohibition of torture, the most significant of which is the Torture Convention[7]. This Convention was adopted by the General Assembly on 10 December 1984 and has been ratified or acceded to by many states, including the SFRY, representing more than half of the membership of the United Nations. It was preceded by the Declaration on the Protection from Torture, which was adopted by the United Nations General Assembly on 9 December 1975 without a vote.

The Trial Chamber Judgment notes that the prohibition contained in the international instruments is absolute and non-derogable in any circumstances.

Despite the clear international consensus that the infliction of acts of torture is prohibited conduct, few attempts have been made to articulate a legal definition of torture. In fact, of the instruments prohibiting torture, only three provide any definition. The first such instrument is the Declaration on Torture, article 1 of which states:

> torture means any act by which severe pain or suffering, whether physical or mental, is intentionally inflicted by or at the instigation of a public official on a person for such purposes as obtaining from him or a third person information or confession, punishing him for an act he has committed or is suspected of having committed, or intimidating him or other persons. . . . Torture constitutes an aggravated and deliberate form of cruel, inhuman or degrading punishment.

This definition was used as the basis for the one subsequently articulated in the Torture Convention, which states, in article 1 that,

> the term 'torture' means any act by which severe pain or suffering, whether physical or mental, is intentionally inflicted on a person for such purposes as obtaining from him or a third person information or a confession, punishing him for an act he or a third person has committed or is suspected of having committed, or intimidating or coercing him or a third person, or for any

6   *Prosecutor v. Z. Delalic et al.*, Case No. IT-96-21-T, 16 November 1998, para. 454
7   The Convention against Torture and Other Cruel, Inhuman or Degrading Treatment or punishment. As of 2008 the Torture Convention has been ratified by 145 states.

reason based on discrimination of any kind, when such pain or suffering is inflicted by or at the instigation of or with the consent or acquiescence of a public official or other person acting in an official capacity.

This differs from the formulation used in the Declaration on Torture in two ways. First, there is no reference to torture as an aggravated form of ill-treatment in the Torture Convention. However, this quantitative element is implicit in the requisite level of severity of suffering. Secondly, the examples of prohibited purposes in the Torture Convention explicitly include 'any reason based on discrimination of any kind', whereas this is not the case in the Declaration on Torture.

Having in mind also the third such instrument, the Inter-American Convention, the Trial Chamber Judgment concludes that the definition of torture contained in the Torture Convention reflects a consensus which the Trial Chamber considers to be representative of customary international law.

Having reached this conclusion, the Trial Chamber considers in more depth the requisite level of severity of pain or suffering, the existence of a prohibited purpose, and the extent of the official involvement that are required in order for the offence of torture to be proven.

2. Severity of Pain or Suffering

Although the Human Rights Committee, a body established by the ICCPR to monitor its implementation, has had occasion to consider the nature of ill-treatment prohibited under article 7 of the ICCPR, the Committee's decisions have generally not drawn a distinction between the various prohibited forms of ill-treatment. However, in certain cases, the Committee has made a specific finding of torture, based upon the following conduct: beating, electric shocks and mock executions, *plantones*, beatings and lack of food; being held incommunicado for more than three months whilst being kept blindfolded with hands tied together, resulting in limb paralysis, leg injuries, substantial weight loss and eye infection.

The European Court and the European Commission of Human Rights have also developed a body of jurisprudence that deals with conduct constituting torture, prohibited by article 3 of the European Convention. As with the findings of the Human Rights Committee, it is difficult to obtain a precise picture of the material elements of torture from the decisions of these bodies, although they are useful in providing some examples of prohibited conduct[8].

The Trial Chamber Judgment notes that the Special Rapporteur on Torture, in his 1986 report, provided a detailed, although not exhaustive, catalogue of those acts which involve the infliction of suffering severe enough to constitute the offence of

---

8   The Judgment discusses in detail the *Greek Case*, (1969) 12a Yearbook of the European Convention of Human Rights, the Northern Ireland Case (*Ireland* v. *UK* (1979-80) 2 E.H.R.R. 25), and *Aksoy* v. *Turkey* (1997) 23 E.H.R.R. 553.

torture, including: beating; extraction of nails, teeth, etc.; burns; electric shocks; suspension; suffocation; exposure to excessive light or noise; sexual aggression; administration of drugs in detention or psychiatric institutions; prolonged denial of rest or sleep; prolonged denial of food; prolonged denial of sufficient hygiene; prolonged denial of medical assistance; total isolation and sensory deprivation; being kept in constant uncertainty in terms of space and time; threats to torture or kill relatives; total abandonment; and simulated executions.

The conclusion is made that the most characteristic cases of torture involve positive acts. However, omissions may also provide the requisite material element, provided that the mental or physical suffering caused meets the required level of severity and that the act or omission was intentional, that is an act which, judged objectively, is deliberate and not accidental. Mistreatment that does not rise to the threshold level of severity necessary to be characterized as torture may constitute another offence.

It is difficult to articulate with any degree of precision the threshold level of suffering at which other forms of mistreatment become torture. However, the existence of such a grey area should not be seen as an invitation to create an exhaustive list of acts constituting torture, in order to neatly categorize the prohibition.

3. Prohibited Purpose

Another critical element of the offence of torture is the presence of a prohibited purpose. The list of such prohibited purposes in the Torture Convention expands upon those enumerated in the Declaration on Torture by adding 'discrimination of any kind'. The use of the words 'for such purposes' in the customary definition of torture, indicate that the various listed purposes do not constitute an exhaustive list, and should be regarded as merely representative. Further, there is no requirement that the conduct must be solely perpetrated for a prohibited purpose. Thus, in order for this requirement to be met, the prohibited purpose must simply be part of the motivation behind the conduct and need not be the predominating or sole purpose.

A fundamental distinction regarding the purpose for which torture is inflicted is that between a 'prohibited purpose' and one which is purely private. The rationale behind this distinction is that the prohibition on torture is not concerned with private conduct, which is ordinarily sanctioned under national law. In particular, rape and other sexual assaults have often been labeled as 'private', thus precluding them from being punished under national or international law. However, such conduct could meet the purposive requirements of torture as, during armed conflicts, the purposive elements of intimidation, coercion, punishment or discrimination can often be integral components of behavior, thus bringing the relevant conduct within the definition.

II. *The Prosecutor v. Furundzija*[9]

The approach of the Trial Chamber Judgment differs: it discusses first international humanitarian law and after that international human rights law.

The judgment cites the relevant articles of the Geneva Conventions and the Additional Protocols, which explicitly prohibit torture in times of armed conflict[10].

The Trial Chamber also noted that torture was prohibited as a war crime under article 142 of the Penal Code of the Socialist Federal Republic of Yugoslavia and that the same violation has been made punishable in the Republic of Bosnia and Herzegovina by virtue of the decree-law of 11 April 1992.

The Trial Chamber agrees that a general prohibition against torture has evolved in customary international law. This prohibition has gradually crystallized from the Lieber Code and The Hague Conventions, in particular articles 4 and 46 of the Regulations annexed to Convention IV of 1907, read in conjunction with the `Martens clause' laid down in the Preamble to the same Convention. Torture was one of the acts expressly classified as a crime against humanity under article II(1)(c) of Allied Control Council Law No. 10. As stated above, the Geneva Conventions of 1949 and the Protocols of 1977 prohibit torture in terms.

All these treaty provisions have ripened into customary rules and it is evinced by various factors. The Trial Chamber Judgment goes on:

> First, these treaties and in particular the Geneva Conventions have been ratified by practically all States of the world. Admittedly those treaty provisions remain as such and any contracting party is formally entitled to relieve itself of its obligations by denouncing the treaty (an occurrence that seems extremely unlikely in reality); nevertheless the practically universal participation in these treaties shows that all States accept among other things the prohibition of torture. In other words, this participation is highly indicative of the attitude of States to the prohibition of torture. Secondly, no State has ever claimed that it was authorised to practice torture in time of armed conflict, nor has any State shown or manifested opposition to the implementation of treaty provisions against torture. When a State has been taken to task because its officials allegedly resorted to torture, it has normally responded that the allegation was unfounded, thus expressly or implicitly upholding the prohibition of this odious practice. Thirdly, the International Court of Justice has authoritatively, albeit not with express reference to torture, con-

---

9   Trial Chamber Judgment, 10 December 1998
10   Under the Statute of the International Tribunal, as interpreted by the Appeals Chamber in the Tadic Jurisdiction Decision, these treaty provisions may be applied as such by the International Tribunal if it is proved that at the relevant time all the parties to the conflict were bound by them. In this case, Bosnia and Herzegovina ratified the Geneva Conventions of 1949 and both Additional Protocols of 1977 on 31 December 1992. Accordingly, at least common article 3 of the Geneva Conventions of 1949 and article 4 of Additional Protocol II, both of which explicitly prohibit torture, were applicable as minimum fundamental guarantees of treaty law in the territory of Bosnia and Herzegovina at the time relevant to the Indictment. In addition, in 1992, the parties to the conflict in Bosnia and Herzegovina undertook to observe the most important provisions of the Geneva Conventions, including those prohibiting torture. Thus undoubtedly the provisions concerning torture applied as treaty law in the territory of Bosnia and Herzegovina as between the parties to the conflict.

firmed this custom-creating process: in the Nicaragua case it held that common article 3 of the 1949 Geneva Conventions, which *inter alia* prohibits torture against persons taking no active part in hostilities, is now well-established as belonging to the corpus of customary international law and is applicable both to international and internal armed conflicts.

The Trial Chamber Judgment concludes that the treaty and customary rules impose obligations upon States and other entities in an armed conflict, but first and foremost address themselves to the acts of individuals, in particular to State officials or more generally, to officials of a party to the conflict or else to individuals acting at the instigation or with the consent or acquiescence of a party to the conflict. Both customary rules and treaty provisions applicable in times of armed conflict prohibit any act of torture. Those who engage in torture are personally accountable at the criminal level for such acts.

Under current international humanitarian law, in addition to individual criminal liability, State responsibility may ensue as a result of State officials engaging in torture or failing to prevent torture or to punish torturers. If carried out as an extensive practice of State officials, torture amounts to a serious breach on a widespread scale of an international obligation of essential importance for safeguarding the human being, thus constituting a particularly grave wrongful act generating State responsibility.

When discussing international human rights law the Trial Chamber Judgment notes that the prohibition of torture laid down in human rights treaties enshrines an absolute right, which can never be derogated from, not even in time of emergency (on this ground the prohibition also applies to situations of armed conflicts). This is linked to the fact, that the prohibition on torture is a peremptory norm or *jus cogens*. This prohibition is so extensive that States are even barred by international law from expelling, returning or extraditing a person to another State where there are substantial grounds for believing that the person would be in danger of being subjected to torture.

These treaty provisions impose upon States the obligation to prohibit and punish torture, as well as to refrain from engaging in torture through their officials. In international human rights law, which deals with State responsibility rather than individual criminal responsibility, torture is prohibited as a criminal offence to be punished under national law; in addition, all States parties to the relevant treaties have been granted, and are obliged to exercise jurisdiction to investigate, prosecute and punish offenders. Thus, in human rights law too, the prohibition of torture extends to and has a direct bearing on the criminal liability of individuals.

The Trial Chamber Judgment points that the prohibition against torture exhibits three important features:

1. The Prohibition Even Covers Potential Breaches

States are obliged not only to prohibit and punish torture, but also to forestall its occurrence: it is insufficient merely to intervene after the infliction of torture, when the physical or moral integrity of human beings has already been irremediably harmed

In the case of torture, the mere fact of keeping in force or passing legislation contrary to the international prohibition of torture generates international State responsibility.

2. The Prohibition Imposes Obligations *Erga Omnes*

Furthermore, the prohibition of torture imposes upon States obligations *erga omnes*, that is, obligations owed towards all the other members of the international community.

Where there exist international bodies charged with impartially monitoring compliance with treaty provisions on torture, these bodies enjoy priority over individual States in establishing whether a certain State has taken all the necessary measures to prevent and punish torture and, if they have not, in calling upon that State to fulfill its international obligations. The existence of such international mechanisms makes it possible for compliance with international law to be ensured in a neutral and impartial manner.

3. The Prohibition Has Acquired the Status of *Jus Cogens*

While the *erga omnes* nature appertains to the area of international enforcement, the other major feature of the principle proscribing torture relates to the hierarchy of rules in the international normative order. Because of the importance of the values it protects, this principle has evolved into a peremptory norm or *jus cogens*, that is, a norm that enjoys a higher rank in the international hierarchy than treaty law and even 'ordinary' customary rules. The most conspicuous consequence of this higher rank is that the principle at issue cannot be derogated from by States through international treaties or local or special customs or even general customary rules not endowed with the same normative force.

Clearly, the *jus cogens* nature of the prohibition against torture articulates the notion that the prohibition has now become one of the most fundamental standards of the international community. Furthermore, this prohibition is designed to produce a deterrent effect, in that it signals to all members of the international community and the individuals over whom they wield authority that the prohibition of torture is an absolute value from which nobody must deviate.

Some of the consequences include the fact that torture may not be covered by a statute of limitations, and must not be excluded from extradition under any political offence exemption.

The broad convergence of the aforementioned international instruments and international jurisprudence demonstrates that there is now general acceptance of the main elements contained in the definition set out in article 1 of the Torture Convention.

The Trial Chamber concludes that it is appropriate to identify or spell out some specific elements that pertain to torture as considered from the specific viewpoint of international criminal law relating to armed conflicts. The Trial Chamber considers that the elements of torture in an armed conflict require that torture:

(i) consists of the infliction, by act or omission, of severe pain or suffering, whether physical or mental; in addition;

(ii) this act or omission must be intentional;

(iii) it must aim at obtaining information or a confession, or at punishing, intimidating, humiliating or coercing the victim or a third person, or at discriminating, on any ground, against the victim or a third person;

(iv) it must be linked to an armed conflict;

(v.) at least one of the persons involved in the torture process must be a public official or must at any rate act in a non-private capacity, e.g. as a de facto organ of a State or any other authority- wielding entity.

III. *Prosecutor* v. *Dragoliub Kunarac et al.*[11]

In the Judgment of the Appeals Chamber in *Kunarac* further clarification is provided as to the nature of the definition of torture in customary international law as it is given in the Torture convention, in particular with regard to the participation of a public official or any other person acting in a non-private capacity. The Appeals chamber agrees that the definition of the crime of torture, as set out in the Torture Convention, may be considered to reflect customary international law.

The Torture Convention was addressed to States and sought to regulate their conduct, and it is only for that purpose and to that extent that the Torture Convention deals with the acts of individuals acting in an official capacity. Consequently, the requirement set out by the Torture Convention that the crime of torture be committed by an individual acting in an official capacity may be considered as a limitation of the engagement of States; they need prosecute acts of torture only when those acts are committed by a public official or any other person acting in a non-private capacity

11 Appeals Chamber, 20 June 2002

In the *Furundzija* Trial Judgment, the Trial Chamber noted that the definition provided in the Torture Convention related to the purposes of the Convention.

The accused in that case had not acted in a private capacity, but as a member of armed forces during an armed conflict, and he did not question that the definition of torture in the Torture Convention reflected customary international law. In this context, and with the objectives of the Torture Convention in mind, the Appeals Chamber in the Furundzija case was in a legitimate position to assert that at least one of the persons involved in the torture process must be a public official or must act in a non-private capacity.

This assertion, which is tantamount to a statement that the definition of torture in the Torture Convention reflects customary international law as far as the obligation of States is concerned, must be distinguished from an assertion that this definition wholly reflects customary international law regarding the meaning of the crime of torture generally.

The Trial Chamber Judgment in *Kunarac* was right to say that the public official requirement is not a requirement under customary international law in relation to the customary responsibility of an individual for torture outside of the framework of the Torture Convention. This is confirmed by the Appeals Chamber Judgment.

IV Conclusions

Having reviewed these three cases, it is possible to conclude that two trends could be observed in the ICTY jurisprudence.

Firstly, this is the expansion of the list of prohibited purposes as well as the deletion of the specific purpose requirement.

Secondly, the removal of the official sanction requirement. All three judgments accept that the term torture can encompass non-state actors. The first two judgments qualify this by requiring that such non-state actors act in an official capacity for a state-like entity. Kunarac accepts that torture can be committed by private individuals in violation of international humanitarian law, regardless of official capacity. It rejects any requirement relating to the status of the perpetrator, considering that torture is defined solely by the nature of the act committed.

C. Constitutive elements for the crime of torture at present

The constitutive elements required for the crime of torture at the ICTY are:
- the infliction, by act or omission, of severe pain or suffering, whether physical or mental;
- the act or omission must be intentional; and
- the act or omission must be for a prohibited purpose, such as obtaining information or a confession; or punishing, intimidating or coercing the

victim or a third person; or discriminating, on any ground, against the victim or the third person.[12]

Here is a more detailed explanation of the constitutive elements.

I. Severe Pain or Suffering

The threshold level of suffering that is necessary to meet the definition of torture is difficult to articulate with any degree of precision.[13] Moreover, existing case-law has not determined the absolute degree of pain required for an act to amount to torture.[14] However, the Trial Chamber in *Kvočka* articulated the following approach:

> [i]n assessing the seriousness of any mistreatment, the Trial Chamber must first consider the objective severity of the harm inflicted. Subjective criteria, such as the physical or mental effect of the treatment upon the particular victim and, in some cases, factors such as the victim's age, sex or state of health will also be relevant in assessing the gravity of the harm.[15]

The articulation by the *Kvočka* Trial Chamber has received the endorsement of the Trial Chambers in other subsequent judgements.[16] One such judgement provided a further detailed articulation:

> When assessing the seriousness of the acts charged as torture, the Trial Chamber must take into account all the circumstances of the case, including the nature and context of the infliction of pain, the premeditation and institutionalization of the ill-treatment, the physical condition of the victim, the manner and method used, and the position of inferiority of the victim. In particular, to the extent that an individual has been mistreated over a prolonged period of time, or that he or she has been subjected to repeated or various forms of mistreatment, the severity of the acts should be assessed as a whole to the extent that it can be shown that this lasting period or repetition of acts are inter-related, follow a pattern or are directed towards the same prohibited goal.[17]

Mistreatment that does not rise to the threshold level of severity necessary to be characterized as torture may constitute another offence.[18]

The physical or mental suffering need not be visible after the commission of the crimes in question.[19] Though torture often causes permanent (physical or mental)

---

12 Kunarac Appeal Judgment, paras. 142 and 144; *see also Prosecutor* v. *Miroslav Kvočka et al.*, Case No. IT-98-30/1-T, 2 November 2001 ('Kvočka Trial Judgment'), para. 141, cited with approval in Kvočka Appeal Judgment, para. 289.
13 Čelebići Trial Judgment, paras. 461-469.
14 Kunarac Appeal Judgment, para. 149.
15 Kvočka Trial Judgment, para. 143.
16 See *Prosecutor* v. *Milorad Krnojelac*, Case No. IT-97-25-T, Judgment, 15 March 2002 ('Krnojelac Trial Judgment'), para. 182; Brđanin Trial Judgment, para. 484.
17 Krnojelac Trial Judgment, para. 182.
18 Čelebići Trial Judgment, para. 469.

damage to the health of the victims, permanent injury is not a requirement of torture.[20]

The act of rape, once it has been proved, necessarily implies the pain or suffering as required by the definition of the crime of torture.[21]

II   Intentional Act or Omission

Most characteristic cases of torture involve positive acts. However, omissions may also provide the requisite material element, provided that the mental or physical suffering caused meets the required level of severity and that the act or omission was intentional, that is an act which, judged objectively, is deliberate and not accidental.[22]

There is an important distinction between 'motivation' and 'intent.' For instance, in torture of sexual nature, the Appeals Chamber has held that even if the perpetrator's motivation is entirely sexual, it does not follow that the perpetrator does not have the intent to commit an act of torture or that his conduct does not cause severe pain and suffering, whether physical or mental, since such pain or suffering is a likely and logical consequence of his conduct. ... In view of the definition, it is important to establish whether a perpetrator intended to act in a way which, in the normal course of events, would cause severe pain and suffering, whether physical or mental, to his victims.[23]

III. Prohibited Purpose

The prohibited purposes listed in the definition of torture 'do not constitute an exhaustive list, and should be regarded as merely representative.'[24]

Humiliation of a victim has been included as a prohibited purpose by some Trial Chambers, while other Trial Chambers have rejected this notion.[25] The Appeals Chamber has not clearly taken a position with respect this question.[26]

19   Kunarac Appeal Judgment, para. 150. In the appellate brief, the Applicant-Accused had argued that the evidence from his expert medical witnesses showed that there were no severe consequences to the victims thereafter.
20   Kvočka Trial Judgment, para. 148.
21   Kunarac Appeal Judgment, para. 151.
22   Čelebići Trial Judgment, para. 468.
23   Kunarac Appeal Judgment, para. 153.
24   Čelebići Trial Judgment, para. 470.
25   Kvočka Trial Judgment, para. 152; Furundžija Trial Judgment, para. 162 (specifically including the humiliation of the victim among the possible purposes of torture). *But see* Krnojelac Trial Judgment, *supra* n. 15, para. 186 (explicitly rejecting the Trial Chamber's dicta in *Kvočka* and *Furundžija*).

Acts need not have been perpetrated solely for one of the purposes prohibited by international law.'[27] According to the Appeals Chamber, 'if one prohibited purpose is fulfilled by the conduct, the fact that such conduct was also intended to achieve a non-listed purpose (even one of a sexual nature) is immaterial.'[28]

The prohibited purpose need not be the predominating purpose.[29]

---

26   The Appeals Chamber endorsed the Trial Chamber definition given in Furundžija. However, the Appeals Chamber has also endorsed a definition given by the Trial Chamber in *Kunarac*, which specifically did not include humiliation of a victim as a prohibited purpose. *See* Furundžija Appeal Judgment, para. 111; Kunarac Appeal Judgment, , paras. 142-144.

27   Kunarac Appeal Judgment, para. 155.

28   Kunarac Appeal Judgment, para. 155.

29   Čelebići Trial Judgment, para. 470; *Prosecutor* v. *Dragoljub Kunarac et al*, Case No. IT-96-23-T & IT 96-23/1-T, 22 February 2001 ('Kunarac Trial Judgment') para. 486. The Appeals Chamber has been silent as to whether the prohibited purpose must be predominating.

6. English Law and Evidence Obtained by Torture: Vindication of Basic Principle or Judicial Abnegation? Implications of *A* v. *Secretary of State for the Home Department.*

Patrick Birkinshaw

> There can be few issues on which international legal opinion is more clear than on the con-
> demnation of torture.[1]

> Unhappily, condemnatory words are not always matched by conduct.[2]

Many of the chapters in this book deal with the question of torture in a philosophical, pragmatic, jurisprudential, socio-cultural or broad contextual sense. The present
chapter deals with a specific point of law raised in the case *A(FC)*[3] but to understand
what was involved in resolving that point of law, it is necessary to outline some features behind the background to present terrorist activity and the UK government's
response to international terrorism. The point of law raised is of vital importance.
Furthermore, if the arguments of Dershowitz are supported, namely as torture is
widely practised in 'civilized states' we should stop being hypocritical and torture
should be made lawful under strict judicial conditions,[4] it would be difficult to see
why the next step should not be taken: that statements extracted by torture should be
admissible in judicial proceedings – the point at issue in *A(FC)*. And if statements,
why not confessions? The universal condemnation of torture since the Second
World War would then count for nothing.[5] Behind the judgment of the appellate
committee of the House of Lords is a warning from Holdsworth: 'Once torture has
become acclimatized in a legal system it spreads like an infectious disease. It saves
the labour of investigation. It hardens and brutalizes those who have become accus-
tomed to use it.'[6]

---

1 *A (FC)* v. *Secretary of State for the Home Department* [2005] UKHL 71 per Lord Bingham
   para. 33.
2 Ibid, per Lord Nicholls para. 67.
3 See note 1 above.
4 A. Dershowitz *Shouting Fire: Civil Liberties in a Turbulent Age* (Boston, Little Brown and
   Company, 2002). The debate about torture is legion but an antidote to Dershowitz is J.
   Waldron's 'Torture and Positive Law: Jurisprudence for the White House' *Columbia Law
   Review* 105 (2005): 1681-1750.
5 See D. M. Rejali *Torture and Democracy* (Princeton, Princeton University Press, 2008).
6 W. F. Holdsworth *History of English Law* (London, Methuen, 1922), vol 5 pp. 194-95.

A. Terrorism in the UK

Despite the long history of Irish Republican terrorism within the United Kingdom it is surprising that the decision in *A(FC)* raised points of law that had not previously been addressed by British or Northern Irish courts. Were statements obtained by torture admissible before a judicial tribunal in the UK? Previous case law and legislation had focused upon the admissibility or otherwise of *confessions* obtained by improper means and s. 76 of the Police and Criminal Evidence Act 1984 excluded such confessions. The situation in *A(FC)* raised the question of the admissibility of evidence from a third party, which had allegedly been obtained by torture overseas without the involvement of British agents and which had been used as intelligence to order executive detention of suspected terrorists within the UK. That novel point had arisen because of the global context in which terrorism operated and because of the contention that national security was now an internationally influenced concern and not simply a national one. That was the result of the House of Lords decision in *Rehman* v. *Secretary of State for the Home Department* which had given a new meaning to terrorism and actions contrary to the interests of national security.[7]

Within this evolving context, governments faced the problem of having within their jurisdiction individuals suspected of terrorist activity who were not citizens of the UK but who could not be deported to their place of origin or elsewhere because of the risk of breaches of the European Convention on Human Rights (ECHR) in the way they would be treated in those countries, specifically torture or inhuman and degrading treatment under Article 3 ECHR. This was the effect of the Strasbourg Court of Human Rights judgment in *Chahal* v. *UK*.[8] There was correspondingly not enough evidence to bring before a criminal court to offer the prospect of a successful prosecution for criminal offences. Forms of executive detention were therefore introduced in the UK under the Anti-terrorism, Crime and Security Act 2001 s.23.[9] It was in procedures leading to such detention before the Special Immigration Appeal Commission (SIAC) that the issue of admissibility of the evidence was called into question.

The present war on terrorism had therefore raised the question of detention and admissibility of evidence. However, the British government had a long history of involvement in counter terrorist activities and the strain that such involvement exerted on values of liberal democratic society and security. The conflict brought about by British involvement in Ireland has a long heritage. Internment (detention without trial) in Northern Ireland was re-introduced between 1971-75 and powers of detention without trial were introduced in 1975;[10] Diplock Courts (a criminal trial without a jury for 'scheduled' offences) operated for over thirty years until 2007.

---

7   [2002] 1 All ER 122 (HL).
8   (1996) 23 EHRR 413 – there was intervention by UK in July 2007 to overrule this decision in *Ramzy* v. *The Netherlands* Application No. 25424/05.
9   Detention followed certification by the Secretary of State under s. 21.
10   Removed by the Northern Ireland (Emergency Provisions) Act 1998 s. 3.

Although the question in *A(FC)* had not been squarely confronted by British courts, the use by British forces and officials of techniques for questioning interned suspects in Northern Ireland had attracted the attention of the European Commission and Court of Human Rights. In *Ireland* v. *UK*[11] five techniques of sensory deprivation practised on internees amounted to degrading and inhumane treatment but, by majority, they did not amount to torture. The former European Commission on Human Rights did establish unanimously that the combination of techniques amounted to torture.

B. Further Developments

Before examining how the operation of procedures introduced in 2001 precipitated the legal challenge in *A(FC)*, some other important developments have to be examined. The UK Security and Intelligence Services had been brought within the remit of statutes beginning in 1989 and continuing with legislation in 1994, 1996 and the Regulation of Investigatory Powers Act 2000. Some limited forms of Parliamentary oversight via the Security and Intelligence Committee were introduced in 1994. Until this legislation, the services operated clandestinely under the royal prerogative with only minimal statements concerning them made to Parliament. Information about operations and identities were strictly prohibited. Under the prerogative, the services as intelligence gathering bodies had no executive powers and the security service acted through the agency of domestic police forces where necessary. As well as allowing some more information to be published about the services, albeit very limited, the legislation was necessary to give the services powers to carry out what would otherwise be unlawful actions, both at home and abroad. In order not to allow the operations of the services to be exposed, evidence obtained by telephone or email intercepts cannot be admitted as evidence in a court of law. The Anti-terrorism, Crime and Security Act 2001 does allow evidence which is otherwise inadmissible to be used in proceedings before SIAC which hears appeals from suspected terrorists and this was seen as crucial in the Court of Appeal judgment in *A(FC)*. This special dispensation was given, as we shall see, a wider significance.

The further development was the decision in *Pinochet (No. 1)*.[12] The case involved the former dictator and president of Chile, Pinochet. As is widely known, a Spanish prosecutor sought his extradition from England to Spain to face various charges covering murder, torture and kidnapping of Spanish citizens resident in Chile during Pinochet's dictatorship. The case made three appearances in the House of Lords. The first case provided a wide ranging judgment to the effect that *ius cogens* (binding and generally accepted norms of international law) and customary in-

---

11 (1978) 2 EHRR 25: these involved 'wall-standing' under stress, hooding, subjection to noise, deprivation of sleep and deprivation of food and drink.
12 *R* v. *Bow Street Metropolitan Stipendiary Magistrate ex p Pinochet Ugarte (No. 1)* [1998] 4 All ER 897 (HL).

ternational law determined that a former head of state could not be immune from prosecution for acts for which he was responsible and which did not form a part of his official functions – immunity only applied to acts performed by him in the exercise of his official functions as a Head of State – acts of torture and hostage taking could not be so regarded. The judgment imposed no limits in relation to the time of Pinochet's lack of immunity while in office. The judgment was nullified by a different panel of the appellate committee of the House of Lords because of the association of one of the judges with a body that had intervened in the case. This was unprecedented. In *Pinochet (No. 3)*,[13] the Law Lords ruled that the combined effect of s.134 Criminal Justice Act 1988[14] and the Convention against Torture meant that there would be no immunity from charges of torture for a former head of state of Chile after Chile signed the Convention in 1988. While many of the offences ruled extraditable in the first hearing were now inoperative, some were still 'live' and Pinochet's extradition was ordered for these offences.[15] Because of intervention by the Home Secretary, he was not, however, extradited to Spain.[16]

C.   Special Immigration Appeals Commission (SIAC)

SIAC was introduced by legislation in 1997 as a response to the decision in *Chahal* by the Court of Human Rights (above).[17] That case centred on the inadequacy of the procedures adopted by the British authorities to determine whether a person whose presence in the UK was deemed not to be conducive to the public good on the grounds of national security should be deported. The procedure amounted to a breach of Art 5(4) ECHR[18] so that Chahal's detention was unlawful. He could not be deported because this would amount to a breach of Art 3 ECHR.[19] The SIAC was influenced to some extent by Canadian procedures. The rules of procedure of SIAC had the imprimatur of no less a figure than Lord Lester QC – a long standing champion of human rights protection. He described them in Parliamentary proceedings as 'a fair compromise' between the liberties of an individual and national security.[20] The Commission is chaired by a High Court judge and since 2001 is a superior court

---

13   *R v. Bow Street Metropolitan Stipendiary Magistrate ex p Pinochet Ugarte (No. 3)* [1999] 2 All ER 97 (HL).

14   S. 134 implemented the Convention against Torture in the UK.

15   [1999] 2 All ER 97 (HL) by virtue of s. 2 Extradition Act 1989.

16   *Pinochet (No. 3)* was distinguished in *Jones* v. *Kingdom of Saudi Arabia* [2006] UKHL 26 when the House of Lords refused to allow the Kingdom of Saudi Arabia and its officials from being sued in civil law in English courts for damages for alleged acts of torture inflicted on British citizens in Saudi Arabia. The court ruled this would be contrary to state immunity.

17   Special Immigration Appeals Commission Act 1997 and the procedural rules contained in SI 1034/2003 and SI 1285/2007.

18   The right to a 'speedy challenge' before a court.

19   T. Poole 'Courts and Conditions of Uncertainty in "Times of Crisis"' LSE Legal Studies Working Paper No. 7/2007.

20   HL Debs. vol 580 cols. 1437-38.

of record. SIAC had been criticized by the House of Lords in *Rehman* for taking too prescriptive an approach when reviewing decisions by the Secretary of State on questions of 'the interests of national security' lying behind a deportation or detention -- this was a matter of judgement peculiarly within the area of expertise of the Secretary of State and those who advised him although a decision could be reviewed on grounds of unfairness or perversity.[21] SIAC's task is to establish: were there reasonable grounds for the Secretary of State's belief or suspicion and *not* whether the latter had made a proper judgement call on what the interests of national security required and what amounted to terrorism? As we shall see below, the procedures in SIAC weigh heavily against the appellant and are heavily compromised because of national security implications. This is common throughout administrative decisions in the war on terror.[22]

The 1997 Act witnessed the introduction of 'special advocates' or counsel to deal with sensitive evidence that could not be disclosed to the suspected terrorist 'deportee'. Special counsel cannot meet or have contact with the 'client' after the special counsel has seen the closed evidence. Although such a meeting was stated to be theoretically possible it was not allowed as a practice. Examination and cross examination of witnesses may take place in the absence of the appellant. The appellant may receive a summary of evidence but this will not include items that should remain 'closed'. The limitations of special counsel procedure from the point of view of fairness were graphically illustrated by Lords Bingham and Steyn in *Roberts* v. *Parole Board*[23] although the two judges were in the minority in the decision. The security and intelligence parties involved in SIAC proceedings operate under internal guidance on what should be disclosed and material helpful to the appellant should be disclosed, but not to the appellant or his lawyers. This self-regulating ordinance operated under the control of one of the parties to the process.[24] SIAC can hear evidence which is not otherwise admissible in legal proceedings.[25] This would

21   [2001] 4 All ER 122 (HL).
22   *R (Gillan)* v. *Commissioner of Metropolitan Police* [2006] UKHL 12 where in making decisions in relation to security and individual liberties Lord Bingham said there are 'what appear to be considered and informed evaluations of the terrorist threat on one side and effectively nothing save a measure of scepticism on the other. There is no basis on which the respondents' (Government's) case can be rejected. This is not a question of deference but of "relative institutional competence"' (at para. 17).
23   [2005] UKHL 45. Lord Woolf ruled use of special counsel in Parole Board hearings was permissible, providing 'If a case arises where it is impossible for the Board both to make use of information that has not been disclosed to the prisoner and, at the same time, protect the prisoner from a denial of his fundamental right to a fair hearing then the rights of the prisoner have to take precedence, but we have not in my view reached the stage in this case where we can say this has happened' (paras. 78 and 62).
24   *A* v. *Secretary of State for the Home Department* [2004] EWCA Civ 1123 per Laws LJ paras. 278-280.
25   SIAC (Procedure) Rules 2003, SI 1034, r. 44(3).

be directed to the exclusion in English law of 'hearsay' evidence in criminal trials.[26] Some of this, however, was the evidence allegedly obtained by torture. An exception was made so that evidence obtained by intercepts was allowed to be heard.[27] The procedures represent an attempted balance between the requirements of justice and fairness and secrecy in the public interest. The names of witnesses or informers or agents or the latter's methods for instance could not be disclosed.

D. Detention and Control Orders

It should be noted that the proceedings in *A(FC)* had been preceded by a decision of the House of Lords concerning the same appellants in which the UK government's post 9/11 reaction to the shocking events in the United States, the Anti-terrorism, Crime and Security Act 2001 s.23 and indefinite detention without trial for being a suspected terrorist had been challenged.[28] This involved an appeal from the decision of SIAC which had allowed the appellants' appeal against detention. The House of Lords in the detention case reversed the Court of Appeal which had upheld the legality of the detentions.[29] The Law Lords declared that s.23 was incompatible with the Convention because it amounted to breaches of Articles 5 (unlawful detention) and 14 (discrimination in enjoyment of protection of rights) of the ECHR on the grounds of proportionality and that they were discriminatory. The orders derogating from Art 5 ECHR were quashed although apart from one judge the Law Lords upheld the Home Secretary's declaration of a state of emergency which was a necessary condition for derogation.

The government's eventual response to this adverse decision on detention was to introduce a regime of control orders (CO) under the Prevention of Terrorism Act 2005. These are subject to the Secretary of State having reasonable grounds for believing that an individual is or has been involved in terrorism related activity and the Secretary of State considers a CO necessary for purposes connected with protecting members of the public from a risk of terrorism. They involve confinement to one's home for a fixed period each day and other restrictions such as electronic tagging. In certain circumstances, the Court of Appeal ruled that they may amount to a breach of Article 5.[30] This ruling on control orders caused the then Home Secretary to suggest that protection of the ECHR should be removed in some areas. If there were a

---

26   Under special circumstances, hearsay may be admitted in criminal trials: ss. 114-118 Criminal Justice Act 2003.
27   RIPA s. 18(1)(e).
28   *A v. Secretary of State for the Home Department* [2004] UKHL 56. These powers were subject to annual renewal. They are now replaced by control orders as explained which are also subject to annual renewal. An independent reviewer is appointed under the Prevention of Terrorism Act to review the operation of the Act.
29   *A v. Secretary of State for the Home Department* [2002] EWCA Civ 1502.
30   *Secretary of State for the Home Department* v. *JJ* [2006] EWCA Civ 1141; see also *Secretary of State for the Home Department* v. *E* [2007] EWHC 233 (Admin)

derogation from the Convention, only the courts could make a control order. Otherwise they are made by the Secretary of State and challengeable in the Administrative Court of the High Court. The Court of Appeal, however, ruled separately that the procedures involved in making control orders, very similar to the SIAC procedures, which used closed evidence which was not shown to the subject of the order and the use of special counsel did not constitute a breach of Article 6 ECHR which provides a right to a fair trial in the determination of one's civil rights.[31] The Administrative Court originally ruled that there had been a breach of Article 6 but was overruled by the Court of Appeal.

The House of Lords subsequently upheld the decision of the Court of Appeal in holding that a non derogating control order of 18 hours did amount to detention and breached Article 5 ECHR.[32]

However, in relation to Article 6, the majority of Law Lords disagreed with the Court of Appeal and were not convinced that the prohibition on disclosing 'closed material' to the subject of a control order would allow a fair procedure to take place within the terms of Article 6 and the civil limb of justice. There may be cases where the use of special advocates and other devices could not overcome a basic lack of fairness.[33] Each case would have to be dealt with carefully to ensure existing procedures comply with fairness and with Article 6.[34] The Council of Europe Commissioner for Human Rights and UK Parliamentary Joint Committee on Human Rights 'had difficulty in accepting that a hearing could be fair if an adverse decision could be based on material that the controlled person had no effective opportunity to challenge or rebut.'[35] Para 4(3)(d) of the Schedule to the 2005 Prevention of Terrorism Act (which requires a court not to order disclosure of material which it would be against the public interest to disclose) should be read and given effect under s.3 HRA 1998[36] 'except where to do so would be incompatible with the right of the controlled person to a fair trial' said Baroness Hale.[37] She emphasized that evidence used against the subject of the order may be obtained by torture and as we shall see the burden is upon the challenger to prove that the evidence was obtained by torture. It is particularly difficult for a person subject to a CO to do this.[38] Intercept material may be used on CO proceedings and the features involved in SIAC proceedings will be present, ie secrecy. At para 66 of her judgment, she gave examples of how the judge and special advocate should stringently test the material and the advocate should be allowed to call witnesses to rebut the closed material noting the tendency

31 *Secretary of State for the Home Department* v. *MB* [2006] EWCA Civ 1140.
32 *Secretary of State for the Home Department* v. *JJ* [2007] UKHL 45.
33 See note 22 above.
34 *Secretary of State for the Home Department* v. *MB (FC)* [2007] UKHL 46. The procedures are in the Prevention of Terrorism Act 2005 Schedule para. 4 and Part 76 CPR.
35 Per Lord Bingham in *MB* at para. 41.
36 Which states that legislation shall be interpreted in so far as this is possible to be consistent with the ECHR.
37 Para. 72.
38 Para. 73.

to over emphasize the claim for secrecy in terrorist cases.[39] Some of these instructions seem to contradict the wording of Civil Procedure Rules 76.25 which govern CO procedures and the Secretary of State can object to the special advocate communicating with the subject of the CO. The case was remitted to the Administrative Court for reconsideration in the light of this guidance.

E.   A(FC) *in SIAC and the Court of Appeal*

Having set the context of the *A(FC)* decision we come to the crucial point of law. Can evidence obtained by torture be admissible before SIAC? SIAC itself decided that torture only went to the 'weight' of evidence, i.e. its reliability, not its admissibility.[40] The Court of Appeal upheld this ruling.[41] The court ruled that there was no precedent against it; the authorities only covered confessions extracted from the defendant. International prohibitions (Art 15 Covenant against Torture (CAT)) concerning non admissibility of evidence extracted by torture) had not been implemented to that extent in domestic law and did not amount to *ius cogens*. SIAC was not in breach of Article 6 ECHR because of the nature of its task – it was not determining a fact: was the detainee a terrorist? It was asking: were there reasonable grounds for the Secretary of State's belief or suspicion that the detainee was a terrorist and his presence in the UK was against the interest of national security? How this can be interpreted as a non judicial act carried out by a judicial tribunal chaired by a High Court judge beggars belief although the criticism of the House of Lords in *Rehman* had emphasized the limits of the capability of SIAC in second guessing judgements about national security. This was noted above. The receipt of evidence by torture was not 'offensive' under Article 6 given the limited nature of the SIAC's review of the Secretary of State's belief or suspicion and its support by 'reasonable grounds'.[42] Article 6 ECHR was not subject to Article 15 CAT because 'a general requirement to interpret Article 6 in harmony with other rules of international law does not make compliance with those other rules a condition of compliance with Article 6.' That, said Laws LJ 'proves too much'.[43] There are objections to these points that were considered by the House of Lords on appeal, and some that were not (see below) but one of the most telling points was raised by Neuberger LJ, the dissenting judge, who saw disparities between the common law and the position under the European Convention in the judgment of the majority:

39   Citing S. Turner and S. Schulhofer *The Secrecy Problem in Terrorism Trials* (New York, Brennan Centre for Justice, NYU School of Law, 2005).
40   29 October 2003. SIAC gives open judgments and closed judgments.
41   *A* v. *Secretary of State for the Home Department* [2004] EWCA Civ 1123: a 2-1 majority decision. The decision was made after the Court of Appeal decision involving detention of the parties involved in A(FC) but before the House of Lords decision reversing the Court of Appeal ruling detention was unlawful.
42   Para. 260.
43   Para. 270.

If my [dissenting] conclusions on the issue so far are correct, they may be said to be somewhat ironic: the common law of England, which has a particularly good record as to the vice of torture since 1640, does not exclude evidence obtained by torture, whereas the law of Europe, where the abolition of torture is rather more recent, would exclude such evidence.[44]

The judgment was met with disbelief, shock and even horror. There was certainly criticism of the majority judgments in the House of Lords but Lord Rodger did spring to the defence of the majority.

F. A (FC) *in the House of Lords.*[45]

The large part of the remainder of my chapter will focus on this immensely important case and the separate judgments of the Law Lords who decided unanimously that such evidence could not be admissible in a judicial forum in the UK.

The appeal was heard by a seven judge panel of the appellate committee (usually it is five) denoting the importance of the question at stake. Can a judicial body receive evidence obtained by torture administered by foreign agents or is it inadmissible under the common law or otherwise? Torture itself was outlawed in 1640 (by implication) and no known warrants had been issued in England by the Crown to extract torture since that date. Although, victims were sent to Scotland after that date to be tortured -- an early form of 'extraordinary rendition' – until cessation of this practice in 1708 after union with England.[46]

There was unqualified criticism by several of the Law Lords of the majority in the Court of Appeal where the matter had been approached as a technical point of evidence and where one might add the matter of substance was defeated by technicalities. 'This condemnation [of torture by the common law] is more aptly categorized as a constitutional principle than as a rule of law' declared Lord Bingham.[47] 'It trivialises the issue ... to treat it as an argument about the law of evidence. The issue is one of constitutional principle.'[48] For Lord Hoffmann: 'Rejection of torture has a constitutional resonance for English people which cannot be overestimated.'[49]

Before examining the arguments under the various heads of law presented to the Law Lords, Lord Bingham noted that since 2001 SIAC had been a superior court of record by virtue of amendments introduced by the Anti-terrorism etc Act. The fact

44   Para. 474
45   [2005] UKHL 71.
46   S. 5 Treason Act 1708 disallowed admission of confessions extracted by torture. The UK Joint Parliamentary Committee on Security and Intelligence has reported on *Rendition* Cm 7171 (2007) Government Response Cm 7172 and *The Handling of Detainees by UK Intelligence Personnel in Afghanistan, Guantanamo Bay and Iraq* Cm 6469 (2005) and Government Response Cm 6511.

47   Para. 12.
48   Lord Bingham at para. 52.
49   Para. 93.

that the majority of the Court of Appeal therefore ruled that SIAC was not a judicial body for the purposes of Article 6 ECHR is remarkable. The argument as to the inadmissibility of such evidence was made under three heads: common law, the ECHR and international law.

I. The Common Law

The common law had long established that statements by an accused are inadmissible if improperly obtained: the common law authority is *Ibrahim* v. R^{50} although there are numerous examples and ss. 76 and 78 Police and Criminal Evidence Act 1984 have confirmed the route taken by the common law in legislation. The latter section does provide a *discretion* to exclude evidence where in all the circumstances its admission would have such an adverse effect on the fairness of proceedings that the court ought not to admit it.[51] But this would not apply to inadmissible evidence – the very question at issue in *A(FC)*. What the House of Lords noted, unlike the Court of Appeal, was that the question had not been tested in English courts (unlike confessions) because evidence of statements of others was hearsay and thereby inadmissible in any event. The rules of criminal evidence in English law prevented the issue from being discussed until SIAC was allowed to hear evidence which was otherwise inadmissible. How, asked Lord Bingham, could evidence obtained by torture be admissible when common lawyers regarded torture as 'totally repugnant to the fundamental principles of the common law' and as a creature of royal prerogative. It was a 'revolting brutality of the [erstwhile] continental criminal procedure'.[52] This sounds admirable, but punishment ordered by common law courts could have amounted to torture or at least inhumane and degrading treatment until comparatively recently even though the Bill of Rights 1688 prohibited 'cruel and unusual punishment'. Flogging may have been cruel but it was not unusual. For Lords Hope and Carswell, if the position re statements was not authoritatively stated as inadmissible, it was a 'small but certain step' and a 'modest but logical extension' of the rule against admitting confessions' obtained by torture.[53] The House of Lords is to be applauded for placing a prohibition on the reception of statements obtained by torture in judicial proceedings and for re-asserting the common law repugnance of torture. More widely still, courts have a discretion, which they must exercise, to prevent an abuse of their process brought about by a threat to basic human rights or the rule of law.[54] The judgment is a fitting tribute to the judicial development of the

---

50 [1914] AC 599 (PC).
51 D. Ormerod and D. Birch 'The Evolution of the Discretionary Exclusion of Evidence' *Criminal Law Review* (2004): 767-788.
52 Lord Bingham, para. 12 citing W. F. Holdsworth *History of English Law*, (3rd ed., 1945) vol. 5 pp. 194-195.
53 Paras. 110 and 152 respectively.
54 *R* v. *Horseferry Road Magistrates Court ex p Bennett* [1994] 1 AC 42 at 61-62. In *R (Ramda)* v. *Secretary of State for the Home Department* [2002] EWHC (Admin) 1278 extradition to

'common law of human rights'. However, the judgment leaves many holes in the common law as we shall see.

II. The European Convention on Human Rights

Several of the judgments presume that the Court of Human Rights (CHR) at Strasbourg which adjudicates on claims to breaches of the ECHR against member states of the Council of Europe would reject such evidence. Lord Bingham's judgment gives this subject the fullest analysis. In *Soering* v. *UK*[55] the CHR described Article 3 and its absolute prohibition of torture as 'one of the fundamental values of the democratic societies making up the Council of Europe.' But the issue was whether Article 6 would be breached by admitting such evidence. Would it be a denial of a fair hearing? The Convention against Torture is emphatic in its denunciation of torture as is the CHR; would the CHR be any less so in such a case as the present under Article 6, queried Lord Bingham? For the point is that the issue has not as of writing been dealt with directly by the CHR. 'Had the CHR found (in *Harutyunyan* v. *Armenia*[56]) that the complaints of coercion and torture appeared to be substantiated, a finding that Article 6(1) had been violated would .. have been inevitable'.[57] But there is no authority on the question. The Jalloh case[58] left the issue open, even if it seems clear that torture will more or less automatically invalidate the use of the information as evidence under the Convention. The issue is however squarely before the court in the *Gäfgen* case.[59] The Convention itself had to be interpreted under relevant rules of international law applicable in the relations of the parties (Vienna Convention Art 31(3)(c)). One of these would be the Convention against Torture. This was the very point rejected by the majority of the Court of Appeal.

III. Public International Law

The third ground of attack lay under public international law. Lord Bingham's judgment in particular is an articulate and glowing tribute to the universal condemnation of torture and again he dealt most extensively with the discussion on this point under international law. The other judges concentrated on the common law.

France was resisted where it was alleged that evidence to be admitted against R in France had been obtained by torture. The principle also covers prosecuting authorities: *R (CH Research & Campaign against Arms Trade)* v. *Director SFO and BAE Systems* [2008] EWHC 714 (Admin.).
55   (1989) 11 EHRR 439.
56   App. No. 36549/03 (5 July 2005).
57   Lord Bingham, para. 26.
58   *Jalloh* v. *Germany* App. No. 54810/00 (11 July 2006). See I. Cameron 'European Court of Human Rights: April 2006 – March 2007' *European Public Law* (2007) 533-568.
59   Application (pending); see decision for App. No. 22978/05 (10 April 2007).

The 'prohibition of torture enjoys the highest normative force recognised by international law.'[60] It is present in the UN Declaration on Human Rights, the International Covenant on Civil and Political Rights and the Convention Against Torture including Art 15 which requires the exclusion of statements made as a result of torture as evidence in *any* proceedings. The UN Resolution on Prohibition concerns evidence and not just confessions. The language of international law is not simply the prohibition of torture but the full implementation of legislative, judicial and administrative means to suppress it and any encouragement to it. 'States must act positively to suppress torture'.

Lord Bingham accepted that outlawing torture was *ius cogens* – peremptory norms of behaviour deemed to be worthy of a special status because of their importance.[61] Even the Court of Appeal decision acknowledged such a status[62] but that court would not hear an argument about Article 15 CAT being a principle of customary international law and therefore applicable in domestic proceedings because it had not been raised as an argument before SIAC or in the appeal. But Bingham also accepted that the *ius cogens* nature of the norm also forbade the use of evidence obtained by torture.

In assessing the impact of these international developments on English law and on the European Convention, Bingham was at his most creative and helped in drawing new inspiration from international legal principles for the development of the common law in particular. Both the common law and ECHR should and would be developed and influenced under international law. English law has traditionally been firmly based on a dualist tradition in relation to international law and municipal law. They operate in different spheres affecting parties in different ways. International norms cannot be binding in municipal law unless implemented by municipal law or have effect unless they are accepted as principles of customary international law or as part of *ius cogens*.[63] There was a very important practical consequence of this duality when it came to interpreting domestic statutes in England. The orthodox position could be summed up by saying that a treaty could be examined in order to interpret an implementing statute that was unclear or ambiguous and where the treaty might confer that clarity or assist in establishing it.[64] The more recent approach, one would not refer to it as apostasy but it is certainly not conventional, is that a judge should not interpret a statute in a manner inconsistent with treaty obligations where such an interpretation was possible. If more than one interpretation is possible, adopt that which fulfils international obligations.

In *A(FC)* the appellants 'rely on the well established principle that the words of a UK statute, passed after the date of a Treaty and dealing with the same subject mat-

---

60   Para. 28.
61   Vienna Convention Art 53: *Prosecutor* v. *Furundzija* [1998] ICTY 3 (International Criminal Tribunal for the former Yugoslavia).
62   Paras. 112 and 267.
63   The precise scope of customary international law is subject to qualifications.
64   *J. Buchanan & Co. Ltd* v. *Babco etc Ltd* [1978] AC 141 (HL). The case law also discussed *travaux préparatoires*.

ter, are to be construed, if they are reasonably capable of bearing such a meaning, as intended to carry out the treaty obligation and not to be inconsistent with it'.[65] This is not confined to implementing measures and nor to provisions that are unclear or ambiguous but where more than one interpretation is possible – a frequent occurrence in legislation. The universal condemnation of torture and the use of evidence obtained by torture enshrined in these international norms set the context in which the domestic legislation had to be interpreted.

> I am startled, even a little dismayed, at the suggestion (and acceptance by CA majority) that this deeply rooted tradition and an international obligation solemnly and explicitly undertaken can be overridden by a statute and a procedural rule which make no mention of torture at all.[66]

For Lord Hoffmann, a power to admit evidence obtained by torture would have to be given *expressly* in primary legislation so that Parliament could be notified and debate the point.[67] Were Parliament to authorize such a development in flagrant breach of international law it would doubtless put the doctrine of Parliamentary sovereignty under the severest of scrutiny. But in reality that would seem to be an event for a class-room discussion and not a prospect that we would face. It has come close to occurring in the USA where the President vetoed a bill outlawing use of waterboarding and other practices. In setting up SIAC to act 'like a court' and to review the Secretary of State's decision Parliament expected it to act like a court, said Lord Hoffmann.[68] For him, it had become a general rule that evidence obtained by torture was inadmissible.[69]

All the judges therefore condemned torture and the use of statements obtained by torture although Lord Rodger said he found the case very difficult because of the nature of decision-making by the Secretary of State and SIAC and not because he did not share the revulsion of torture.[70]

The judgments nonetheless leave many questions unresolved and which are examined below.

G. Problems?

There are several difficulties resulting from *A(FC)*.

---

65   Para. 27 citing *Garland* v. *British Rail Engineering Ltd* [1983] 2 AC 751, 771.
66   Lord Bingham, para. 51.
67   Para. 96, and see Lord Rodger, para. 137.
68   Para. 95.
69   Para. 97.
70   Para. 129.

I.   The use of statements obtained by torture by the executive in non judicial processes, or to defend itself against an allegation of unlawful action.

Such statements may not be used to establish guilt or innocence but, Lord Nicholls believed, they could be used to defend officials against an allegation of unlawful action (for example, if the police were sured for wrongful arrest and some of the information on which they had acted had been obtained by torture) although public interest immunity may require the information be kept secret.[71] Information obtained by torture can still be used providing it is not led or used directly in evidence before a judicial tribunal. But using such evidence to defend actions one took would be direct use. Could such evidence be used by the executive to issue a control order, or to make an order for deportation such as *Rehman* above? Lord Hope believed the answer to this is for another day – it was not ruled out. Lord Hoffmann said:

> It is not the function of the courts to place limits upon the information available to the Secretary of State, particularly when he is concerned with national security. Provided that he acts lawfully, he may read whatever he likes. In his dealings with foreign governments, the type of information that he is willing to receive and the questions that he asks or refrains from asking are his own affair.[72]

The answer seems to be 'Yes' and Lord Rodger answers this point affirmatively[73] pointing out that a Secretary of State's certificate of suspected terrorism under s.21 of the Anti-terrorism etc Act 2001 may last for six months if no appeal is made and until SIAC reviews the certificate under s.26(1). In other words Parliament allowed a significant period of detention in the absence of an appeal. Lord Brown also answers the question affirmatively.[74] But they would not be admissible before a judicial body. Nothing seems to prevent them being used by lawyers in a way that intercept intelligence is used: the intelligence cannot be admitted but it will be used to formulate the argument and assist the case. Foreign intercepts incidentally are not inadmissible.[75] Indeed, Lord Brown was at pains to point out that the decision would not undermine the fight against terrorism.

> Your Lordships' decision on these appeals should not be seen as a significant setback to the [executive's] necessary efforts to combat terrorism. Rather it confirms the right of the executive to act on whatever information it may receive from around the world, while at the same time preserving the integrity of the judicial process and vindicating the good name of British justice.[76]

This brings into focus the role of the intelligence and security services which I address below.

---

71   Para. 72
72   Para. 93
73   Paras. 132-133.
74   Para. 169.
75   *R* v. *P* [2001] 2 All ER 58 (HL).
76   Para. 171.

II. Could evidence obtained as a result of the torture apart from statements and confessions be used in judicial proceedings?

This is graphically known as the fruits of the poisoned tree doctrine. In the USA the fourth amendment to the constitution has been used to exclude such evidence. In England, the approach has not been as restrained and evidence illegally obtained may be admitted if it is relevant.[77] English law places ultimate reliance upon the probative quality of the evidence. Here we have the topic so beloved by supporters of torture; finding the ticking bomb after a statement by a third party or accused extracted by torture? Finding finger prints upon the bomb and using that evidence. How independent is the evidence of the torture? How tainted is it by the 'corruption and stench of torture'? How far removed is it from the core evidence which is inadmissible – the confession or statements of a third party? There is a reason to regard it as a duty of states, save perhaps in limited and exceptional circumstances, as where immediately necessary to protect a person from unlawful violence or property from destruction, to reject the fruits of torture inflicted in breach of international law, said Bingham.[78] So his powerful judgment acknowledges exceptions.[79] Could the police implead such evidence to make an arrest and defend an allegation of false arrest in a court? Lord Brown (a former treasury counsel ie advocate for government) was clear that the 'forbidden fruits' may be used, as were Lords Hope and Hoffmann.

III. The burden of proving torture.

This is absolutely crucial. The procedures involving control orders as well as proceedings before SIAC which use closed material and special advocates should be recalled and the difficulty in which the appellant is placed. Given the circumstances it is not a procedure in which all the cards are face up. Much of the evidence would not be seen by the appellant or his lawyers. Nonetheless, the majority decided that the burden of proving torture lies on the appellant. The judges concluded differently on the reliance to be placed on two cases in which this question was relevant. One came from Germany[80] where evidence was admitted even although the United States officials refused to give evidence of interrogation practices conducted by them. The other was a decision of the Strasbourg Court of Human Rights *Mamatkulov and Asharav* v. *Turkey* which dealt with related themes where a breach of Article 3 ECHR was not found when a receiving state made assurances about treatment despite widely recorded evidence of torture.[81] The court could not make a finding of

---

77 *R* v. *Sargent* [2001] UKHL 54.
78 At para. 34. And paras. 46, 47.
79 S. 76 Police and Criminal Evidence Act 1984 provides that evidence may be admitted under s. 76(4) where a confession is excluded.
80 *El Motassadeq* NSW 2005 2326 (Hamburg).
81 CHR App. Nos. 46827/99 and 46591/99 (4 February 2005).

fact but placed its emphasis on Uzbekistan's assurances. One finds it difficult not to side with Bingham in his criticism of the reliance of the majority on these cases both of which he felt to be of 'questionable value' at best.[82]

The minority (and incidentally the three most senior judges) Bingham, Nicholls and Hoffmann – agreed that the Secretary of State must show that once it is alleged that evidence was obtained by torture, he must establish that it was not. It would be absurd to require the appellant to prove that evidence was obtained by torture when he knows little of the evidence against him.[83] 'If SIAC is unable to conclude that there is not a real risk that the evidence has been obtained by torture, it should refuse to admit the evidence.'[84] Lord Hope's test is said Bingham, a test which in the real world can never be satisfied.[85] Hope's test runs as follows: 'Is it *established,* by means of such diligent unquiries into the sources that it is practicable to carry out and on a balance of probabilities, that the information relied on by the Secretary of State *was* obtained under torture?'[86] The court should not set up 'insuperable barrier[s]' to the use of information from foreign regimes. To trigger the exclusion, it must be shown that the statement in question was obtained by torture – I repeat on a balance of probabilities. For Lord Rodger the statement must be shown (by the appellant) to have been obtained by torture.[87] Lord Carswell said: 'If SIAC is unable to conclude that there is not a real risk that the evidence has been obtained by torture, it should refuse to admit the evidence.'[88] The onus of proving torture was on the appellant and the quantum appears to be 'a balance of probabilities'.

SIAC should make its own inquiries where the appellant raised plausible reason for thinking that a statement was obtained by torture. This was a crucial point in *Othman* v. *Secretary of State*[89] where the Court of Appeal discussed what 'diligent enquiries' by SIAC entailed. The Court of Appeal held that this duty of inquiry had not been properly discharged by SIAC in a situation where the appellant would have faced so many barriers to establishing the test.[90]

The Court of Appeal ruled that a Jordanian, Mr Othman, could not be deported to Jordan where he would face terrorist charges on the grounds that his presence in the UK represented a threat to national security. The court accepted that it was open to SIAC to find that the appellant would not be ill-treated in Jordan, based on a memorandum of understanding between the Kingdom of Jordan and the UK that Jordan would desist from such treatment.[91] Nor was he likely to be tried by a court – the

---

82   Paras. 54-60.
83   Lord Hoffmann, para. 98.
84   Lord Bingham, para. 56
85   Para. 59.
86   Para. 121, but see paras. 116-122.
87   Para. 138.
88   Para. 156.
89   [2008] EWCA Civ 290.
90   *Othman,* para. 61; and see para. 439 of SIAC's decision.
91   Such agreements had passed judicial scrutiny in the case of Algeria but had been ruled invalid in relation to Libya.

Jordanian State Security Court (SSC) – that was not independent and impartial.[92] But the Court of Appeal differed from SIAC in its finding that SIAC applied an 'insufficiently demanding test to determine the issue of whether Article 6 rights would be breached' by the SSC hearing evidence obtained by torture.[93] The SIAC had misunderstood and misinterpreted the speeches of the law lords in *A(FC)* and had placed mistaken reliance upon the case. SIAC had not satisfied itself by proper enquiry that evidence obtained in breach of a fundamental principle of the Convention would not be acted upon by the SSC. The outcome of such admission would 'constitute a total denial of justice in *Soering* terms'.[94] In short, the SIAC had not paid sufficient regard to the *constitutional* and *fundamental* nature of the ruling in *A(FC)*. The test set by the Court of Appeal is very high and given the tone of the majority decision on this point is surprising. They seem to have placed the threshold higher than the majority in *A(FC)*.

However expressed, the burden is on the person alleging torture. We shall have to see whether the higher courts adopt as strict a test on the nature of SIAC's inquiries as the Court of Appeal.

IV   What amounts to torture?

The question of what amounts to torture was addressed by the judgment. There is not the immediacy of the red hot poker and the pliers but there are well documented practices which are barbaric. A major plank in America's war on terror involved clear breaches of the prohibition of inhuman and degrading treatment and even torture. George Bush's has famously called for 'unprecedented severity' in the methods of interrogation. There was a statutory redefinition of torture and authorized techniques.[95] The President in 2008 vetoed an Interrogation Authorization Bill outlawing 'specialized techniques' and which would have restricted interrogation to those in the Army Field Manual. The legal justification and argument from officials supporting such practices as legal within existing restraints were farcical were it not so desperately serious an issue. It had the stench of perversion and lickspittle.

Does inhuman and degrading treatment automatically exclude statements in the way torture would? Bingham said there is a difference in quality but lesser may become the greater over time and would thereby become excluded. Otherwise such evidence is subject to ss 76 and 78 Police and Criminal Evidence Act. Hoffmann believed the interrogation techniques in *Ireland* v. *UK* (above) would meet the defini-

---

92   See *Soering* v. *UK,* (1989) 11 EHRR 439.
93   *Othman,* para. 46.
94   Ibid., para. 41.
95   P. Sands, *Torture Team: Deception, Cruelty and the Compromise of Law* (London, Penguin, 2008); P. Gourevitch and E. Morris *Standard Operating Procedure: A War Story* (London, Pan Macmillan, 2008). M. Lazreg, *Torture and the Twilight of Empire* (Princeton, Princeton University Press, 2008).

tion of torture set out in s.134 Criminal Justice Act: severe pain and suffering administered by officials in the exercise of their duties or purported duties and these would be unlawful and inadmissible. But not *all* conduct ruled against Article 3 in *Ireland* would be caught by s.134, he believed.

Lord Hope saw the distinction as 'fluid' but 'we should apply the standards that we wish to apply to our own citizens and not accept a foreign definition'. US practices, he exclaimed 'shock the conscience'.[96]

V.. Intelligence and the secret services.

This is the most important dimension to the war on terror. The Crown accepted that any British agents using torture would be acting unlawfully and the evidence would be inadmissible before judicial hearings. The question was to what extent this prohibition affected foreign security and intelligence services. The security and intelligence communities are networked like ground elder. And as Lord Hope observed: 'Information – the gathering of intelligence – is a crucial weapon in the battle by democracies against international terrorism.'[97]

It was noted above that secret intelligence services in the UK had been placed under a legislative framework since the late 1980s. There is oversight by the Intelligence and Security Committee established under the Intelligence Services Act 1994 which is a joint committee of both houses of Parliament (members are 'notified' under the Official Secrets Act 1989 (OSA) s.1 so they are subject to the absolute duty of secrecy under that Act (below)). Information may be refused by service chiefs if it is deemed 'sensitive' (Sch 3(4)), or it may be refused on the determination of the Secretary of State. Sensitive includes that which is about operations, which might lead to the identity of the provider or is provided by foreign government or its agency and it does not consent although the Secretary of State may override this if 'desirable in the public interest'. The Prime Minister may exclude matters from being published in annual reports published by the committee under s.10(7) after consulting the committee.

The OSA s.1 places an absolute prohibition on disclosure by security and intelligence officers and others who are 'notified' by a Minister of information from their work and about the special investigation powers in s.4(3) – intercepts, entering property etc. The House of Lords ruled in Shayler[98] that s.1 OSA did not constitute a breach of Art 10 ECHR – the free speech provision. Secrecy for intelligence gatherers was necessary and not disproportionate and there were a variety of internal and external mechanisms through which a security or intelligence officer could raise

96   *A (FC)*, para. 126.
97   Ibid., para. 105.
98   [2002] 2 All ER 477 (HL). The courts have ruled that under civil law, security and intelligence officers are under a 'life-long' duty of confidence: *Attorney General* v. *Blake* [2001] 1 AC 268.

their concerns. 'Whistleblowing' is not necessary and the members of the services are not protected by the legislation that introduced whistleblowing into UK law, the Public Interest Disclosure Act 1998. Ultimately, a refusal to allow publication by the authorities of the disclosure of an officer may be challenged by judicial review.

Finally, under Freedom of Information Act 2000 in the UK, the security and intelligence services and GCHQ are *excluded* from the statutory provisions on access to information held by public authorities. An absolute exemption protects their information from disclosure when it is held by another public body. In other words, neither officials nor the Information Commissioner can order disclosure in 'the public interest'.

As one imagines the position is cocooned in secrecy without any effective outlet for an officer troubled by what he or she knows about the provenance of intelligence and how it was extracted.

The Butler Report on the use of intelligence and weapons of mass destruction in Iraq was not dealing with the problem of torture but the manipulation and malleability of intelligence for political purposes.[99] If intelligence is to be used more widely by governments in public debate, its uses and limitations must be carefully explained and there must be clearer division between assessment and advocacy.[100] Nonetheless, there were some compelling conclusions on the uses of intelligence. There were world-wide networks of intelligence communities but procedures are 'still not sufficiently aligned to match the threat'.[101]

> These limitations [in intelligence transforming mysteries into knowable secrets] are best offset by ensuring that the ultimate users of intelligence, decision makers at all levels, properly understand its strengths and limitations and have the opportunity to acquire experience in handling it. It is not easy to do this while preserving the security of sensitive sources and methods. But unless intelligence is properly handled at this final stage, all preceding effort and expenditure is wasted.[102]

Does the 'proper handling' of intelligence include use of that by the UK executive which has been procured by torture, no matter how unreliable? The answer from *A(FC)* appears to be 'yes'.

H.   Some comparisons between the UK and USA courts in the war on terror

There is a self congratulatory tone in some of the judgments in *A(FC)* about the virtues of British justice but the general condemnation of torture by the law lords was

---

99   Lord Butler (Chair), *Review of Intelligence on Weapons of Mass Destruction* (HC 898, London, The Stationery Office, 2004).
100   Ibid., para. 468.
101   Ibid., para. 136
102   Ibid., para. 52.

114

nonetheless invigorating. The case also has to be seen in company with its predecessor *A etc* in which detentions under s.23 Anti-terrorism etc Act were declared unlawful and the more recent control order case in which the law lords ruled very strictly on the fairness of control order procedures.[103] It has displayed the appellate committee of the House of Lords as a robust tribunal defending human rights and civil liberties. The Human Rights Act has been a central feature in that defence. This deserves applause.

Until the judgment in *Boumediene* by the Supreme Court (below) the position compared very favourably to the role of US courts and their relationship to oversight of executive powers in the war on terror and the President's promotion of legislation to enhance the executive primacy, to exclude the role of the ordinary courts in oversight of executive detentions and to have cases heard before military commissions. I can only make fleeting references to this widely reported saga. Although *Hamdi* v. *Rumsfeld*[104] and *Rasul et al* v. *Bush*[105] supported the application of habeas corpus following executive detentions, the justifications required by the courts from the executive were criticized for requiring only the thinnest of evidence.[106]

The Military Commissions Act 2006 provides for military commissions to try 'enemy unlawful combatants' and prohibits challenge in ordinary courts of matters before military commissions and any use of the Geneva Conventions before a court proceeding seeking habeas corpus. The MCA makes clear that statements procured by torture are inadmissible. Statements produced by treatment 'short of torture' can be admitted if a military judge finds that 'the totality of the circumstances renders the statement reliable and possessing sufficient probative value; and the interests of justice would best be served by admission of the statement into evidence.'[107]

After an initial refusal to hear the case challenging the constitutionality of the Act, the Supreme Court ruled that an appeal concerning this legislation would be heard. Commentators were sanguine that the court would rule that a constitutional right to habeas corpus applies in such cases but the procedure before the Commissions and the right of appeal to the 'DC circuit' may satisfy those requirements. Furthermore, the view has been expressed that the MCA will have successfully excluded the operation of the Geneva Convention in Commission hearings.[108] The Supreme Court, however, ruled that the MCA had not removed the right of those detained in Guantanamo to seek habeas corpus before the federal courts and the inadequate and ineffective procedures in use before the Commissions meant the MCA op-

---

103 See n. 34 above.

104 542 US 507 (2004).

105 542 U. S. 466 (2004).

106 There was greater sophistication shown in *Hamdan* v. *Rumsfeld* 126 S. Ct. 2749 (2006) where the Supreme Court held that the Geneva Convention was not removed in hearings before military commissions and the federal courts' jurisdiction was not removed by the Detainee Treatment Act 2005.

107 S. 948r.

108 C. Bradley 'The Military Commissions Act, Habeas Corpus, and the Geneva Conventions' Duke Law School Working Paper No. 96/2007.

erated as an 'unconstitutional suspension of the writ'.[109] The 5-4 judgment has done much to repair the reputation of the judicial branch in the USA and its vindication of the rule of law.

Conclusion

Despite its limitations *A(FC)* will doubtless be added to the lexicon of great statements of principle from the courts in protecting the individual against arbitrary action. It stands beside the *Public Committee against Torture in Israel* case[110] where interrogation techniques based on torture and inhumane treatment were outlawed and where the court noted:

> Although a democracy must often fight with one hand tied behind its back, it nonetheless has the upper hand. Preserving the rule of law and recognition of an individual's liberty constitutes an important component in its understanding of security. At the end of the day, they strengthen its spirit and allow it to overcome its difficulties.

Committee against Torture left open the necessity argument to justify torture which did not apply in that case. Despite its great constitutional resonance, *A(FC)* has left largely unchanged the reliance by 'civilized governments' on intelligence extracted by torture. Indeed, the government according to the judgment of some of the Law Lords would be in denial of a fundamental duty of preserving national security were it to ignore such intelligence. The chances of such evidence being admitted before judicial proceedings in the UK depends upon whether the stringent test of the Court of Appeal in *Othman* is upheld by the House of Lords and on whether the self denying ordinance of the Home Secretary not knowingly to use such material as *evidence* is maintained.[111] The eradication of the wider practice of using such intelligence to survey, investigate, detain and question is beyond the capability of judicial bodies.[112] Indeed the widespread blanket of secrecy which protects intelligence and security would prevent their effective challenge in any representative forum. Life-saving information may be obtained. Is torture a price worth paying in the war

---

109 *Boumediene* et al. v. *Bush* et al. 128 S.Ct. 2229, 171 L.Ed.2d 41 (2008)
110 *Public Committee against Torture in Israel* v. *State of Israel* (1999) 7 BHRC 31 (Supreme Court, Israel) para. 39.
111 That, said Lord Hoffmann, is a policy, not a rule of law: *A(FC)* para. 90.
112 The use of intelligence obtained by torture puts the efforts by Mr Blair and Mr Brown's governments to extend pre-charge detention in the case of suspected terrorists beyond 28 days into perspective. In *R (Binyan Mohamed)* v. *Secretary of State for Foreign Affairs* [2008] EWHC 2048 and 2100 (Admin) the Divisional Court ruled that the claimant,who was a detainee in Guantanamo Bay and who had been subject to torture, was entitled, subject to any public interest immunity pleas, to documents in the possession of the Foreign Office which were relevant to his trial before the US Military Commission outlined above. This was despite the vehement protests of the US government.

against terrorism – a war that seeks to uphold civilized standards and the integrity of the individual?

7. Bush II's Constitutional and Legal Theory: The Constitution of Emergency between Law and Propaganda

Agustín José Menéndez

> Sometimes ... the values to be secured by the genuine Rule of Law and authentic constitutional government are best served by departing, temporarily but perhaps drastically, from the law and the Constitution. Since such occasions call for that awesome responsibility and most measured practical reasonableness which we call statesmanship, one could say nothing that may appear to be a key to identifying the occasion or a guide to acting in it.
>
> John Finnis, *Natural Law and Natural Rights*

> The problem is not renegade actors; the problem, frankly, is renegade lawyers.
>
> Philippe Sands debating John Yoo

A.   Introduction

This chapter analyses the positive and theoretical aspects of the doctrine of constitutional law put forward by the administration of Bush II since the terrorist attacks of September 11th 2001. The chapter is divided into four parts. First, I claim that Bush II's doctrine of constitutional law can be identified by reference to the four amendments to the positive constitutional law of the United States his lawyers have advocated and relied upon when offering legal advice.[1] It has been claimed that the President can establish in a definitive and final manner who poses a threat to national security and deny her some key constitutional rights; in particular her rights to liberty, privacy, life and physical integrity, as the President can order their indefinite arrest, warrantless surveillance, assassination or torture. Second, I maintain that all these amendments are to be understood as the rather consistent application of Bush II's theory of constitutional law, which affirms that there are two US constitutions (one applicable to 'ordinary' citizens and circumstances, the other to enemies and 'emergency' or 'exceptional' circumstances) and that international norms other than bilateral treaties are not real law. Third, I submit that changes in positive constitutional law and in constitutional theory are underpinned by an eclectic, minimalist and decisionistic theory of law, which denies any structural relationship between law and public reason. The minimalism of Bush II's legal theory accounts for the fact

---

1   By the phrases 'Bush II's lawyers' or the 'court lawyers of Bush II', I make reference to the main legal architects of the four constitutional amendments described in section I and in particular to David Addington, Alberto Gonzales, James Bybee, Jack Goldsmith, John Yoo and William Haynes II.

that it relies on an 'overlapping consensus' of three different mainstream legal theories (originalism à la Scalia, 'modern' natural law à la Finnis, and pragmatism à la Posner). Fourth, it seems to me that there are very good reasons to take very seriously the consequences of Bush II's constitutional doctrine and theory, but that should not entail considering them as serious legal and political theories. They have been intended as part and parcel of the propaganda effort to transform constitutional practice. This should make us reflect on the structural similarities between Bush II's constitutional and legal theories and the strategic legal advice characteristically provided by the attorneys of mafia dons and by the 'court lawyers' of Fascist states, all of whom area keen on instrumentalising the form of law at the service of raw power.

B. The four constitutional amendments of Bush II

Bush II has tried to alter key aspects of US constitutional law so as to expand executive power to the detriment of other institutions and decision-making process.[2] Such changes have resulted in a constitutional doctrine which seriously infringes the rights to freedom, privacy, physical integrity and life of both non-citizens and citizens, and openly infringes international legal standards.

The four constitutional amendments described below are said to temporary and narrow deviations from ordinary constitutional standards exclusively applicable to 'enemy combatants'. However, it would be wrong to take such characterization at its face value. On the one hand, the affirmation that the 'war on terror' is a 'long war' which will last for at least one generation[3] implies that the changes could be as permanent as formal amendments to the Constitution. On the other hand, the term 'enemy combatant' designates anybody deemed by the President to be a threat to US national security.[4] The vagueness of the standard and the lack of any review whatsoever render fully uncertain who would be fall under the description.

All four amendments are defended on three concurrent grounds, namely: (1) a 'dogmatic' interpretation of the legal texts, based on the search for the 'literal' and 'original' meaning of the provisions; (2) peculiar normative arguments which focus on the morality of acting unmorally under extreme circumstances; (3) prudential arguments, concerning the consequences of interpreting constitutional norms one way

---

2   The best overall description is to be found in C. Savage, *Takeover* (Boston, Little, Brown & Co., 2007).
3   By declaring 'war on global terror' and defining the scope as to stop and defeat 'every terrorist group of global reach', Bush II clearly indicated that the war on terror was bound to be a very long war. See Address to a Joint Session of Congress and the American People, 20 September 2001, available at http://www.whitehouse.gov/news/releases/2001/09/20010920-8.html.
4   A comprehensive analysis of how the category has been defined by the Bush II Administration can be found in P. J. Honigsberg, 'Chasing 'Enemy Combatants' and Circumventing International Law: A Licence for Sanctioned Abuse' *UCLA Journal of International Law and Foreign Affairs* (2007): 1-74.

or the other in the 'post 9/11' world in which we are 'one bomb away' from disaster. While the specific dogmatic arguments employed vary from one amendment to the other, in all cases Bush II's lawyers rely on close readings of the literal tenor of legal provisions and make extensive (and exclusive) use legislative materials, while teleological arguments and systemic interpretation are formally discarded. This results in wider discretion for the interpreter. As regards normative arguments, two are frequently invoked. The first goes that the legality and morality of given acts cannot be determined during emergencies by reference to what positive law prescribes, but by the 'practical' judgment of leaders. In brief, not only *inter armas silent leges*, but *inter armas silent mores*. The second is that the existential threat to the political community posed by terrorism entitles the political community to deny all rights to those (generally, aliens) who make use of such rights to threaten the life of the republic. The typical prudential argument is that the nature of the 'new' terrorist threat requires replacing criminal procedure, with its simultaneous affirmation of liberty to do wrong and retroactive punishment, with 'preemptive' justice, aimed at rendering impossible the commission of the crime. This entails that constitutional rights should be redefined (and weakened) so as to render possible the efficient gathering of information from suspected terrorists.[5]

Before considering Bush II's constitutional amendments in detail, it is important to notice that the radical character of his constitutional agenda stems from the fact that it aims at changing the very content of constitutional law. We are not dealing with unconstitutional acts undertaken in the 'dark side'; what we face is the explicit promotion of the 'dark side' to constitutional normality.[6] There is a world of difference between the two projects.

I.   No habeas corpus for enemy combatants

Bush II's first constitutional amendment affirms the inherent power of the President to order the detention of any person (including a US citizen), who has been previously certified as an enemy combatant. The decision of the President to either confine enemies within military facilities in the United States, or order their transfer to a location abroad is final and cannot be reviewed by any other institution or decision-making process.[7] This is the same as denying the privilege of habeas corpus to enemy combatants.

This first amendment is the result of three closely interrelated decisions.

---

5   Gonzales memorandum of 25 January 2002, available at <http://www.gwu.du/~nsarchiv/NSAEBB/NSAEBB127/02.01.25.pdf>, p. 2.
6   Cheney interviewed in Russert's *Meet the Press*, 16 September 2001.
7   See B. Egelko, 'Gonzales says the Constitution doesn't guarantee habeas corpus', *San Francisco Chronicle*, 24 January 2007, available at <http://www.sfgate.com/cgi-bin/article.cgi?f=/c/a/2007/01/24/MNGDONO11O1.DTL>.

First, enemy combatants were denied the right of access to a US ordinary court or to a standard military court; instead, they were expected to be brought before a 'military commission', and denied basic legal guarantees.[8] Although the original text of the executive order excluded from its scope US citizens, two of them were later deemed to be enemy combatants and arrested on the sole authority of the President.[9]

Second, enemy combatants were denied the protection of the Geneva conventions, because they were found to be inapplicable to the 'war on terror' as 'quaint' and 'obsolete' norms.[10]

Third, the allegedly more 'valuable' enemy combatants were transferred to 'law-free zones' such as Guantanamo,[11] 'black sites' in Iraq, Poland, Romania, Diego García and Djibouti (among others)[12], or prisons in third countries (Morocco, Syria, Egypt and others, all characterized by their appalling treatment of detainees), in the latter case after being 'extraordinarily rendered'.[13]

All this was advocated on the grounds that the fight against Al Qaeda and other terrorist organizations was a war and thus enemy combatants could be indefinitely arrested until the war ended; and that this was such a radically novel type of war that fundamentally new legal norms should be devised for it, overcoming the quaint and obsolete norms contained in the Geneva Conventions and in the Code of Military Justice.[14] In concrete, Bush II's lawyers denied both that the Fourth Amendment

8 'Detention, Treatment, and Trial of Certain Non-Citizens in the War Against Terrorism', Executive Order of 13 November 2001, available at <http://www.presidency.ucsb. edu/ws/index. php?pid=63124>.

9 On Padilla and Hamdi, see B. Ackerman, *Before the Next Attack* (New Haven, Yale University Press, 2006), pp. 24ff.

10 On 18 January 2002 Bush issued an executive order accepting the legal advice put forward by Office of Legal Counsel which denied Geneva rights to enemy combatants (J. Yoo and R. J. Delahunty to W. J. Haynes II, 'Application of Treaties and Laws to al Qaeda and Taliban Detainees', 9 January 2002, available at: http://www.gwu.edu/~nsarchiv/NSAEBB/ NSAEBB127/02.01.09pdf>. This was followed by the Bybee memorandum of 22 January 2002, available at: <http://www.gwu.edu/~nsarchiv/NSAEBB/NSAEBB127/02.01.22.pdf> and the Gonzales memorandum of 25 January 2002: <http://www.gwu.edu/~nsarchiv/ NSAEBB/NSAEBB127/02.01.25.pdf.

11 See 'Memorandum for William J. Haynes, 'Re: Possible Habeas Jurisdiction Over Aliens Held in Guantanamo Bay' (signed by J. Yoo and P. Philbin), of 28 December 2001, available at <http://www. pegc. us/archive/DOJ/20011228_philbinmemo pdf>.

12 D. Priest, 'CIA Holds Terror Suspects in Secret Prisons', *The Washington Post*, 2 November 2005. Bush II openly admitted the existence of secret prisons on 6 September 2006 (http://www.whitehouse.gov/news/releases/2006/09/20060906-3.html).

13 Legal memorandum by J. Yoo 'The President Power as Commander in Chief to Transfer Captive Terrorists to the Control and Custody of Foreign Nations', 13 March 2002, which remains classified. On the rendition program, see *CIA above the law? Secret detentions and unlawful inter-state transfers of detainees in Europe* (Strasbourg, Council of Europe, 2008); and the 'report on the alleged use of European countries by the CIA for the transportation and illegal detention of prisoners' from the Committee of the European Parliament, 26 January 2007 (A6-9999-2007) available at: http://www.statewatch.org/news/2007/jan/ep-cia-rendition-cttee-report.pdf. See also S. Gray, *Ghost Plane* (New York, St Martin Press, 2006).

14 J. Yoo, *War by Other Means* (New York, Atlantic Press, 2006), p. 36.

provided a universal right of judicial protection and that the Geneva Conventions (especially Common Article III) reflected a mandatory norm of international law. By means of an allegedly literal interpretation of these norms, they concluded that positive US law only granted protections to those who were part and parcel of the political community, from which those aiming at undermining it should be excluded.[15] The Geneva Conventions were only applicable to the community of, one guesses, civilized nations, from which Al Qaeda and the Taliban were excluded (the latter as rulers of a 'failed state', a legal concept used for the occassion).

Judges Advocates General and the State Department expressed their firm disagreement. This explains why it took so long to draft the actual rules governing military commissions. The long saga of decisions of the Supreme Court[16], and the reactions by Congress[17] seem to have resulted in the (at least temporary) reversal of Bush II's first amendment.

II. Warrantless surveillance of enemy combatants

Bush II's second constitutional amendment affirms that the President has the power to order the warrantless surveillance of enemy combatants, and incidentally, of US residents or even citizens. This entails a redefinition of the scope of the right to privacy, as enshrined in the Fourth Amendment as usually interpreted (in particular, on the basis of the rulings of the Supreme Court in *Katz*[18] and *Keith*,[19] and of the 1978 Foreign Intelligence and Security Act).[20]

Bush II's lawyers have argued that the Fourth Amendment only requires that surveillance is conducted in 'reasonable' ways. A court warrant is not the most reasonable way to protect the rights of citizens against state intrusion when it comes to intelligence gathering during a war; reasonableness is then better guaranteed by trusting the President or his Attorney General to take the right decisions.[21] Explicit statu-

---

15 Ibid., pp. 16, 23 and 33.
16 In particular, *Rasul*, 542 US 466 (2004), *Hamdi*, 542 US 507 (2004), *Hamdan*, 548 U. S. 557 (2006) and *Boumediene* 128 S. Ct. 2229 (2008)
17 The Detainee Treatment Act 2005, 119 Stat 2680, at 2739 (see also the signing statement of President Bush, available at <http://www.whitehouse.gov/news/releases/2005/12/20051230-8.html> and the Military Commissions Act 2006, 120 Stat 2600.
18 *Katz* v. *U. S.* 389 US 347 (1967).
19 *U. S.* v. *District Court for the Eastern District of Michigan, Southern Division, et al.* 407 US 297 (1972).
20 92 Stat 1783. FISA did not govern physical searches until 1994. See 108 Stat 3423, section 807, at 3443. For the practice before 2001 see A. R. Cinquegrana, 'The Walls (and Wires) have Ears: The Background and the First Ten Years of The Foreign Intelligence Surveillance Act of 1978', *University of Pennsylvannia Law Review* 137 (1989): 793-828.
21 President Bush's Radio Address of 17 December 2005, available at: <http://www.whitehouse.gov/news/releases/2005/12/20051217.html>. See also 'Legal Authorities supporting the activities of the National Security Agency described by the President,

tory limitations of the powers of the President (such as those contained in FISA) are to be deemed unconstitutional if they encroach upon his power to do so.

Bush II's second amendment resulted in the Terrorist Surveillance Program started in October 2001.[22] Although it remains a secret program, we know that it affected all communications in and out the United States in which there was 'reasonable basis' to conclude that one of the parties was a member of 'Al Qaeda'. There are good reasons to suspect that the said program was only one among several similar initiatives.[23] For example, there is a wealth of information indicating that the major switches of telecommunications companies were used for surveillance purposes.[24]

The tragicomic events surrounding the re-certification of the Terrorist Surveillance Program in March 2004[25] proved that there were doubts concerning the legality of the program within the administration, only increased after its existence was publicly revealed.[26] But against some odds, Bush II was rather successful in obtaining the endorsement of Congress in the Protect America Act of 2007.[27] In particular, the requirement of a judicial warrant for each specific surveillance operation was substituted by judicial review of the executive guidelines according to which surveillance of foreign intelligence targets 'reasonably believed' to be outside of the United States was to be conducted. This rendered legal surveillance within the United States and of US persons, even citizens.[28] At the time of writing, Congress had just passed a permanent reform of FISA confirming a good deal of such powers

published on 19 January 2006, available at <http://www.usdoj.gov/opa/ whitepaperonnsalegalauthorities.pdf.>

22 J. Risen and E. Lichtblau, 'Bush Lets U. S. Spy on Callers Without Courts', *The New York Times*, 16 December 2005.

23 The most spectacular of which was without doubt the so-called Total Information Awareness program, based on massive mining of major public and private databases. It is surprising how little effort has been made to elucidate the relationship between such plans and intelligence activities realized under the UKUSA Agreement, in particular the so-called Echelon network. See L. D. Sloan, 'Echelon and the Legal Restrains on Signal Intelligence: a Need for Reevaluation', *Duke Law Journal* 50 (2000): 1467-1510.

24 See also the USA today revelations about the government having access to list of phone calls. 'NSA has massive database of Americans' phone calls', USA Today, 5 October 2006. See also the information on the case brought by Electronic Frontier Foundation against AT&T at <http://www.eff.org/nsa/hepting>. The first official acknowledgment of the role played by telecommunications companies can be found in C. Roberts, 'Debate on foreign intelligence surveillance', *El Paso Times*, 22 August 2007.

25 See the definitive account in Savage, *Takeover*, pp. 185-88.

26 For a sample of the scholarly criticism, see C. Bradley, D. Cole, W. Dellinger, R. Dworkin, R. Epstein, P. B. Heymann *et al*, 'On NSA Spying: A Letter to Congress', (2006) 53 *The New York Review of Books*, 9 February 2006, available at: <http://www.nybooks.com/articles/18650#fn1>. It was formally withdrawn in early 2007. See Letter from Attorney General Gonzales to the Senate Judiciary Committee, 17 January 2007, available at <http://www.fas.org/irp/agency/doj/fisa/ag011707.pdf>.

27 12 Stat 552.

28 'Shifting the FISA Paradigm: Protecting Civil Liberties by Eliminating Ex Ante Judicial Approval', *Harvard Law Review* 121 (2008): 2200-21.

(and granting immunity to the companies which have cooperated in the conduct of domestic warrantless surveillance since 2001).

III. Assassination of enemy combatants

The third Bush II amendment says that the President has the power to order the assassination of enemy combatants.

There was a rather world-wide consensus on the legal prohibition of targeted assassinations in the late XXth century,[29] Israel being the exception.[30] In particular, the blatantly illegal actions of the CIA during the Cold War exposed by the Church Committee[31] resulted in a further explicit reinforcement of the legal prohibition in the US legal order, through the Executive Orders of Presidents Ford, Carter and Reagan.[32]

Bush II signed a secret intelligence finding in which he authorized selective assassinations a few days after 9/11.[33] The scope of the order was expanded in 2002.[34] By the spring of 2003 the use of targeted assassinations had become fully normalized, as proved by the far from covert attempt to kill Saddam Hussein immediately before the open war in Iraq.[35] Manifold assassinations have been authorized and conducted since, including assassinations as part of covert operations in Iran.[36]

Although it seems that the decision was so quick as not have left time for previous written legal advice, the man who would have provided it, John Yoo, has claimed that the usual interpretation of the ban on assassinations does not apply to the 'war on terror',[37] a new type of conflict in which enemies will not only be killed

---

29   M. N. Schmitt, 'State Sponsored Assassination in International and Domestic Law' (1992) 17 *Yale Journal of International Law* 609-685.

30   See J. Nicholas N. Kendall, 'Israeli Counter-Terrorism: Targeted Killings under International Law', *North Carolina Law Review*, 80 (2002): 1069-88; K. Eichensehr, 'On target? Israeli Supreme Court and the Expansion of Targeted Killings', *Yale Law Journal* 116 (2007): 1873-82.

31   See Church Committee's report on selective assassinations at <http://www.aarclibrary. org/publib/contents/church/contents_church_reports_ir.htm.>

32   See Executive Order 11905, of 18 February 1976, section 5(9)available at <http://www. presidency.ucsb.edu/ws/print. php?pid=59348>; Executive Order 12036, of 24 January 1978, section 2-305, available at <http://www.presidency.ucsb.edu/ws/index.php?pid=31100>; Executive Order 12333, of 4 December 1981, section 2. 11, available at <http://www. archives.gov/federal-register/codification/executive-order/12333.html>.

33   B. Woodward, 'CIA Told to Do 'Whatever Necessary' to Kill Bin Laden', *Washington Post*, 21 October 2001.

34   J. Risen and D. Johnston, 'CIA Expands Authority to Kill Qaeda Leaders', *New York Times*, 15 December 2002.

35   D. E. Sanger and J. F. Burns, 'Bush Orders Start of War on Iraq: Missiles Apparently miss Hussein', *New York Times*, 20 March 2003.

36   A. Cockburn, 'Secret Bush "Finding" Widens War on Iran', *Counterpunch*, 2 May 2008.

37   Ibid., p. 58 and especially pp. 60 and 63.

in traditional operations, but in 'surgical targeted killings'.[38] The latter are an application of the doctrine of 'collective self-preemption' which also underlies Bush II's first amendment.[39]

IV Torturing enemy combatants

Bush II's fourth constitutional amendment says that the President has the power to choose the techniques with which enemy combatants will be interrogated, even if they are tantamount to torture or cruel, inhuman or degrading treatment according to all other nations parties to relevant international treaties.

As a matter of positive constitutional law, both US statutes (the 1994 Anti-Torture Statute and the 1996 War Crimes Act)[40] and international treaties ratified by the US (more specifically the Convention Against Torture of 1984)[41] establish an absolute prohibition of torture and cruel, inhuman or degrading treatment.

A series of legal opinions from the Office of Legal Counsel reconsidered what was actually forbidden by those norms. Three of them have been rendered public until now.[42] In the three of them, the definition of torture is so narrow as to exclude any act short of the killing of the detainee (and not even that under certain circumstances). Questions concerning the legality of techniques of interrogation employed

---

38   Ibid., p. 54. The force of the argument carries Yoo to claim that the terrorist attacks of 11 September 2001 would have been legal had it not been for the fact that the method of the attack was 'the hijacking of civilian airliners' (Yoo, *War*, p. 64), a very intriguing and in my view ridiculous claim. A similar one is made regarding the eventual capture of Rumsfeld or Tenet on p. 166.

39   Ibid., p. 61.

40   Anti-Torture Statute, 108 Stat 382; War Crimes Act 1996, 110 Stat 2104.

41   See, among others, M. Nowak and E. MacArthur (eds.), *The United Nations Convention against Torture. A Commentary* (Oxford, Oxford University Press, 2008).

42   Jay S. Bybee to Alberto R. Gonzales, 'Standards of Conduct for Interrogation under 18 U. S. C. §§ 2340-2340A', of 1 August 2002, available at <http://www.gwu.edu/~nsarchiv/NSAEBB/NSAEBB127/02.08.01.pdf>; Letter of Yoo to Gonzales, regarding 'the views of our Office concerning the legality, under international law, of interrogation methods to be used on captured al Qaeda operatives', of 1 August 2002, available at <http://www. gwu. edu/~nsarchiv/NSAEBB/NSAEBB127/020801. pdf>; Yoo to Haynes II, 'Memo Regarding the Torture and Military Interrogation of Alien Unlawful Combatants Held Outside the United States', of 14 March 2003, available at <http://www.aclu.org/pdfs/ safefree/yoo_army_torture_memo.pdf.> Bybee had addressed an opinion to Haynes II concerning the interplay between the decision to bring detainees before Military Commissions and the admissibility of evidence obtained through interrogation. See 'Potential Legal Constrains Applicable to Interrogations of Persons Captured by US Armed Forces in Afghanistan', of 26 February 2002, available at <http://www.gwu.edu/~nsarchiv/NSAEBB/NSAEBB127/02.02.26.pdf>.

by military personnel were settled in a series of specific, but closely related (in chronological and substantive terms) opinions.[43]

The core of the defence of the right to torture was a peculiar interpretation of the literal tenor of the law. In particular, it was claimed that an act could only be qualified as torture if it complied simultaneously with two conditions: one objective, the other subjective.[44] The objective condition was the infliction of 'severe harm', either physical or mental. 'Physical harm' amounting to torture was 'death, organ failure or the permanent impairment of a significant body function'.[45] The critical standards for determining the accrual of mental pain or suffering were the lasting character of the harm (to be counted in months or years) and its resulting from the specific actions codified in the US Code.[46] The subjective condition was met when the interrogator 'acted with specific intent', or what is the same, 'he must expressly intend to achieve the forbidden act'.[47] Thus, it was not sufficient that interrogation results in a prolonged physical or mental pain or suffering; for a crime to be committed, the mental state of the interrogator must be that corresponding to the intentional of *severe and lasting* mental pain or suffering to the concrete detainee.[48]

There was considerable dissent expressed within the ranks of the administration on this definition.[49] During his brief stint as head of the Office of Legal Counsel in 2003-4, Jack Goldsmith (assistant to Haynes II until he was promoted to the OLC)

43 Diane Beaver to General James T. Hill, 'Legal Brief on Proposed Counter-Resistance Strategies', and 'Legal Review of Aggressive Interrogation Techniques', of 11 October 2002; Haynes II to Rumsfeld, 'Counter-Resistance Techniques', of 27 November 2002, and approved 2 December 2002 by Rumsfeld. The three documents are available at <http://www.gwu.edu/~nsarchiv/NSAEBB/NSAEBB127/02.12.02.pdf>. A compilation of opinions and decisions which helps understanding who and why took decisions has been posted by Senator Levin of the Armed Services Committee, and is available at <http://levin.senate.gov/newsroom/supporting/2008/Documents.SASC.061708.pdf>.

44 Bybee to Gonzalez, 'Standards of Conduct', p. 3.

45 Ibid., p. 6. This phrase derives from the definition of severe physical pain triggering compulsory health assistance of uninsured people. It was used to define torture, despite the lack of comparability of the two situations, because allegedly it was the only positive definition of 'severe physical pain' which could be found in the US Code.

46 Ibid., pp. 9-12. Namely (a) intentional infliction or threatened infliction of severe physical pain or suffering; (b) administration or application, or threatened administration or application, of mind-altering substances or other procedures calculated to disrupt profoundly the senses or the personality; (c) threat of imminent death; (d) the threat that another person will imminently be subject to death, severe physical pain or suffering, or the administration or application of mind-altering substances or other procedures calculated to disrupt profoundly the senses or personality.

47 Ibid., p. 3.

48 Ibid., p. 8.

49 See Alberto J. Mora's memo of 18 June 2004, 'Statement for the Record: Office of General Counsel Involvement in Interrogation Issues', available at <http://www.aclu.org/pdfs/safefree/mora_memo_july_2004.pdf>.

withdrew Yoo's and Bybee's opinions.[50] Still, Bush II's fourth amendment has not been abandonded.[51] The President himself has opposed any attempt by Congress to reaffirm the prohibition of the use of torture (in particular, through his signing statement added to the 2005 Detainee Treatment Act and his recent veto of the bill reiterating the prohibition of any interrogation technique beyond those contained in the Army Field Manual).[52] Moreover, the director of the CIA has explicitly admitted that at least three detainees were waterboarded, while it is now accepted that the National Security Council explicitly discussed and approved specific techniques of interrogation before the interrogation of concrete detainees, and that was approved by Bush II himself.[53]

C. The constitutional theory of Bush II

The four amendments proposed and relied upon by Bush II's lawyers are to be constructed as specific concretizations of the constitutional theory to which Bush II's lawyers subscribe. This constitutional theory rests upon two key premises which reinterpret the legal meaning of the two main sources of limits to presidential action, namely, the US Constitution and international law. First, the US Constitution is said to contain two different sets of fundamental norms: the ordinary constitution *and* the emergency constitution. The latter is said to vest massive powers in the President which entitled him to override limits to his action set by other institutions. Second, international law, and very especially, multilateral treaties and international manda-

---

50 J. L. Goldsmith, *The Terror Presidency* (New York, Norton, 2007), pp. 144 ff (especially p. 155). Yoo, *War by Other Means*, pp. 185-6 seems to have resented that, although he (in my view, rightly) claims that changes have been more aesthetical than substantive.

51 J. Mayer, 'The Memo: How an Internal Effort to Ban the Abuse and Torture of Detainees was Thwarted', *The New Yorker*, 27 February 2006, reports that Mora was shown by late January a draft – one guesses, given the dates – of Yoo's legal opinion on specific interrogation techniques. The said opinion had been solicited by Haynes in what seems hard not to believe was an effort at influencing and perhaps rendering moot the Working Group itself. Mora kept on arguing that both Yoo's memo and the draft report of the Working Group were flawed. And so had done Judges Advocate General Romig, Bohr, Sandkhuler and Rives when proposing changes to the draft (their opinions are available at <http://www.dod. mil/pubs/foi/detainees/05-F-2083_JAGmemos. pdf>). Even if it was not rendered public, not even known within Army circles, the Working Group produced a final report by 4 April (available at <http://www.gwu.edu/~nsarchiv/NSAEBB/NSAEBB127/03.04.04.pdf>), which only became declassified after the Abu Grahib scandal broke out. Rumsfeld issued new guidelines concerning interrogation methods by 16 April; available at:
    <http://www.gwu. edu/~nsarchiv/NSAEBB/NSAEBB127/03.04.16.pdf>.

52 The full text of the bill can be found at <http://www.opencongress.org/bill/110-h2082/text>.

53 S. Shane, 'C. I. A. Chief Doubts Tactic To Interrogate Is Still Legal', *New York Times*, 8 February 2008; J. C. Greenburg, H. L. Rosenberg and A. de Vogue,. 'Top Bush Advisors Approved 'Enhanced' Interrogation', *ABC News*, 9 April 2008; J. C. Greenburg, H. L. Rosenberg and A. de Vogue, 'Bush Aware of Advisers' Interrogation Talks', *ABC News*, 11 April 2008.

tory norms are said to lack legal bite and to be properly described as congeries of behavioural regularities.

I.   The dual constitution

The theory of the dual constitution affirms that there is not but two US constitutions. Along with the ordinary constitution, applicable during the times in which the life of the republic proceeds normally, we find an emergency constitution, applicable during crisis situations. The 'ordinary' constitution is enshrined in the vast majority of the provisions of the 1787 Constitution, formal amendments, and constitutional conventions developed over time. The key provisions of the emergency constitution are contained in the written text of the US Constitution. The most important one is the first sentence of Article II. 2 of the Constitution, which establishes that

> The President shall be Commander in Chief of the Army and Navy of the United States, and of the Militia of the several States, when called into the actual Service of the United States.

Additionally, we find bits and pieces of the emergency constitution in the express limits to constitutional applicable during emergencies.[54] The remaining content of the emergency constitution result from the constitutional practice during previous emergencies (in particular, the War of Independence, the Civil War and the three World Wars, including the Cold War). The core provisions of the emergency constitution are those concerning the allocation of power, not its substantive provisions. The vast variety of possible threats to the republic explain why the written constitution limits itself to determine in an unambiguous and definite manner *who* should be in charge of establishing how the core principles of the constitution are to be operationalized in emergency situations.

Emergency powers are said to be vested almost exclusively in the President as Commander in Chief. This is grounded on the claim that the President is the institutional actor best placed to take decisions during extraordinary constitutional times, for three reasons. He is the head of the most hierarchical branch of government, he is invested with direct democratic legitimacy, and he is used to exercising key powers on the decisive policies during emergencies (foreign policy, defence and intelligence).

The terrorist attacks of September 2001 were tantamount to a declaration of war against the government and the people of the United States, something which by itself activated the inherent emergency powers of the President; the actuality of his inherent emergency powers is said to have been further confirmed by Congress's Authorization to Use Military Force of September 18th, 2001.[55] Moreover, the radi-

---

54   Thus, the Second Amendment establishes that the privilege the writ of habeas corpus should not be suspended but 'in cases of rebellion or invasion' if moreover 'the public safety' may require it.

55   115 Stat 224. See Yoo's Memo of 25 September 2005, available at <http://www.justice.gov/olc/warpowers925.htm>.

cally new character of the threat posed by 'Al Qaeda' implied that this emergency was like no others. The nature of 'Al Qaeda' resulted in a global combat where cheap weapons of mass destruction might be used with unprecedented lethal consequences. Because this was a war like no others, the emergency constitution might have to be revised and most of the norms established in previous emergencies set aside as they had been rendered 'obsolete' and 'quaint'. The President could and should rewrite the constitution of emergency to adapt it to the new circumstances. This indeed amounts to claiming that the President has a power functionally akin to the *puovoir constituent* residing in the People, only the chief of the executive holds it as regards the emergency constitution, not the ordinary constitution.[56] In particular, the emergency version of the 'unitary doctrine of the executive' vests the President with the power to review the constitutionality of the statutes passed by Congress, and eventually to set them aside if unconstitutional; and also to ignore and left without application the rulings of the Supreme Court concerning the constitutionality of a given norm. This power is singularly exerted through a peculiar source of law, the signing statement.[57] Using them, Bush II has indeed contested the constitutionality of more than seven hundred legal provisions[58] by typically claiming that '[t]he executive branch shall construe [section, title and name of the act] in a manner consistent with the constitutional authority of the President to supervise the unitary executive branch and as Commander in Chief'.[59]

II. International law as behavioural regularities

The second element of Bush II's theory of constitutional law is his theory of international law, according to which international norms other than bilateral treaties are merely behavioural regularities, and not a source of legal obligations.

The argument is three-pronged.[60] First, it is claimed that only a fraction of international norms can be characterized as legal norms proper. In particular, customary

---

56 Or does he? If the constitution of emergency is to remain activated for as long as the 'war on terror' lasts, and that could well be an awful long time, the difference between the two constitution-making powers becomes very diffuse indeed.

57 See American Bar Association, 'Recommendation of the Task Force on Presidential Signing Statements and the Separation of Powers Doctrine', available at <http://www.abanet.org/ leadership/2006/annual/dailyjournal/20060823144113.pdf>. On the literature, see P. J. Cooper, *By Order of the President* (Lawrence, University Press of Kansas, 2002), ch. 7; P. J. Cooper, 'George W. Bush, Edgar Allan Poe and the Use and Abuse of Presidential Signing Statements' *Presidential Studies Quarterly* 35 (2005): 515-32.

58 See American Bar Association, 'Recommendation of the Task Force on Presidential Signing Statements and the Separation of Powers Doctrine'; Cooper, 'Bush, Poe and Presidential Signing Statements'. See also Cooper, 'Bush, Poe and Presidential Statements'.

59 See for example the signing statement attached to the Detainee Treatment Act 2005.

60 Even more radical criticisms have been expressed by other Bushite lawyers. See for example J. R. Bolton, 'Is There "Really" Law in International Affairs?' *Transnational Law and Contemporary Problems* 10 (2000): 1-48.

norms and multilateral treaties are not law in a strict sense, because states comply with them only if the national interest or the threat of coercion of powerful states (and not any autonomous institution constituted by international law) coerce them into compliance.[61] Customary international law is thus better understood as a set of behavioural regularities stabilized by mutual interest, cooperation in a prisoner's dilemma situation, or coercion exerted by a hegemonic state;[62] while multilateral treaties are instruments through which states spread information about their mutual intentions.[63] Second, the only international customary norms with legal bite are those supported by the United States. This claim derives from a rather idiosyncratic understanding of how the *opinio juris* which underlies international customary norms is forged, in concrete, by transforming the *de facto* preminence of the United States in world affairs in a law-making power.[64] Third, the President as the *pouvoir constituent* of the constitution of emergency can decide in a final and unreviewable manner whether or not a given international standard should be followed by US authorities; so that even if customary norms or multilateral treaties have legal bite, they can be override by the President.

The utmost expression of Bush II's theory of international law is the neologism 'lawfare', intended to mean 'the strategy of using or misusing law as a substitute for traditional military means to achieve an operational objective.'[65] Thus, international law is not only denied legal force, but stigmatized as one of the weapons of terrorists.

D. The minimalist and eclectic legal theory of Bush II

Bush II's legal theory is not the result of a systematic effort at answering the trade questions of legal theorists (what law is, in what relationship it stands with morality, what are the basis of validity of positive norms, etc.) but a minimal theory sufficient to provide support to the radical changes in positive law and constitutional theory advanced and relied upon the court attorneys of the President.

Bush II's legal theory is minimalist and eclectic. The key premise of this theory is that law is the ultimate source of validity of legal norms is the will of the sovereign.

---

61 E. Posner and J. Goldsmith, *The Limits of International Law* (Oxford, Oxford University Press, 2005), p. 10.

62 Ibid., p. 39.

63 Ibid., p. 105.

64 Yoo, *War*, pp. 33 and 37.

65 Charles J. Dunlad Jr, at present Deputy Judge Advocate, in 'Law and Military Interventions: Preserving Humanitarian Values in 21st Conflicts', a lecture delivered at the Kennedy School of Government on 29 November 2001, available at <http://www.duke.edu/~pfeaver/dunlap.pdf>.

66 Donald Rumsfeld and Jack Goldsmith expanded the concept and shifted its target, now 'European and South American allies and the human rights industry (sic) that supported their universal jurisdiction aspirations', see Goldsmith, *Terror Presidency*, pp. 59ff.

We the People acting through its representatives is the sovereign under the ordinary constitution, and We the People as represented by the President is the sovereign under the emergency constitution. Bush II's legal theory is thus a prescriptivist conception of law, which rejects the notion that legal reasoning should be viewed as a special case of critical practical reasoning (and thus, neither as a fully discretionary activity, in which moral and prudential arguments can be freely invoked to defeat positive legal norms; nor as a fully autonomous, technical activity; but one which in limited but decisive ways incorporates critical normative reasoning).[66] And consequently, the legal theory of the attorneys of the White House assumes that the interpretation of legal norms, and very especially constitutional norms, is a matter of *decision*, not a matter of *reasoning*.

The minimalist character of Bush II's legal theory is closely related to its eclecticism; as a 'thin' legal theory, it can rely on an 'overlapping consensus' of 'thick' legal theories to the extent that they subscribe, one way or the other, to the core prescriptivist assumption, even if they are antagonistic and contradictory when we consider them as 'thick' theories. This is indeed very convenient in strategic terms, as it seems to provide an expanded 'base' of support for the concrete constitutional changes being advocated.[67] And indeed, Bush II's lawyers have borrowed from three distinct theories of law, namely: (1) the peculiar bred of positivism that originalist theories endorse (exemplified by the originalism of Scalia); (2) the bred of 'modern' iusnaturalism concerned with the nature of positive law (exemplified by Finnis's legal theory); (3) pragmatist theories of law which characterize law as an instrument for other social ends (exemplified by Richard A. Posner's legal theory, applied and developed to emergencies by Eric Posner and Adrian Vermeule).

It may be necessary to underline that I am not claiming that all of these authors would fully agree with either the constitutional amendments or the constitutional theory of Bush II. Rather, I make three far more modest claims. First, the eclectic and incomplete theory of law put forward by Bush II's lawyers has been built with bits and pieces of the said three legal theories; whether it makes sense to take bits and pieces from the original complete legal theory or not is a different question, which is irrelevant to the court attorneys of the White House, but may be critical to the original authors of the bit or piece. Second, these borrowings reveal that

---

66 As Robert Alexy, Ronald Dworkin or Neil D. MacCormick, to name only three outstanding contemporary legal theories, conceptualize the law. This is not alien in any sense to the US constitutional tradition; just the contrary; see M. J. Horwitz, *The Warren Court and the Pursuit of Justice* (New York, Hill and Wang, 1999).

67 This strategy has structural parallelisms with that underlying the pragmatic legal theory developed by Cass Sunstein over the years, and very especially on his 'Incompletely Theorized Agreements', *Harvard Law Review* 108 (1995): 1733-72; and now in his 'Incompletely Theorized Agreements on Constitutional Law', *University of Chicago Public Law Working Paper, no 147*, available at <http://papers.ssrn.com/sol3/Delivery.cfm/SSRN_ID957369_code 249436.pdf?abstractid=957369&mirid=1>. Its political equivalent is 'government by fringes' as mastered by Karl Rove; see G. Wills, 'Fringe Govermment', *New York Review of Books*, 6 October 2005.

originalism à la Scalia, pragmatism à la Posner and (modern) natural law à la Finnis have a common prescriptivist foundation, even if the way in which law is reduced to power in each case is very different, and has different consequences. But even then, the ultimate endorsement of prescriptivism creates a potential affinity with theories such as Bush II's constitutional and legal theory. Third, the affinity between all these theories has occasionally led to a partial, even if qualified, endorsement of some of the most controversial aspects of the four constitutional amendments put forward by Bush II in all three cases.

I.   Originalism à la Scalia.

Originalism is a breed of legal positivism that affirms that there is an objective meaning of legal norms, to be determined by reference to the authoritative constitutional will.[68] Although the term and the contours of the debate have been shaped in relation to the US Constitution,[69] it is obvious that similar debates concerning the canons of interpretation are endemic to all legal systems.

Originalism is an attractive theory of law and legal interpretation for Bush II's lawyers because it can be used to weaken the constraints that constitutional law imposes upon the executive. Although formally speaking it offers criteria to determine in an objective and fixed manner what the constitutional law says, in substantive terms not only the subjective or intersubjective will of the constitution-makers may be extremely difficult to ascertain in an objective manner (thus inviting discretionary interpretation), but also the identification of law with the will of a given authority (even if power has obtained in 'democratic' competition among elites) cracks the door open for the characterization of law as a congeries of norms, only tied together by their being willed by the sovereign; consequently, the ruling few have a larger discretion to determine what the law is.[70]

Originalism supports Bush II's constitutional amendments and his constitutional and legal theory in two concrete ways.

First, it allows the attorneys of the White House to present revolutionary judgments as conservative ones. By pretending to ground their claim on a 'lost' constitutional norm, they obtain a conservative wrapping for claims that advance an interpretation of positive constitutional law radically deviant from existing constitutional

---

68   The 'loci classici' are A. Scalia, 'Originalism: The Lesser Evil' (1989) 57 *University of Cincinnati Law Review* 57 (1989): 849-65 and A. Scalia, *A Matter of Interpretation: Federal Courts and the Law* (Princeton, Princeton University Press, 1997).

69   See for example S. G. Calabresi (ed), *Originalism, A Quarter-Century Debate* (New York, Regnery, 2007).

70   Cf. R. Dworkin, 'On Gaps in the Law' in P. Amselek and N. D. MacCormick (eds.), *Controversies on Law's Ontology* (Edinburgh, Edinburgh University Press, 1991), pp. 84-90; 'The Ardous Virtue of Fidelity: Originalism, Scalia, Tribe and Nerve' *Fordham Law Review* 65 (1997): 1249-1268; and also R. A. Posner, *How Judges Think*, (Cambridge, MA, Harvard University Press, 2008), pp. 103-4.

practice (for example, if the President orders the warrantless surveillance of a US citizen within US territory in open breach of FISA, they claim that FISA was unconstitutional because it breached inherent executive powers; so true compliance with the Constitution requires allowing the President to order the warrantless surveillance) Indeed, the attorneys of the White House have frequently claimed that they were just rolling back the unconstitutional limits on executive action set by Congress in the seventies.

Second, originalism helps claiming that the four constitutional amendments are democratically legitimate. After all, it is generally assumed that the Constitution was authored by the people, and that it should not be changed but by the people. So to the extent that the President is faithfully restoring the true meaning of the constitution against meddling and elitist judges, and irresponsible notables in Congress, he is actually advancing the cause of democracy.

II.   Legal Pragmatism à la Posner

Posnerian legal pragmatism claims that law is to be understood as a set of behavioural regularities concerning the use of state power. Denying any clear-cut distinction between what law is and what should be, Posner adds that officials should regard law as a means to achieve specific social ends, and thus are well-advised to take decisions in such a way that they maximize social welfare.[71] The alleged 'pragmatic' character of this theory derives from its antifoundational, even antitheoretical stand and its companion emphasis on practice.[72]

Legal pragmatism à la Posner is attractive to Bush II's lawyers because it weakens constitutional constrains upon executive action to the extent that it emphasizes the decisionistic and particularistic character of legal reasoning; not only must each specific context indeed be thoroughly considered if the ultimate end is to maximize social welfare through legal adjudication; but law is the result of *action*, of the *action taken by officials*.

Still, the 'standard' view of Posner's theory comes hand in hand with an institutional theory which expands the role of courts, and dramatically constrains the legislators and the executive. This is because judges, contrary what is the case with the other two branches of government, proceed by means of incremental concrete decisions to settle particular and specific problems, and not by sweeping general decisions abstracted from any specific context. Judicial rulings are less prone to have massive unintended consequences, not only because of their narrower scope, but also because rectification is easier and speedier. How could it then be claimed that Posner's legal pragmatism serves the cause of aggrandisement of the executive

---

71   R. A. Posner, *The Problems of Jurisprudence* (Cambridge, Harvard University Press, 1990), p. 26; and *Economic Analysis of Law* (Boston, Little and Brown, 1972).

72   See 'The Problematics of Moral and Legal Theory' *Harvard Law Review* 111 (1998): 1637-1717.

power? The explanation lies in the fact that Posner in *Not a Suicide Pact* (and, as already said, Posner and Vermeule in *Terror in the Balance*) have assigned a key role to the distinction between ordinary and emergency politics, and have claimed that the benign role played by courts during ordinary times is actually to be played by Presidents during emergencies.[73] In concrete, they claim that the executive is the best-placed institution to preserve the republic during emergencies, on account of the speed, secrecy and decisiveness of its actions.[74] If this premise is true in general, is even truer if the emergency poses a radically new threat, as the present one does, because everything must be rethought from the scratch. Because new measures must have a chance to 'prove themselves',[75] monitoring or surveillance by other branches of government or by citizens themselves is unadvisable.[76]

Legal pragmatism offers support to Bush II's constitutional amendments because it justifies the four constitutional amendments in the name of the different weight to be given to the collective interest in national security under emergencies, thus requiring a new 'weighing and balancing' of subjective rights to freedom and the collective good of security.[77] In the book that ironically marked the launching of the Oxford series on inalienable rights (*sic*), Posner claims that because 'the law of necessity supersedes the Constitution',[78] the scope of fundamental rights should be made less extensive.[79] The reason is a simple calculus: the people at risk of being victims of a terrorist attack are far more numerous than those whose liberties may be curtailed; so the interest of the greatest number should prevail over that of the lesser. Posner adds that subjective rights to freedom should be only 'modestly' curtailed,[80] but then does endorse (with some qualifications, but also with some additions) Bush II's four constitutional amendments.[81]

---

73 R. A. Posner and A. Vermeule, *Terror in the Balance: Security, Liberty and the Courts* (Oxford, Oxford University Press, 2007), p. 21
74 Ibid., p. 16 and 30.
75 R. A. Posner, *Not A Suicide Pact* (New York, Oxford University Press, 2006), p. 31.
76 Posner and Vermeule, *Terror in the Balance,* pp. 16 and 45.
77 Posner, *Not A Suicide Pact*, p. 31.
78 Ibid., p. 70
79 Ibid., p. 8.
80 Ibid., p. 41.
81 Ibid. In concrete: (1) all rights (not only habeas corpus, but *all* rights) could be denied to a foreigner enemy combatant seized abroad and brought into the United States (reservations should be held on whether foreign residents already present in the US could be treated similarly (pp. 41 and 58); (2) the right to judicial protection is to be redefined, increasing the length of time during which people could be arrested and held incommunicado on the sole authority of the executive (pp. 65 and 73; with reasonable remaining undetermined); even citizens could be detained indefinitely if they are deemed to be terrorists (pp. 67 and 73); (3) trial by military commission is fine even when there is no war (p. 73); (4)Individuals could be required to prove they are not terrorists, rendering unnecessary that prosecutors prove it (p. 58); (5) torture could be resorted to if there is a 'state of necessity' (pp. 12 and 81).

134

It may seem counterintuitive to claim that modern natural law theory is one of the house legal theories of Bush II's lawyers. Leaving aside the fact that the main exponents of modern natural law theories may share with the administration similar views on sexual morality and bioethics,[82] it is well-known that modern natural law offers a sophisticated account of the relationship between legal and practical reason.[83] One would then suppose that the structural and substantial connection between law and objective principles of morality defended by Finnis and other modern natural lawyers should provide a standpoint from which to criticize (and criticize heavily for that purpose) the practice and theory of constitutional law followed by Bush II's lawyers.

Still, modern natural law offers critical support to Bush II's constitutional and legal theory on one specific (and key) account: its rationalization of the dualistic understanding of the constitution and consequently of the need of unlimited executive power during emergencies, or what is the same, a moral grounded defence of the old principle that *inter armas silent leges*. In a neglected passage in *Natural Law and Natural Rights* reproduced at the beginning of this chapter, Finnis claims that when societies are 'threatened with military, economic or ecological disaster',[84] what the executive decides and pretends to embody into law should be regarded for the time being as a correct moral judgment; 'statesmen' *must* depart, 'temporarily but perhaps drastically' from the ordinary constitution, while presumably both citizens and scholars should simply be silent and comply, because 'one could say nothing that may appear to be a key to identifying the occasion or a guide to acting in it'. Thus, at the critical moments of truth, not only does law cease to be a guide to action, but legally constituted power ceases to be guided by practical reason and must be exercised by reference to individual political judgment.[85] Whatever 'statesmanship' applied to departing from law is, clearly it cannot be the same kind of public reason which underpins ordinary constitutional and statutory norms.

It could be argued that I am making too much out of a short passage in *Natural Law and Natural Rights*. Lack of space prevents me from attempting a deeper analysis of the relationship between Finnis' theory of emergencies and his overall theory, or for that matter, the complex genealogy of this idea, and the relationship in which it stands with Aristotles' and Aquinas' legal theory. I will only claim that Finnis himself seems to have proved that his theory of emergencies is far from being an abstract and marginal annotation in his *Natural Law and Natural Rights* to the extent that it grounds his criticism to the ruling of the House of Lords on the constitutional-

---

82 Including active and passive hostility towards stem cell research, same sex-marriage, abortion and any regulation of the right to die. See C. Tiefer, *Veering Right* (Berkeley, California University Press, 2004).

83 See N. D. MacCormick, 'Natural Law Reconsidered', *Oxford Journal of Legal Studies* 1 (1981): 99-109.

84 J. Finnis, *Natural Law and Natural Rights* (Oxford, Oxford University Press, 1979), p. 246.

85 Ibid., p. 275. The full quote is reproduced at the beginning of this chapter.

ity of the indefinite detention of certain foreign suspected of being terrorists.[86] By claiming that aliens do not have a right to be treated equally when it comes to the modalities of detention,[87] Finnis seems to confirm the central role played by his views on the morality and legality of unconstitutional action during emergencies. Quite obviously, the intriguing question is in which other respects the rights to be acknowledged to foreigners are different.

E. Conclusion: The constitution of emergency between law and propaganda

By holding to the narrative that the terrorist attacks of September 11th, 2001 plunged us into an unbrave new world, Bush II's lawyers have pretended to justify the exertion of the alleged inherent executive power to rewrite the emergency constitution that is said to lurk behind the ordinary US constitution. The recent judgment of the Supreme Court in *Boumediene*, the several investigatory committees set up in Congress, and above all, the progressive change of mind of the US public, seem to indicate that the revolution was close to success, but ultimately failed. But that cannot be taken for granted. *Boumediene* was decided by the narrowest of majorities, Congress lacks a clear goal in its investigations, and the public may get diverted if a new terrorist attack takes place. Moreover, as has been argued in this chapter, the challenge posed by Bush II was not merely one of unconstitutional action in the shadows, but is properly described as a frontal attack aimed at the constitutional doctrines, constitutional theory and legal theories of Bush II's lawyers. Even if the four constitutional amendments are about to be rejected, there are worrying signals that Bush II has been rather successful at transforming the very terms of the debate in constitutional and legal theory, and indeed in public debate in general. Ten years ago, arguments in favour of the juridification of torture would have been regarded as extravagant; today they are regularly taken to be serious propositions on which reasonable people can reasonably disagree. By revealing the interconnections between constitutional doctrine and theory, this chapter shows that the failure of Bush II's constitutional amendments may be temporary if his successes in theoretical terms are not also reversed. This is a very good reason to take very seriously Bush II's constitutional and legal theory, and not be contented to disregard it as fringe thought.

Moreover, evidence is coming to light that proves that there is a causal chain between the blatant violations of constitutional and international law and the legal advice provided by key General Counsels within the Administration, and decisively, from the Office of Legal Counsel in the Departament of Justice. The legal responsibility of Bush II's lawyers is not a partisan question, but a major issue which should be of concern to all jurists, and to all scholars in general. Although Bush II's lawyers have repeatedly claimed that they limited themselves to describing what the law

---

86   *A* v. *Secretary of State for the Home Department* [2004] UKHL 56, [2005] 2 AC 68.
87   J. Finnis, 'Nationality, Alienage and Constitutional Principle' *Law Quarterly Review* 127 (2007): 417-45, p. 438.

said, and consequently, they do not have any legal responsibility for what politicians decided to do *within the bounds of what they were advised was legally permissible*, the contrary is well established in law since the Nuremberg Trials. Specious legal advice leading to blatant violations of the law is part of the legal chain of causation, and thus, lawyers may be brought before criminal courts.[88] There are clear indications indeed that serious crimes have been committed by CIA operatives, military personnel and lawyers.[89]

Still, it would be wrong to analyse Bush II's constitutional and legal theories as if they were simply constitutional and legal theories. By doing that we will not only risk giving them too much undeserved credit, but we will miss the key role they have played in the propaganda effort to transform constitutional and political practice. In short, we have to be aware of the double role of Bush II's theories: as legal theories and as propaganda. The core decisions in the so-called 'war on terror' would not have been feasible if unsupported by well-formed constitutional arguments. They played a decisive role in convincing the restless many that the dissenting voices against the ruling few were not to be listened to. That what was being done was both legally and morally permissible. Because modern societies cannot be integrated by mere force, because most people believe the law is by and large a repository of moral principles, no matter how imperfect, the attempt to place the President above the law has to be legitimized by means other than force, with legal arguments playing a paramount role. But when the legal arguments put forward are merely specious arguments put forward for narrow strategic reasons, when the form of law is placed at the service of power, law is disconnected from public reason and turned into (cheap) propaganda.[90] The propagandistic subversion of law is far from new. It is in a way typical, as Scott Horton has reminded us,[91] of mob lawyers. And indeed the reduction of law to a mere technique cracks the door open to the propagandistic use of law.[92] But more worryingly, there are disturbing structural similari-

---

88   In particular, see the judgment in *US* v. *Alstoetter*, analysed in depth by Matthew Lippman, 'The Prosecution of Josef Alstoetter et al.' *Law, Lawyers and Justice in the Third Reich' Dickinson Journal of International Law* 16 (1997): 343. On Alstoetter and the basis on which Bush II's lawyers could be prosecuted, see Milan Markovic, 'Can Lawyers Be War Criminals?' *Georgetown Journal of Legal Ethics* 20 (2007): 347-68.

89   'A Review of the FBI's involvement and observations of detained interrogations in Guantanamo Bay, Afghanistan and Iraq', available at <http://www.usdoj.gov/oig/ special/s0805/final.pdf>, p. xxii. Four recent books have articulated very cogent legal cases. See M. Ratner, *The Trial of Donald Rumsfeld. A Trial by Book* (New York, The New Press, 2008); P. Sands, *Torture Team* (London, Allen Lane, 2008); E. de la Vega, *US* v. *Bush* (New York, Seven Stories, 2006) and V. Bugliosi, *The Prosecution of George W. Bush for Murder* (New York, Vanguard, 2008).

90   Indeed, it was only to be expected that the main advocates of Bush II's theory of law (including Justices Scalia and Thomas) would have been keen watchers of the TV show *24*. Sands, *Torture Team*; see also Clucas, Ch. 11 below.

91   S. Horton, 'The Green Light', 2 April 2008, available at <http://harpers.org/archive/ 2008/04/hbc-90002779>.

92   B. Z. Tamanaha, *Law as a Means to an End: A Threat to the Rule of Law* (Cambridge, Cambridge University Press, 2006).

ties between the constitutional and legal theory of Bush II's lawyers and the constitutional and legal theory of the court lawyers of Fascism and Nazism. The narrative on the radical new circumstances, and the consequent the need for radically new theories of law, as well as its infiltration of established and respected institutions and bodies of law by raw power leave the reader with a frustrating sense of *déjà-vu*.[93]

All this should make us reflect, and reflect seriously and deeply. Because we had been there already, they (and we) should have known better.

---

93 See S. Levinson, 'Torture in Iraq and the Rule of Law in America' (2004) 133 *DAEDALUS Journal of the American Academy of Arts and Sciences*. 5, available at <http://www. amacad. org/publications/summer2004/levinson.pdf>; and S. Horton, 'The Return of Carl Schmitt', published in *Balkinization*, 7 November 2005, available at <http://balkin.blogspot. com/2005/11/return-of-carl-schmitt.html>. It is not my intention to draw comparisons between the 'war on terror' and other conflicts; or between Bush II and other historical political leaders. My claim is a more modest one and considers the way in which Bush II's lawyers have argued in law. It is they and their arguments that I find pertinent to compare with, say, Carl Schmitt (as Sanford Levinson and Scott Horton have already suggested), Karl Larenz, Alfredo Rocco, Sergio Panunzio or Francisco Javier Conde. On the topic, see C. Joerges and N. Singh (ed.), *Darker Legacies of Law in Europe* (Oxford, Hart, 2003).

8. Torture, between Law and Politics: A Retrospective View

Marina Lalatta Costerbosa

A. Introduction

This chapter contributes to the discussion of torture at the present time from a historical point of view. My contention has always been that the history of modern political thought can offer us a critical understanding of the question of the justifiability of torture, a question that is today again scandalously being raised.

Torture is not only a practice of the past. People continue torturing today, even in democratic countries, and we can see many attempts to justify it today in democratic countries.

In this chapter I will not be directly concentrating on the revived contemporary debate on torture. Rather, my purpose is to focus on the role which torture had in the past and on the presumed change which has occurred in the last decades. For instance, it has recently been argued, for example by Antonio Cassese, that 'today torture is *merely* an instrument of repressing political and ideological dissent. *Through time it has become* the most brutal form of war on political enemies, against those who do not agree with the ideology of the dominant power'.[1] From this angle I will try to throw light on the recent *Rehabilitierung* of torture.

My question is the following: is it true that such a radical change has occurred? Is it true that torture is essentially a political instrument and no longer a judicial instrument? Again, is it true that in the past torture was always something different from today, ignoring of course the changing of the more or less sophisticated, more or less cruel and underhand instruments to perform it in the most effective way? My point is that the argument that the meaning of torture has changed from a judicial to a political one, *pace* the good intentions of its supporters, favours the position of torture's defenders. The reason is that, if we say that today torture has a new face, a political face, people could argue that today we are in an exceptional and dangerous situation indeed, and that for *this* reason torture and in particular the 'new' form of torture is a necessary and adequate reaction to the attack by the 'forces of evil', or something like that. On the contrary, I think that we may reject torture with more force and arguments if we recognize that what we have in front of us really is a *reaction* without precedent, but that does not mean that it is justified by extraordinary international and political circumstances; on the contrary, it presents a regression in terms of liberty and rights, a regression insofar as the democratic process is concerned.

Torture is an old instrument. It was used in the past to defend power through judicial practice, but all of this happened in an age when people were not expected to

---

1   A. Cassese, *I Diritti Umani Oggi* (Laterza, Rom-Bari, 2005), p. 76, italics added.

define themselves as upholders of democracy and human rights. My interpretation tries to show, with, I hope, more evidence than the 'change argument', that torture is unacceptable and incompatible with democracy and human rights, and I think that in the process it may afford a realistic insight into the nature of the *status quo*. Today people are trying to square the circle, so to speak; they support torture and at the same time call themselves democratic. This does not work. Even the arguments which were elaborated during the Enlightenment, for example by Christian Thomasius, Pietro Verri, or Cesare Beccaria, are today misunderstood or simply ignored.[2] Today we are going back to pre-modern forms of law and power.

Two points support this view. The first one goes back to Niccolò Machiavelli, because in his works we can find an idea of torture not only as a legal instrument, but also as a political instrument *stricto sensu*.[3] In Machiavelli's age and thought, torture was already political, just like today, and not only an instrument for judicial inquiry.

The second point deals with Enlightenment thought. If we read books by authors like those mentioned above, we will find some arguments against torture which are used today. Not so much has changed in this respect, and this means that today we are facing a regression (a 'three century regression'), a deeply antidemocratic movement. To a great extent, today we are repeating that old debate, the claim to justice of the Enlightenment has not yet been realized and, in any case, probably never will be realized once and for all. Those thinkers have shown how useless and inhuman torture is, but that is not enough in face of the new ideologies and policies promoted by efficient modern instruments of hegemony designed to shape and shed public consent. As I will try to demonstrate, in Machiavelli's *Discourses* and in Thomasius' essay on torture we can already find clear awareness of the existence of a political sense of torture. Arguments that using torture is pointless are strong arguments only if we are talking about judicial torture, and this is crucial for my analysis. Indeed, if torture is also a political instrument, it can be 'useful', and for that reason – as was already clear to Thomasius – good arguments against torture have to show its injustice, not only its uselessness. Torture cannot be a mere question of utility. This holds today as in the past.

B. From judicial torture to political torture: the Machiavellian view

I prefer for the moment to proceed slowly and talk about a part of the history of torture. In Greek and Roman antiquity torture was an instrument which had a place within a general concept of law and politics. It was a judicial instrument for extort-

---

2   C. Thomasius, *Über die Folter*, ed. by R. Liebewirth (Weimar, Hermann Böhlaus, Nachfolger, 1960); P. Verri, *Osservazioni sulla Tortura*, ed. by C. Gallone (Milan, 1997).

3   N. Machiavelli, *Lettere*, ed. by Giorgio Inglese (Milan, Rizzoli, 1996); N. Machiavelli, 'Discorsi sopra la prima deca di Tito Livio', in Id. , *Opere*, (Rome, Istituto dell'Enciclopedia italiana fondata da Giovanni Treccani, 2006).

ing by violence a confession or piece of information to be used in a trial against the accused, who refused to confess, or a presumed witness, who was reticent about the facts.[4] It was considered an instrument of proof, which was only suited to the lower classes, however, in particular to slaves (with the exception of crimes directly or indirectly against political authority like magic, *falsa moneta* and *majestatis causa*, to punish which cases the Romans also used to torture free people). It was considered an instrument of proof regardless of the principle of the presumption of innocence (as a sort of preventive detention, so-called *mala mansio,* demonstrates) or individual responsibility for having committed the crime in question (it involved witnesses too). Moreover, torture differed from ordeal, which had nothing to do with forcing the will of someone, and was related to the irrational and superstitious conviction that a particular reaction by the accused to a cruel practice, such as bad water,[5] would be a sign of truth. By contrast, torture had a 'rational' (if wrong) connection with truth.

U*nder certain conditions* torture in the pre-modern age was clearly considered legal and right. So it was in theory and in law, so in Antiquity and in the Middle Ages. In practice torture was used not only for judicial reasons, but also for more general purposes. It was applied in order to destroy the enemy, including the ideological or religious enemy, i.e. related to political aims. We may think of the Inquisition or the torture of Christians in Ancient Rome because they were Christian.[6]

If this is true, and if my interpretation of Machiavelli is correct, as early as the 16th century, for instance in Machiavelli's *Discourses*, we can find a political justification of extreme punishments including torture. Machiavelli was not a precursor, but a good interpreter of his age. In this sense Machiavelli is important for my purpose; to reflect on his theory and later on some Enlightenment thinkers seems to me interesting for the present.

Focusing on Machiavelli's thought is particularly interesting for two different reasons. For one thing, after he was accused of conspiracy and arrested, he was himself tortured. And then again, he explicitly revealed the true nature of torture, its double face: the political and the judicial.

So, a word about Machiavelli. On 18 February 1512, Niccolò Machiavelli was accused as a presumed partner of Pier Paolo Boscoli and Agostino Capponi in their conspiracy against the De Medici cardinal who would later become Pope Leone X. After his arrest he was tortured, as he told Francesco Vettori in a letter dated 13 March 1513, when he left prison. This was the traditional use of torture. Judges tried to obtain his confession. He was innocent and did not confess anything. But that is not the most interesting thing as such. What I find more relevant is the reaction and the opinion Machiavelli seems to have on torture *in general*, because – as we can see in the correspondence with Vettori – he did not condemn the event in itself, he did not reject torture, but the way in which in *that* (his) particular situation it was used.

---

4   P. Fiorelli, *La tortura giudiziaria nel diritto comune* (Milan, Giuffrè, 1954) Vol. I.
5   See *Numbers* 5:4-31
6   Fiorelli, *La tortura giudiziaria nel diritto comune*, p. 45.

In Machiavalli's opinion, torture can be unfairly suffered, that is, it can be *fairly* suffered. When is torture unjust? When it is used against people that are only suspected and not only against people who are seriously suspected or considered guilty.[7] The point at issue and the reason for his bitterness are not connected with the injustice of that institution; on the contrary, they depend on the fact that a non-liberal and suspicious political and social context make application of it unfair. But the reason for this justification of torture is not the traditional one: the reason grounded on the need to expiate someone's extreme guilt or to receive confession and information about a crime. Moreover, Machiavelli seems to know that in particular this way of obtaining a confession is dangerous and problematic in itself (as his biography shows).

The 23rd chapter of his *Discourses* is of capital importance in this context. The title is 'How much did the Romans avoid using moderation in judging their subjects'. Machiavelli's thesis is that Romans used no moderation and they were right in so doing. In fact extreme punishments are the necessary instrument not for justice (justice is not the end of adjudication), but for ' control over subjects which cannot and must not be offensive any more'.[8] 'That is possible – Machiavelli continues – in two ways, either by eliminating every possibility of being harmful, or giving them everything they desire'.[9] With Livy, Machiavelli concludes: 'you have to annihilate them, making them totally dependent on your power, either by punishment, or by inducements.[10]

First of all, here extreme punishments are not a judicial instrument, but punishments. They are not the outcome of applying the criterion of proportionality between crime and punishment. They are related to *political reasons*, which can justify the absence of penal proportionality as the criterion of fairness. Machiavelli thinks that the independence of punishment from a proportional relationship with crimes and even from application of the criterion of retribution has to be rightly understood. It is here fundamental to look at the relationship between punishment and the political circumstances. Punishment has to satisfy the political needs and requirements of the ruler. In 1502 Florentine people made exactly this mistake: They looked at proportionality and respected moderation in their judgements after the rebellions of Arezzo and Val di Chiana. By contrast, the right criterion is for Machiavelli the criterion of political efficacy. 'They used,' he tells us, 'the criterion of moderation which is very dangerous in judging people'.[11]

Here we see the primacy of politics over law, the priority of efficacy of political decision over moral and legal correctness. For these reasons Machiavelli defends extreme punishments like torture, and supports rulers and judges in using them for political ends, in particular to stabilize power.

---

7   Machiavelli, *Lettere*, p. 99.
8   Machiavelli, *Discorsi sopra la prima deca di Tito Livio*, p. 280.
9   Ibid.
10   Ibid.
11   Ibid., p. 283.

In paragraph 16 of the rightly famous *Dei delitti e delle pene* (1764) by Cesare Beccaria the argument on torture presupposes an idea of torture as judicial torture, which was considered a useful instrument for obtaining a confession or good information, or for discovering the truth before a trial, or an extreme punishment suited to very serious crimes, purifying the accused from the infamy deriving from heavy guilt.[12]

In order to condemn torture and demonstrate its incompatibility with legal order, Beccaria produces four interrelated arguments.

The first argument corresponds to the principle of the presumption of innocence. 'A person cannot be considered guilty and the state cannot refuse him its public protection until it is demonstrated by trial that he has violated the social contract. What sort of law can authorize a judge to punish a citizen before the sentence? Only a law such as force'.[13] The second argument concerns the usefulness of torture. It is not only true that torture is unjust in itself, but it is also useless and a source of mistakes:

> The offence is certain or uncertain. If it is certain, the punishment that law prescribes in each case is enough, and torture is useless, because judges do not need a confession. If it is uncertain, it is wrong to torture an innocent person, because they are innocent until proven guilty. And I add that it goes against all reasons to expect that a person be at the same time the accused and the accuser, and that pain should be the test of truth, as if truth resided in the muscles and fibres of a wretch under torture. That is an instrument for acquitting criminals and condemning feeble innocents.[14]

The third argument is related to the intrinsic irrationality of torture as a judicial instrument. Torture presupposes a factual levelling between the criminal and the innocent, and this is contrary to every conception of justice and to the principle of individual responsibility. For this reason it is also incompatible with legality, because it is irrational and unacceptable that the same consequences should derive from being guilty or innocent. Furthermore, Beccaria underlines that a very strange consequence comes from applying torture, because the innocent is put in a worse condition than the criminal. Indeed, either the former confesses and is accused, or he is recognized innocent and has suffered unfair torments. By contrast, the criminal in any case has an advantage. If he confesses, he is condemned for his guilt, but he has a chance of avoiding this. If he resists torture with determination, he has to be acquitted. He has exchanged a bad punishment for a better one. In the end, an innocent person can only lose, the criminal can only win.

When Beccaria refers to torture as the punishment for an infamous act, he presents his fourth argument, based on a principle of justice, because in this case the problem consists in the abuse of power that torture implies. In torturing, the political

---

12   C. Beccaria, *Dei delitti e delle pene*, ed. by A. Burgio (Milano, Feltrinelli, 2007).
13   Ibid. p. 60.
14   Ibid.

authority exceeds its constitutive limits. And that is nonsense again, because 'infamy would be eliminated through infamy'!

Let me now briefly turn to another Italian philosopher, Pietro Verri. When he writes on torture and its intrinsic injustice Verri is thinking about judicial torture, which is usually justified by the argument of public security and the common good. As is well-known, this sort of justification will be very clearly elaborated by Utilitarianism. In this regard a passage from the Manuscripts by Jeremy Bentham is paradigmatic. Here the utilitarian philosopher points out two cases in which torture may be applied:

> There seem to be two Cases in which Torture may with propriety be applied. 1. The first is where the thing which a Man is required to do being a thing which the public has an interest in his doing, is a thing which for a certainty is in his power to do; and which therefore so long as he continues to suffer for not doing he is sure not to be innocent. 2. The second is where a man is required what probably though not certainly it is in his power to do; and for the not doing of which it is possible that he may suffer, although he be innocent; but which the public has so great an interest in his doing that the danger of what may ensue from his not doing it is a greater danger than even that of an innocent person's suffering the greatest degree of pain that can be suffered by Torture, of the kind and in the quantity permitted to be employed[15]

In order to favour general interests – that is the argument – it would be justified to sacrifice the interest of a single individual.

Against this common opinion, Verri's arguments are partially Beccaria's arguments (… we know how bitter Verri's feelings were against Beccaria, who was accused of having plagiarized arguments by other authors, in particular by Verri himself). In any case, polemics apart, it is worth concentrating on Verri's arguments against torture, because some of them are very interesting, original, and in my opinion, strong.

The first of Verri's arguments is the well-known argument of the usefulness of torture as an instrument of truth. The other four arguments are specifications of the general argument of injustice. They are answers to the question: Why is torture unjust as such? Here Verri's considerations are very fertile.

First of all, torture exhibits an excessive nature. It is essentially excessive and for this reason it is impossible to limit and moderate it through laws or judicial practices. Torture is excessive or it is not torture. Torture is efficacious and extreme or it is not torture at all. Torture is structurally unjust: it is a form of injustice. Pretending to avoid this excessive character is like pretending to avoid the excessive character in something that is *by nature excessive*. It would become something radically different.

A second argument concerns the injustice peculiar to every act which is superabundant in doing evil. Torture, in other words, has some psychological implications, because it reveals the obscure sadistic face of human nature. Verri stresses that after

---

15   J. Bentham, Manuscripts, University College, London 46/63-70, in W. L. and P. E. Twining, 'Bentham on Torture' *Northern Ireland Legal Quarterly* 24 (1973): 307-356, pp. 312-313.

the initial disgust, torturers take pleasure from torturing; compassion and humanitarian feelings fade away. The third argument is the one already mentioned: the presumption of innocence. The fourth one consists in recognition of the contra-naturam character of torture. Forcing a confession, forcing one's own confession, forcing the principle of self-conservation to be violated, that is, the fundamental right to life prescribed by natural law, is an action against nature itself. This argument of the contra-naturam character together with the argument of the excessive nature of torture is peculiar and fundamental, because it insists on an evident violation of the basic individual right to life.

At this point, the German philosopher of law Christian Thomasius is very helpful for my chapter, and may bring us to a conclusion.

Thomasius writes on torture in his essay *Dissertatio de Tortura* (1705, more than three centuries ago). It is an essay in two parts. In the first part the author presents some historical-reconstructive reflections. In the second part he presents his normative and critical theories. His first argument is the last one we described in talking about Verri: the argument of the contra-naturam character of torture. The second one is the usually recognized argument of the presumption of innocence. The third one is the frequently maintained argument of the usefulness of torture and of its paradoxical character so well described by Beccaria, as we have just seen: judges lose rather than gain certainty in finding judicial truth.[16] The fourth argument is new and relevant in this context. It deals with conventions and tradition. For Thomasius it is not a good argument to justify torture on the grounds of its antiquity. History is not a principle of justification at all. In this regard we may remember the poor eels of Benjamin Constant's French cook and his connected argument against slavery: for injustice there is no justification through time.[17]

But another argument by Thomasius is decisive for us. He dedicates an entire paragraph (number 4 of the second part) to the *political nature* of torture. Here he writes: 'Punishments give an opportunity to all tyrants to act cruelly towards their subjects, misrepresenting justice. Torture gives the more powerful an instrument by which to harm innocent and hated people'.[18] It is a very clear passage. Torture is a judicial instrument but also a *political* one, because this is an instrument for fighting efficaciously against ideological and political enemies – a very significant aspect of the current application of torture.

D: Concluding remarks

Such was Thomasius' criticism three centuries ago. Old arguments supporting torture such as the Benthamite argument, and old practices such as torture in its different applications are unfortunately recurring.

16 Part B, §§ 2 and 3
17 Thomasius, *De l'Esprit de conquête et de l'usurpation*, chap. XIII, fn. 2
18 Thomasius, *Über die Folter*, p. 164

The 'old' counter-arguments are therefore still valid and have not lost their argumentative force.

Torture has a dual nature: it is judicial *and* political.

Torture is useless in terms of public interest and produces paradoxical outcomes for any trial.

Torture is unjust for at least four main reasons: (i) *it violates* the principle of *the presumption of innocence*; (ii) it implies depreciation of fundamental rights, in particular and first of all *the right to life*; (iii) it is essentially excessive and *cannot be moderated* by legal norms; (iv) finally it *cannot be justified by tradition*.

All this was already clear and evident to Enlightenment thinkers. But these ideas no longer seem so evident today; they are again under debate. They have a worrying topicality, because torture is a cogent reality as a political instrument, as a judicial instrument, and, last but not least, as a practice prejudicial to prisoners, immigrants, and refugees. My impression is that these circumstances show the regressive character of the present, in which subjective rights seem to 'have a price': the price of so-called public security: people expect to legitimize something that is a contradiction in itself, since in a democracy law and torture cannot go together. Torture supporters expect to transform subjective rights into relative rights, which can be sacrificed in the name of public utility and the common interest; relative rights which cannot be defined – borrowing Ronald Dworkin's metaphor – as 'trumps' anymore, but simply as good cards, whose importance depends on contingent conditions; they are always held in reserve.

We may hope that the democratic crisis is only temporary, that the modern democratic process forms part of a general dialectical dynamic. We may hope that the present time is a moment in a progressive process. But for that very reason we have to reflect on the Enlightenment theses and take them seriously. We must not ignore the real meaning of Verri's words with regard to the present situation: they sound, to my mind, like a warning against indifference, against the current risk of underestimating the immorality of torture and what is at stake in terms of constitutional rights.

'It seems impossible to me,' Verri wrote in 1770, 'that torturing could have persisted for so long': never has a prediction erred more than this on the side of optimism.

9. Nursing During National Socialism: Complicity in Terror, and Heroism

Alison J. O'Donnell, Susan Benedict, Jochen Kuhla and Linda Shields

A.   Introduction

In 1933, Adolf Hitler came to power in Germany bringing with him the beliefs, policies and doctrines of National Socialism. All Germans, and many others in the occupied countries of Europe, had their lives controlled by the Nazis until mid-1945. Nurses, like their colleagues in medicine, were important in the implementation of the genocidal goals of the Nazis.

This paper describes the way nursing was organized, regulated, controlled, and practiced during the era of the Third Reich. Using primary sources of legislation, interviews and trial transcripts, and supported by secondary sources which explain the development of the laws surrounding nursing, we present a description and explanation of nursing practice during this unique era.

Nursing in Germany had had a long history, but was changed dramatically by the prevailing philosophies of eugenics and National Socialism. In some institutions, egregious crimes such as the murder of psychiatric patients were carried out by nurses who subscribed to these philosophies or who believed they would be punished if they did not. However, some nurses, at great personal risk, were able to resist, often saving the lives of their vulnerable patients. The organizational structure of the various organizations made nursing a decentralized profession without a unified and powerful voice contributing to the lack of any but individual resistance.

B. The Development of Nursing in Germany

Germany made an important contribution to the development of the nursing profession worldwide. The deaconess schools and motherhouses which saw the education of young women to care for the sick and needy, begun in the late 1700s (1782 Franz Anton Mai in Mannheim), were the first formal schools of nursing.[1]

German nursing was organized according to the *Mutterhaus* (mother house) concept which was an outgrowth of the religious order of St. Vincent de Paul. In the first half of the 19th century, Theodor Fliedner, an Evangelical pastor of the Rhineland, founded a community which resembled in several ways the Mutterhaus of St. Vincent. Women, known as 'Deaconesses' lived together in a motherhouse where they received education in both nursing care and religion. These Deaconesses came to be regarded as the exemplar of nursing. Florence Nightingale came from England

---

1   M. P. Donahue, *Nursing: the Finest Art* (St Louis, MO, Mosby, 1985).

to spend time with the Deaconesses in Kaiserwerth in 1850, which at the time was regarded as the center of nursing education in Europe. At Kaiserwerth, Nightingale was impressed with Fliedner but found the nursing standards there to be inferior to those she observed at the Sisters of Charity hospital in Paris.[2]

By the end of the 19th century, a 'good trained nurse' was one who was unquestioning in her obedience and selfless in her service to others.[3] Obedience and self-denial were paramount in Nightingale nurses who were 'reared in an atmosphere of obedience and conformity'.[4] A secular approach to caring was advocated as Germany, like other nations, experienced socio-economic and cultural changes which accompanied rapid industrialization and urbanization, advances in medicine, philanthropic initiatives in welfare and the emancipation of women. Increasing sophistication in medicine led to a demand for a better class of nurses.[5]

Before World War One (WW1), population growth and development of a growing industrial proletariat, coupled with a rising middle class, altered the health needs of the people and increased the need for nurses both in hospitals and private homes. Increasing demands for nurses enabled some of them to become independent, to separate themselves from restrictive regimes of their training schools, and for the first time to work privately. Nurses who chose to work independently were called 'free' *frei* or 'wild' *wilde* nurses,[6] and often worked in poor conditions, accepting low wages in return for independence.[7]

Changing views of women's roles in society enabled nurses to gain economic independence.[8] Consequently, nursing began to be perceived as a more socially acceptable occupation.[9] Women began to search for new roles outside the traditional confines of *'Kind, Küche, Kirche'*, (children, kitchen, church).

At the beginning of the 20th Century, German nurses sought to establish themselves as members of a profession rather than a charitable and religious enterprise.

2   L. McDonald, *The Collected Works of Florence Nightingale* (Waterloo (Ontario), Wilfrid Laurier University Press, 2001).

3   C. Maggs, *The Origins of General Nursing* (London, Croom Helm, 1983); S. M. Collins and E. R. Parker 'A Victorian Matron; No Ordinary Woman. Eva Charlotte Ellis Lückes (8 July 8 1854-16 February 1919)', *International History of Nursing Journal* 7 (2003): 66-74.

4   M. Baly, *Florence Nightingale and the Nursing Legacy* (London, Croom Helm, 1986), p. 34.

5   C. Helmstadter, "A Real Tone': Professionalizing Nursing in Nineteenth-Nentury London', *Nursing History Review* 11 (2003): 3-30.

6   S. Hahn, 'Nursing Issues in the Third Reich', in J. J. Michalczyk (ed.), *Medicine, Ethics and the Third Reich: Historical and Contemporary Issues* (Kansas City, Sheed and Ward, 1994).

7   G. Boschma, 'Agnes Karll and the Creation of an Independent German Nursing Association', 1900-1927', *Nursing History Review* 4 (1996): 51-168.

8   L. Dock, 'Nursing Organization in Germany', (1901) *ICN Report* 443; L. Dock, *A History of Nursing: Volume IV* (New York, Putman, 1912); Boschma, 'Agnes Karll'; Hahn, 'Nursing Issues'.

9   E. R. Benson, 'Nursing in Germany: a Historical Study of the Jewish Presence', *Nursing History Review* 3 (1995): 189-202; H. Steppe, 'Nursing in Nazi Germany', *Western Journal of Nursing Research* 14 (1992): 744-753; K. M. Klindt, "Gender', and 'Class', as Categories of Nursing History: Male Nurses in the Professionalization of Nursing in the Late Imperial Germany', *Pflege* 9 (1998): 35-42.

Such ambitions reflected the growing international women's movement.[10] Similarly to the United Kingdom (UK), professional registration initiatives were instituted and by 1907 the 'Regulations of a State Examination for Nursing Personnel in Prussia' was in place. In order to take the examination, one had to provide an elementary school certificate, be 21 years of age, physically and psychologically fit and show proof of participation in a one-year nursing course.[11] Similar regulations were enacted in 1908 in Württemberg and Hesse, 1909 in Saxony, 1919 in Baden and 1920 in Bavaria. After WW1, Prussia, Saxony, Hesse, Thuringia, Hamburg and Braunschweig increased the length of required training to two years and lowered the mandatory age to 20 years. Bavaria, Baden, Württemberg, Bremen and Mecklenburg retained the one-year training period. Inherent within German nurses at this time was a strong commitment to the idea of care, service, duty, obedience and unquestioning loyalty to the (usually male) physician.[12] The virtue of obedience extended to obeying orders issued by senior nurses and hospital administrators.[13]

After WW1, developments in nursing were set in a changing and unstable political situation. Germans resented the perceived unfairness of post-war reparations and the Treaty of Versailles. Rampant inflation, industrial collapse and extreme levels of unemployment caused political turmoil. In 1928 a key event occurred. In the general election, the Nazi Party won 12 seats in the German parliament, the *Reichstag*. Societal problems such as unemployment and inflation continued to favour the Nazis and their denunciation of Jews as the cause of the economic problems. In September 1930, an election was called and the number of Nazi seats in the *Reichstag* increased from 12 to 107. The Nazi party was now the second largest party in Germany. In the June 1932 presidential election, Field Marshal Hindenburg, the incumbent, won with 53% of the vote. Hitler garnered over 36%, coming in second. By 31 July 1932, the Nazi Party held 230 seats, giving Hitler enough strength to establish a coalition government. He, however, refused to do so unless he was Chancellor. Lengthy political crises led to negotiations and Hitler was appointed Chancellor on 30 January 1933 at the age of 43 years.[14]

Coupled with the rise to power of Adolf Hitler was the surge of anti-Semitism across Germany. From the beginning of the 20th Century, anti-Semitism had been an integral part of the conservative political platform. Jews had been successful in German academic, professional, and business circles in Germany. As the economy

10   M. Lungershausen, *Agnes Karll, Her Life, Works and Inheritance* (London, Elwin Staude, 1964).
11   E. von Abendroth and M. T. Strobl, 'Nursing in Germany and Austria', *American Journal of Nursing* 50 (1950): 728-730.
12   D. Mansell and J. Hibberd, 'We Picked the Wrong One to Sterilize: the Role of Nursing in the Eugenics Movement in Alberta, 1920-1940', *International History of Nursing Journal* 4 (1998): 4-11.
13   B. R. McFarlane-Icke, *Nurses in Nazi Germany: Moral Choices in History* (Princeton, Princeton University Press, 1999); E. W. Kintner (ed.), *The Hadamar Trial* (London, William Hodge and Co, 1949); S. Benedict 'Killing While Caring: the Nurses of Hadamar', *Issues in Mental Health Nursing* 24 (2003): 59-79.
14   M. Gilbert, *The Holocaust* (New York, Henry Holt and Company, 1985).

declined and unemployment rose, they became the scapegoats. Where once assimilated with a fairly high rate of intermarriage with non-Jews,[15] they soon found themselves to be the objects of social and economic discrimination. Thus with Hitler coming to power, the smoldering anti-Semitism of the Nazis and right-wing political groups ignited.

C.   Eugenics, health and nursing

In the late 19th and early 20th centuries, a new movement gained credence in Europe and the United States (USA). The 'science' of eugenics influenced political thought and became an integral, if perverted, platform of Nazi thinking. Its influence on German nursing was profound.

Eugenic theories derived from Charles Darwin's Theory of Evolution.[16] However, the idea of being able to manipulate survival of the most desirable human qualities was further developed through the teachings of the founder of eugenics and cousin of Charles Darwin, Sir Frances Galton (1822-1911).[17]

Galton suggested the term 'eugenic' in 1883. He further developed his theories while working in the overcrowded slums of London, where he observed the rise of what he perceived as an underclass, an 'undesirable' race, and formulated a theory of heredity in which improvements in the human race could be obtained by 'selective breeding', rather than by natural inheritance. As this term became incorporated into academic debate, its use by physicians as advocates of social hygiene had authoritarian (and ultimately murderous) implications.[18]

Galton believed that Mendelian laws should be applied not only to physical characteristics but also to human intelligence and ultimately, ominously, to fecundity.[19] He suggested that those who had influence in society, namely medical men, support notions of social purity and racial hygiene through therapeutic and medical intervention, thereby preserving a race's hereditary worth. In 1905, Professor Albert Ploetz (1860-1940) founded the German Society for Racial Hygiene in Berlin, which

15   C. Browning, *The Origins of the Final Solution* (Lincoln, University of Nebraska Press, 2004).

16   P. Weindling, *Health, Race and German Politics Between Unification and Nazism 1870-1945* (Cambridge, Cambridge University Press, 1989); International Medical Editorial Bulletin, 'Contemporary Lessons from Nazi Medicine', *International Medical Editorial Bulletin* 6 (1989): 13-20.

17   M. Baly, *Nursing and Social Change* (London, Routledge, 1995 (3rd ed.)); Mansell and Hibberd, 'We Picked the Wrong One to Sterilize'.

18   Weindling, *Health, Race and German Politics*; R. S. Cowan, 'Nature and Nurture: the Interplay of Biology and Politics in the Thoughts of Francis Galton', *Studies in the History of Biology* 9 (1977): 133.

19   Baly, *Nursing*; M. Burleigh, *Death and Deliverance* (Cambridge, Cambridge University Press, 1994).

funded racial hygiene chairs in prominent medical schools.[20] 'Racial hygiene' began to be widely supported as physicians sought to halt what they perceived to be the biological and psychological deterioration of the German *Volk*.[21] In 1907, the medical profession drew further inspiration from the radical and pioneering sterilization programs of the mentally disabled in Indiana, USA.[22]

In Germany and the UK, as a consequence of these views, numbers of patients admitted to psychiatric institutions increased. Reasons for admission varied from mental illness, to vagrancy, prostitution, theft, production of an illegitimate child, political crimes, congenital physical and mental handicaps in children, or being a Jew, Jehovah's Witness, *Sinti* or *Roma,* or homosexual.[23] Anyone deemed not able to make a meaningful contribution to German society was *lebensunwertes Leben,* 'life not worth living'.[24]

World War One further concentrated this eugenic ethos as numbers of perceived 'good healthy Germans' perished in combat,[25] while 'incurables' were cared for in institutions.[26] Between 1914-1919 over 45,000 of the pre-war institutional population died as a result of deliberate starvation, neglect and extreme privations of war.[27] With severe monetary problems following WW1, psychiatric patients were moved into rural areas in an effort to decentralize the cost of care.[28] In these areas, the number of people perceived to be abnormal escalated and eugenic theory increasingly became the accepted norm, offering an apparently rational solution to a growing problem. Instead of providing further support in community settings, psychiatrists created a two-tier system with intensive therapy for acute cases and minimal therapy

20   R. J. Proctor, *Medical Killing in the Nazi Era* (New York, Basic Books, 1986); Weindling, *Health, Race and German Politics.*

21   M. J. Franzblau, 'Ethical Values in Health Care in 1995: Lessons from the Nazi Period', *The Journal of the Medical Association of Georgia* 6 (1995): 161-164.

22   M. Gwyther and S. McColville, 'Nazi Experiments; Can Good Come from Evil?', (19/11/1989) *Observer Magazine* 18.

23   R. C. Baum, *The Holocaust and the German Elite Genocide and the National Suicide in Germany, 1871-1945* (New York, Totowa Rowman and Littlefield, 1981); R. Plant, *The Pink Triangle: the Nazi War Against Homosexuals* (New York, Henry Holt and Company, 1986); J. Chicago, *Holocaust Project from Darkness into Light* (New York, Viking, 1993); United States Holocaust Memorial Museum, Holocaust Museum – permanent exhibition: display case 13 (Washington DC, United States Holocaust Memorial Museum Washington DC, 2000).

24   J. A. Burgess, 'The Great Slippery Slope Argument', *Journal of Medical Ethics* 2 (1991): 169-174; R. J. Lifton, *The Nazi Doctors: Medical Killing and the Psychology of Genocide* (New York, Basic Books, 1986); G. Aly, P. Chroust and C. Pross, *Cleansing the Fatherland: Nazi Medicine and Racial Hygiene* (Baltimore, John Hopkins University Press, 1994).

25   J. E. Gardella, 'Medicine in Nazi Germany: 1933-1945', *North Carolina Medical Journal* 5 (1994): 188-192.

26   M. Burleigh, 'Racism as a Social Policy: the Nazi 'Euthanasia', Programme 1939-1945', *Ethnic and Racial Studies* 14 (1991): 453-473; M. Burleigh, 'Euthanasia in the Third Reich: Some Recent Literature', *Social History of Medicine* 4 (1991): 317-328.

27   J. S. Kestenberg, 'Children Under the German Yoke', *British Journal of Psychotherapy* 8 (1992): 374-390.

28   B. Geary, *Hitler and Nazism* (London, Routledge, 1993).

for chronic patients, coupled with sterilization of those discharged from institutions.[29]

By the late 1920s, the eugenics movement was gaining strength. Influential academics adopted and supported these views in Germany and other countries. In the UK, the prominent birth control campaigner Marie Stopes stated: 'for the careless, stupid or feeble-minded who persist in producing infants of no value to the State and often a charge upon it, the right course seems to be sterilization'.[30] Eminent German geneticists Erwin Baur, Eugen Fisher, Fritz Lenz, Theodor Mollison, and Ernst Rüdin promoted the definition of different human phenotypes; health, sanity and intelligence were considered positive and superior (*höherwertig*) while sickness, insanity and mental retardation were negative attributes (*minderwertig*).[31] During the 1920s, these scientists colluded with the rising Nazi Party in order to promote 'eugenics' legislation, which they redefined 'race hygiene'.[32]

D.   Implementation of eugenic theories

Physicians' responsibility to promote the health of society and the nation included the ethos of survival of the best or fittest; therefore medicine and nursing should act in the interests of future generations. In the 1920s, the Nazis combined these concepts of health and eugenics with anti-Semitism into their ideology.[33] Genetic health courts enforced the involuntary sterilization of people by vasectomy or tubal ligation; physicians were required to report every case of genetic illness or be fined 150 Reichsmark (RM).[34] Midwives and doctors were compelled to report any infant born with an abnormality, and community nurses had to report people who were considered 'unfit' under the racial codes. Racial hygiene was perceived as a cost-effective solution to escalating welfare costs, specifically targeting psychiatric patients in hospitals.[35] Society had the right and the responsibility to exterminate the unworthy,

---

29   Burleigh, 'Euthanasia'.
30   M. C. Stopes, *Wise Parenthood* (London, Pitman's and Sons Ltd, 1927), p. 42.
31   B. Müller-Hill, *Murderous Science: Elimination by Scientific Selection of Jews, Gypsies and Others, Germany 1933-1945* (Oxford, Oxford University Press, 1992). (Phenotype: the way in which the genotype, or genetic makeup, is expressed in the body. For example, the gene for blue eyes as a unit of inheritance would provide the genetic makeup for that gene and if inherited, would be expressed as the phenotype for the individual having blue eyes or not depending on the dominance of the trait of the gene: see B. Gates, *Learning Disabilities*, 3rd ed., New York, Churchill Livingstone, 1997).
32   Weindling, *Health, Race and German Politics*; Müller-Hill, *Murderous Science*.
33   R. J. Evans, *In Defence of History* (London, Granta Books, 1997).
34   Gardella, 'Medicine in Nazi Germany'; M. Burleigh, *Death and Deliverance* (Cambridge, Cambridge University Press, 1994).
35   Aly, Chroust and Pross, *Cleansing the Fatherland*; Gardella, 'Medicine in Nazi Germany'.

individuals who could not contribute to society, and to protect and preserve those deemed worthy, and nurses played an important role.

Lebensunwertes Leben (life unworthy of life) ideology was promoted widely in literature, the popular press and films. School textbooks featured mathematical exercises based upon the cost of care of the mentally ill.[36] During the 1930s the public were encouraged to visit psychiatric hospitals to view the disabled.[37] Visits were organized with nationalistic groups, including Hitler Youth, League of German Maidens, Nazi Women's organization, nurses, lawyers, teachers, midwives and members of the SA *(Sturmabteilungen)* and SS *(Schutzstaffel)*. Institutions themselves organized these visits to emphasize their positive role in institutional care.[38] In reality, the tours disseminated racial hygiene propaganda[39] by placing on display those patients with the most visible and severe disabilities.

E. Nursing and National Socialism

Pioneering educational and practice partnerships were created in the form of newly established training schools for nurses and community nursing posts, as the Nazi Party idealized feminine and motherly roles of the nurse. The National Socialist Physicians' League *(Nationalsozialistischer Ärztebund,* NSDÄB), founded in 1929 at the Nuremberg Nazi Party Congress, had the express goal of promoting racial hygiene, racial science and eugenics in public health. National Socialism was openly endorsed and supported by the traditionally nationalistic medical profession. Jewish physicians lost their academic appointments and had their practices limited to Jewish patients.

The ability to influence the security and tenure of colleagues' positions coincided with a rise in the popularity and membership of the NSDÄB. As doctors worked at the edge of life and death, it was they who controlled and influenced the creation of a purified, scientific and superior *Volk* population.[40] The ethos of National Socialism combined with the ethical and established values of German nursing, served as an ideal platform from which the NSDAP promoted nurses as their 'political soldiers' of healthcare, and through this 'heroic service', nurses had a direct influence on the German people with whom they came into contact.[41] In preparing for impending war, tensions developed. The NSDAP tried to influence the nursing profession by

36   A. Donner (1935), *Mathematik im Dienste der nationalpolitischen Erziehung*, in R. Proctor 'The Destruction of "Lives not Worth Living"', in R. Proctor, *Racial Hygiene: Medicine Under the Nazis* (Cambridge (Massachusetts), Harvard University Press, 1998) 184.
37   Burleigh, *Death and Deliverance*; McFarlane-Icke, *Nurses in Nazi Germany*.
38   Burleigh, *Death and Deliverance*.
39   Burleigh, 'Racism as a Social Policy'.
40   Proctor, *Medical Killing*.
41   Steppe, 'Nursing in Nazi Germany'.

suggesting that the number of nurses to be trained annually should be increased. Traditional nursing virtues of obedience, unquestioning loyalty, duty and conformity which had become internalized amongst some middle class German women were adopted and transferred as the new authority to the Nazi women's movement within the NSDAP.[42]

F. The organization of nursing under National Socialism

In 1903, the Association of the Nursing Professionals in Germany (*Berufsorganisation der Krankenpflegerinnen Deutschlands*, BOKD) was founded through the influence of Agnes Karll (1868-1927).[43] Membership comprised *frei* nurses; *Mutterhaus* nurses such as those in the Catholic and Protestant organizations could not be members. BOKD represented interests of nurses including development of professional training and benefits, and it functioned as an employment agency. Soon, BOKD became the supplier of nurses to hospitals and nursing schools as well as providing continuing education. BOKD became a member of the International Council of Nursing (ICN) in 1904.

Karll, although she died prior to 1933, believed that nurses would be promoters of 'hygiene and social progress', and this remained an inherent belief of practicing nurses.[44] With the advent of National Socialism,

> The nurse, who until then had worked quietly and effectively, was now supposed to become aggressive and a political soldier of the health service. ... the well known (nursing) values continued to be valid and were cleverly combined with the ideas of National Socialism.[45]

Political changes following WW1 facilitated further emancipation of nurses. Seventy-five percent of all German nurses belonged to a *Mutterhaus* which provided education, employment, and retirement benefits. Strong unions, the Free Union and the Reich's Union of Nurses, worked for their members, for better pay and decreased working hours. Dictates forbidding marriage were removed from employment contracts. During this time, the organization of nursing as a profession within the parameters of the *Volk* and values of the 'good German woman' was important.[46] With the advent of Nazism, German nurses found themselves with low social standing, no tradition of assertiveness; poorly paid, lacking a supportive professional or-

---

42   R. Bridenthal, A. Grossman and M. Kaplan (eds.), *When Biology Became Destiny: Women in Weimar and Nazi Germany* (New York, Monthly Review Press, 1982).
43   G. Boschma, 'Agnes Karll and the Creation of an Independent German Nursing Association 1900-1927', *Nursing History Review* 4 (1996): 51-168.
44   Ibid.
45   H. Steppe, 'Nursing in the Third Reich', *History of Nursing Journal* 3 (1991): 21-37, pp. 25-26.
46   Mansell and Hibberd, 'We Picked the Wrong One to Sterilize'.

ganization and increasingly dominated by the highly influential physicians of the NSDÄB.

The Nazi government recognized that nursing must be reorganized and controlled in order to implement their racial policies. The NSDAP appointed nursing leaders who fully supported and strongly influenced the pivotal position of nursing. In one of the nursing publications of the time (1934), Jensen wrote:

> I hope that I may be understood when I say that National Socialism cannot do without exercising its influence over such a large and important profession as nursing. Indeed it must irrefutably take on the nursing profession in a special and thorough manner, since nurses belong to that group of persons who, firstly, have important responsibilities to carry out in the area of national health, and, secondly, are in such intimate and direct contact with their national comrades under such special circumstances, that they can have an especially great educational influence on them.[47]

This statement was congruent with the medical profession's prediction of the future of nursing:

> The requirements which German nurses in social and medical service have to meet in the new state are completely different from the previous period in many respects. The new state does not only want to look after the sick and weak; it also wants to secure a healthy development of all national comrades, and also to improve their health, if their inherited biological predisposition allow for it. Above all, the new state wants to secure and promote a genetically sound, valuable race and, in contrast to the past, not to expend an exaggerated effort on the care of genetically or racially inferior people. Of course, such people must be looked after, but no longer be supported and promoted at the cost of the more valuable people.[48]

Occurring concurrently with this reorganization of nursing and hugely influential was emphasis on collective health of the *Volk*, rather than the individual. *Vorsorge* – the notion that the focus of care should be on the promotion of health of the *Volk* rather than on providing for ill individuals (*Fürsorge*) – emerged as the new order.[49] The individual became valued only for his or her contribution to society, while those unable to contribute had no right to be cared for and should be removed for the good of the *Volk*. Public health's new slogan was *Vorsorge statt Fürsorge*.[50]

There were a number of disparate nursing organizations. In 1933, the Red Swastika Nurses (*Roten Hakenkreuzschwestern*), whose function was to care for sick members of the Nazi Party, aid in military operations and political party events, and to care for relatives of members of the Nazi Party who were incarcerated, was

47   Jenson (1934), cited in Steppe, 'Nursing in Nazi Germany', p. 746.
48   F. Bartels (1933), in S. Hahn, 'Nursing Issues During the Third Reich', in J. M. Michalczyk (ed.), *Medicine, Ethics, and the Third Reich: Historical and Contemporary Issues* (Kansas City, Sheed and Ward, 1994) 143, pp. 143-144).
49   W. Reich, 'The Care-Based Ethic of Nazi Medicine and the Moral Importance of What We Care About', *American Journal of Bioethics* 1 (2001): 68-69.
50   H. Steppe, 'Nursing Under Totalitarian Regimes: the Case of National Socialism', a paper presented at the Congress Nursing, Women's History and the Politics of Welfare (Nottingham, England. 23/07/1993), p. 3.

formed. In May 1934, the Red Swastika nursing organization was dissolved and the NS *Schwesternschaft* (National Socialist Nursing Organization, NSS), known as the 'Brown' nurses for the color of their uniforms[51] was formed. Their main area was to be community nursing because that is where they could have the greatest influence.[52] A NS *Schwesternschaft* mother house was established in the Rudolf Hess Hospital in Dresden. Eight week courses on National Socialism were held there beginning 1 October 1934.[53]

The *Deutsche Arbeitsfront* (DAF, German Labor Front),[54] consolidated the numerous small nursing organizations in 1933. Nurses previously associated with a union were taken over by a national organization, *Reichsgemeinschaft öffentlicher Betriebe*, which was concerned with wages. Male and female nurses were in different organizations. The organizations for the female nurses were:

1. *der Caritasverband* (the Caritas Organization, the Catholic nurses' organization, 1937)
2. *die Schwestern des Deutschen Roten Kreuzes* (Red Cross, 1934)
3. *der Reichsbund der Freier Schwestern* (Federation of Free Nurses, 1936)
4. *die Diakoniegemeinschaft* (the Protestant Nurses' Organization, 1933)
5. *die NS Schwesternschaft* (National Socialist Nursing Association, 1934)[55]

The majority of nurses belonged to the two religious organizations, the *Caritasverband* and the *Diakoniegemeinschaft* with the Nazi nurses claiming just 1001 nurses in 1934.[56] In 1935, the Reich's Women's Leader Gertrud Scholtz-Klink formed the Expert Committee for Nursing within the Association of Free Welfare Work. Two nursing leaders were appointed by Scholtz-Klink.[57] This reorganization effectively meant that all nurses who wanted to practice had to be a member of one of these organizations. Nevertheless, the appointment of matrons selected by the Nazi party further restricted the role, remit and status of nursing. Under their leadership, National Socialism gained a greater and uncontested influence.[58]

Nursing was perceived by society as being highly disciplined and hierarchical with members who, through self-sacrifice and a religious calling, nursed their pa-

---

51   C. Schweikardt, 'You Gained Honor for Your Profession as a Brown Nurse: the Career of a National Socialist Nurse Mirrored by her Letters Home', *Nursing History Review* 12 (2004): 121-138.

52   H. Steppe, 'Nursing since 1933', *Krankenpflege im Nationalsozialismus* (Frankfurt am Main, Mabuse-Verlag, 1996 (8th ed.)).

53   R. J. Proctor, *Racial Hygiene: Medicine under the Nazis* (Cambridge, MA, Harvard University Press, 1988).

54   *Deutsche Arbeitsfront* (DAF) was an organization established in 1933 to replace all labour unions, guilds, and professional organizations. 'Its goal was to organize all German labor (mental and physical) and to train all authentic Germans into an effective work community'. See R. Michael and K Doerr. 2002. *Nazi-Deutsch, Nazi German.* (Westport, CT, Greenwood Press, 2002), p. 119.

55   Steppe, 'Nursing since 1933', p. 65.

56   Ibid.

57   McFarlane-Icke, *Nurses in Nazi Germany*.

58   Proctor, *Medical Killing*.

156

tients.[59] However, nurses in psychiatric institutions were different from the motivated young people portrayed in Nazi propaganda films. Some came into nursing via an in-house staff shuffling,[60] usually from being a kitchen worker or cleaner.[61] Their capacity to care for the sick was not a pre-requisite.[62] If individuals were members of the Nazi Party, their membership permitted them to secure work in the public sector through the German Labour Front and the National Socialist Cell Organization, which was directly involved in employing workers.[63]

Female nurses were required to have one year of domestic service, either in their own homes or in those of someone else, as a prerequisite to nursing.[64] Male caregivers often were older than females, from lower social classes and, prior to the between-war economic crisis, most had been in unskilled employment.[65] Nonetheless, in spite of an ethos of subordination, insecurity and persistently low status for many nurses, others still believed that nursing was a worthwhile career.[66] Under the Nazi biomedical vision, nursing as a profession was given key recognition. With government support, an independent Nazi community nursing service was established to directly influence public health, health education, counselling and health care in rural communities.[67]

Community and Nazi nurses were ordered to actively promote Nazi doctrine as part of their culture, values and working practices.[68] Nurses instructed on the important role of 'Aryan' motherhood advised on healthy lifestyles and reported to the Public Health Officer, both positively and negatively, on local families.[69]

Recruitment and emergence of newly appointed community nurses enabled the Nazi ideology of 'Health of the Nation' to be disseminated in rural areas. This encompassed eugenic, racist and eventually murderous directives.[70] In 1937, the ICN was told of changes being implemented by the Nazi government.[71] Support was

59   McFarlane-Icke, *Nurses in Nazi German.*
60   Ibid.
61   Burleigh, 'Racism as a Social Policy'.
62   H. Steppe, *Krankenplege im Nationalsozialismus* (Frankfurt am Main, Mabuse-Verlag, 1989 (5th ed.)).
63   M. Broszat, *Hitler and the Collapse of Weimar Germany* (Berghahn, New York, 1987).
64   The Reichs Law Review, Part I, Law for the Reorganization of Nursing of 28 September 1938: *Reichsgesetzblatt.* 1938. Nr 154, *Geset zur Ordnung der Krankenpflege. Ausgegeben zn* Berlin, 30 September. Translation by Anette Hebebrand-Verner.
65   McFarlane-Icke, *Nurses in Nazi Germany*; Steppe, 'Nursing in the Third Reich'.
66   McFarlane-Icke, *Nurses in Nazi Germany*; Hahn, 'Nursing Issues'.
67   Steppe, 'Nursing in the Third Reich'.
68   S. Benedict and J. Kuhla, 'Nurses', Participation in the Euthanasia Programs of Nazi Germany', *Western Journal of Nursing Research* 21 (1999): 246-263.
69   Steppe, 'Nursing in the Third Reich'.
70   Weindling, *Health, Race and German Politics.*
71   J. E. Lynaugh, 'From Chaos to Transformation', in B. L. Brush, J. E. Lynaugh, G. Boschma, A. M. Rafferty, M. Stuart and N. J. Tomes (eds.) *Nurses of All Nations: A History of the International Council of Nurses, 1899-1999* (Philadelphia, Lippincott 1999).

sought by key German nursing leaders to oppose these changes to nurses' working practices, but no objections were noted.[72] A nurse working at the time reflected

> Well, actually, everything went by so quietly, there was nothing special, I cannot remember that we reacted in any particular way, we just continued to do our work, only different people were coming ... no really, I have to tell you honestly, it was not the case that we were in any way concerned with these events, it was simply a transition.[73]

Indisputably, this transformation and shift of power proved to be significant.

G. Laws regulating nursing

The Nuremberg Laws of 1935 prohibited gentiles marrying or having sexual intercourse with Jews, thereby 'protecting' future German citizens as a 'pure blood race' .[74] These laws covered health, and from 1939, citizenship, and civil and racial hygiene laws,[75] which enforced inspection and compulsory sterilization of those of non-Aryan descent. Nurses were overtly involved in advisory and reconciliatory roles with victims of sterilizations[76] and in the subsequent 'euthanasia' program, actually administered lethal injections[77]. Others were involved in care for members of party organizations[78] and some were employed in health education programs in work camps, psychiatric hospitals, SS infirmaries and *Reviers* (infirmaries) in concentration camps.[79] Jewish nurses were transferred to newly created segregated ghetto hospitals.[80] Here they received special training to work with patients who had been

72   International Council of Nurses, *Proceedings, International Council of Nurses, Eighth Congress* (1937).

73   Hahn, 'Nursing Issues', p. 142; Ernst Albers: Interview 04/11/1998.

74   Weindling, *Health, Race and German Politics*; R. C. Baum, *The Holocaust and the German Elite Genocide and the National Suicide in Germany, 1871-1945* (New York, Totowa Rowman and Littlefield, 1981

75   Proctor, *Medical Killing*; G. Bock, 'Equality and Difference in National Socialist Racism', in J. W. Scott (ed.), *Feminism and History* (Oxford, Oxford University Press, 1997).

76   Hahn, 'Nursing Issues'.

77   Benedict and Kuhla, 'Nurses' Participation'; Gardella, 'Medicine in Nazi Germany'; Hahn, 'Nursing Issues'; G. Bock, 'Challenging Dichotomies: Perspectives on Women's History', in K. Offen, R. R. Pierson and J. Rendall (eds.), *Writing Women's History: International perspectives* (London, Macmillan, 1992); G. Bock, 'Equality and Difference in National Socialist Racism', in J. W. Scott (ed.), *Feminism and History* (1997).

78   P. J. Brink, 'When Patientology is Ignored: the Case of Nazi Germany', *Western Journal of Nursing Research* 13 (1991): 162-163.

79   S. Benedict, 'The Nadir of Nursing: Nurse-Perpetrators of the Ravensbrück Concentration Camp *Nursing History Review* 11 (2003): 129-146; S. Benedict and J. Georges, 'Nurses and the Sterilization Experiments of Auschwitz: a Postmodernist Perspective', *Nursing Inquiry* 13 (2006): 277-288; J. Georges and S. Benedict, 'An Ethics of Testimony: Prisoner Nurses at Auschwitz', *Advances in Nursing Science* 29 (2006): 161-169.

80   D. Ofer, *Women in the Holocaust* (New York, Yale University, 1998); Benson, 'Nursing in Germany'.

discharged by their Nazi nursing colleagues from Jewish hospitals outside the ghetto boundaries.[81]

H. The National Socialist Nursing Organization

By 1939, 9.2% of all nurses belonged to the NS nursing organization (Table 1). This percentage, however, is not in agreement with the numbers and percentages cited by Breiding.[82] In 1942, the NS nurses organization joined with *Reichbund der Freien Schwestern* ('Blue' nurses), who comprised 20% of German nurses, to form the *NS Reichbund* of German Nurses.[83] Hahn stated that a third (46,855) of nurses belonged to the *NS Reichbund*.[84] (Allowing for an increase in the numbers of nurses from 1939, as reported by Breiding, to 1942, the numbers provided by Breiding and Hahn would be consistent). They worked in 476 hospitals, 4,450 community health stations, and 300 schools of nursing.[85] Many of the nurses who were not politically oriented found themselves, through this forced union with the NS nurses organization, in an uncomfortable position. They were assumed by many non-nurses to be 'Nazis' and the organization expected them to become 'aggressive and a political soldier of the health service'.[86]

Table 1. Numbers of nurses in respective organizations in 1939

Organization	Membership	% of total nurses
Reichsbund	21,459	14.96
NS nurses	10,880	7.59
Red Cross Nurses	14,595	10.17
Catholic Nurses (*Caritasverband*)	50,000	34.86
Protestant Nurses (*Diakoniegemeinschaft*)	46,500	32.42
TOTAL	143,434	100%

81 S. Hahn, 'Nursing Issues in the Third Reich', (1994).
82 B. Breiding, *Die Braunen Schwestern* (Stuttgart, Franz Steiner Verlag, 1998).
83 S. Hahn, (1989) *Faschistische Ideologie und Krankenpflege in Deutschland von 1933 bis 1945, Geschichte der Medizin*, 1901, p. 359.
84 Ibid.
85 Ibid.
86 Steppe, 'Nursing in the Third Reich', pp. 25-26.

In 1938, a law regulating nursing, *Gesetz zur Neuordnung der Krankenpflege,,* stipulated that the medical training of professional nurses would be sanctioned only in state approved schools.[87]

I. Nurses and the implementation of Nazi ideology

Some German nurses swore a public oath of allegiance to the *Führer*, but some were uncomfortable at having to become political.[88] The *NS Schwesternschaft* members were sworn in under the following oath:

> I swear unswerving loyalty and obedience to my *Führer*, Adolf Hitler. I obligate myself as a National Socialist nurse, to fulfill my professional requirements wherever I will work in a loyal and conscientious manner in my service to the people, so help me God.[89]

Even the Red Cross nurses (*die Schwestern des Deutschen Roten Kreuz*) swore their allegiance to Hitler:

> I swear loyalty to the *Führer* of the German people, Adolf Hitler, I solemnly promise obedience and discharge of duties in the work of the German Red Cross according to the orders of my superior. So help me God.[90]

The Protestant nurses organization (*die Diakoniegemeinschaft*), too, was sympathetic to the ideas of National Socialism and did not identify a conflict with the organization's religious affiliation. For example, in 1934, Deaconess D. Bauer wrote in Service to the People (*Dienst am Volk*):

> National Socialism and Socialism, both are not foreign words to the world of deaconry ... Out of this social movement originates the serving throughout and the duty to the community. Also the totalitarian demand of National Socialism is a term we know well because it is something within us although it is characterized differently. This totality demands fight ... Fight is the basic motive of National Socialism ... The *Führer's* thought has been executed in the deaconry ever since the beginning. Discipline and obedience are promoted in the deaconry. Thus the deaconry has already worked for 100 years on a National Socialistic basis. Therefore it greets National Socialism with an open heart...A nurses' association with this ideology can only strengthen a National Socialistic state.[91]

---

87   The Reichs Law Review, Part I, Law for the Reorganization of Nursing of 28 September 1938: *Reichsgesetzblatt.* 1938. Nr 154, *Geset zur Ordnung der Krankenpflege. Ausgegeben zn* Berlin, 30 September. Translation by Anette Hebebrand-Verner.
88   Steppe, 'Nursing in Nazi Germany'.
89   *Bundesarchiv Koblenz*: Head Office of Public Welfare, November 1936, *Bundesarchives* R 36-1061, cited by H. Steppe in 'Nursing under Totalitarian Regimes: the Case of National Socialism', a paper presented at the Congress Nursing, Women's History and the Politics of Welfare (Nottingham, 23 July 1993), cited in Steppe, 'Nursing since 1933'.
90   Steppe, 'Nursing since 1933'.
91   Ibid.

J. Resistance

There were instances where nurses individually, through their own personal conviction, did try to resist Nazi doctrines; however, documented evidence is sparse.[92] Nurses forged patient records to exaggerate the severity of patients' illnesses to defer discharge, or substituted names of the dead for the living patients so they could hide and escape discharge.[93] If discovered, such actions would have had serious consequences for nurses.[94] Individual nurses entrapped in the killing web of the euthanasia program resisted by seeking transfers to other jobs within the same institution or within other institutions. Others became pregnant or moved away.[95] Those who did request transfers or job changes did not suffer reprisals as a result.[96]

K. Conclusion

As the continuum from the prohibition of marriage and relationships between Jews and Aryans, to the sterilization of the handicapped, to the killing of 'lives unworthy of life' developed in Nazi Germany, nurses were involved in every phase. They identified and reported newborns with 'defects', convinced families to relinquish their children to 'Special Children's Units' where they were eventually killed, and rode with adult psychiatric patients on their transports to the killing centres of the 'euthanasia' program where they were gassed. Nurses, acting both on physicians' orders as well as autonomously, killed psychiatric patients by oral and injected overdoses. Over 10,000 patients were killed by nurses.[97] As Jews, Poles, and others deemed 'inferior' were incarcerated in concentration camps, nurses participated – with varying degrees of willingness – in the medical experiments.[98]

It is vital to acknowledge that not all nurses participated in these dreadful events. It was the minority who were either ideologically committed to National Socialism, or who were employed in institutions that were such an integral part of these actions that it would be been extremely difficult to avoid participation – although some did. Yet, just as it is important to know that most German nurses avoided involvement in these events – either by choice or circumstances – it is equally important to understand how those who were involved came to be either willing or reluctant participants so that nurses may never be in a position to carry out crimes on behalf of the government again.

92 Steppe, 'Nursing in the Third Reich'.
93 Burleigh, *Death and Deliverance*.
94 McFarlane-Icke, *Nurses in Nazi Germany*.
95 Benedict and Kuhla, 'Nurses', Participation'.
96 Meta P. statement 16 Nov 1961, Lunesburg police station. File location: *Staatsarchiv München*, file number 33. 029/3.
97 Benedict and Kuhla, 'Nurses', Participation'.
98 Benedict, 'The Nadir of Nursing'; Benedict and Georges, 'Nurses and the Sterilization Experiments'; Georges and Benedict, 'An Ethics of Testimony'.

Among the most apparent reasons for the nurses' participation are ideological commitment, putative duress, and economic pressure such as fear of termination of employment.[99] Nurse-defendants in post-war 'euthanasia' trials stated that they were convinced of not only the lawfulness of their actions but the requirement that they follow the orders of their administrators, physicians, and superior nurses to carry out killings that were mandated by the government.[100] Given the nurses' involvement in these crimes and the history of the organization of nursing during the years of National Socialism, it is important to look for the interactive effect.

Nursing was hierarchical in its organizational structure and the unifying behavior was obedience. Thus when an order was handed down from government to administrators of institutions, it was to be implemented without question by physicians and nurses. Some nurses who did not wish to kill in the name of the state asked for transfers either within or between institutions. Many of these requests were denied, and nurses became complicit in the killings. A few obtained transfers or resigned to avoid participation. Although there was a stated fear of refusal by some, most who refused were simply moved to other jobs without additional consequence. In fact, in more than 60 years of post-war trials, there is no documented case of a nurse being sent to a concentration camp or otherwise severely punished for refusal.[101]

As described earlier, there were five different nursing organizations active during this era and even non-Nazi organizations such as the Red Cross and the Protestant organization declared allegiance to Hitler and National Socialism. Thus, to voice a complaint about unethical orders to the leaders of these organizations would have been fruitless and possibly dangerous. Because of the encompassing nature of each nursing organization, from training to retirement, it would have been impossible to move membership from one to another. Furthermore, nursing as a whole possessed pitifully little autonomy and was viewed as a subservient group to medicine. Thus, even if unified – which, of course, they were not – the nursing organizations would have had little voice or influence in opposing the physicians. Only by examining the social structure, the place of the health care system within it, and the organization of nursing can we begin to understand nurses being willing to kill for the ideology of the state.

99 Benedict and Kuhla, 'Nurses', Participation'.
100 E. Luise Statement at Wasserburg, Germany, 19 June 1961. File location: *Staatsarchiv München*, file number 33. 029/2; Margarete T. 10 April 1962, *Landesgericht München*. File location: *Staarchiv München*, file number 33. 029/3).
101 H. Friedlander, *The Origins of Nazi Genocide* (Chapel Hill, University of North Carolina Press, 1995); Steppe, 'Nursing in the Third Reich'; M. Lagerwey, 'Nursing ethics at Hadamar', *Qualitative Health Research* 9 (1999): 759-772.

10. Torture and the Paradox of State Violence

Penny Green and Tony Ward

Our approach to torture in this paper is primarily criminological rather than philosophical. We are opposed to torture (and we regret that this should seem worth saying), but we leave it to other contributors to spell out the normative reasons why torture is wrong. What interests us as criminologists is *how* state agencies and individual officials come to order, condone or engage in torture. We draw on sociology, psychology and anthropology to try and understand this phenomenon. We also try to make some connections between the social science literature and the philosophical debate.

This paper derives from a much larger project which centres on the concept of 'state crime' and its place in criminology.[1] Recently we have become interested in the work of Norbert Elias[2] and the light it can shed on both state and anti-state violence.[3] Elias interests us because of the connections he makes between macro-social processes of state formation and individual sensibilities. Specifically, he argues that the development of a state monopoly of violence is linked, in complex ways which we cannot go into here, to the development of sensibilities which increasingly abhor interpersonal violence. Spierenburg drew on Elias's work to explain the abolition of torture in the European enlightenment.[4] Rationalist critiques of torture's ineffectiveness as a truth-finding device, he argues, long predated the abolition of torture but only became effective because a change in sensibilities made cruelty abhorrent.

Elias's theory raises an obvious problem, which we call the 'paradox of state violence'. If states depend on a monopoly of organized violence (using the term, as Elias's translators do, in a broad and morally neutral sense), but cultivate an abhorrence of violence, why does this not lead to abhorrence, or at least deep unease, at the state's own practices? Elias was well aware of this paradox or 'contradiction' (1987: 81) but he says frustratingly little about how it is resolved.

---

1   See P. Green and T. Ward, *State Crime: Governments, Violence and Corruption* (London: Pluto Press, 2004)

2   N. Elias, *The Civilizing Process,* trans. E. Jephcott (rev ed., Oxford, Blackwell, 2000)

3   T. Ward and Young, 'Elias, Organised Violence and Terrorism' in M. Mullard and B. Cole (eds.) *Globalisation, Citizenship and the War on Terror* (Cheltenham, Edward Elgar, 2007), P. Green and T. Ward 'Violence and the State' in J. Sim, S. Tombs and D. Whyte (eds.) *State, Power, Crime* (London, Sage, 2009).

4   P. C. Spierenburg, *The Spectacle of Suffering* (Cambridge: Cambridge University Press, 1984), pp. 188-90.

A.   Three solutions to the paradox

There appear to be three possible resolutions to the paradox, so far as torture or any other type of state violence, is concerned:

(i)   It is incompatible with humane sensibilities and therefore unacceptable;

(ii)   It is compatible with human sensibilities so long as it is used in a rational, rule-bound manner which contributes to the state's overriding goal of maintaining and protecting the pacified social spaces in which 'civilized' life is possible;

(iii)   It is incompatible with humane sensibilities but nevertheless acceptable, because certain persons in certain situations are exempt from civilized restraints.

For the sake of logical completeness we should perhaps add a fourth possibility. Some practices may be seen as compatible with humane sensibilities but nonetheless unacceptable for some other reason, for example because, like the methods of conditioning in Burgess's *A Clockwork Orange,* they deny the value of free will. It is unlikely that many people take this attitude to torture.[5]

Solutions (i) to (ii) seem at first sight to define three clear-cut and mutually exclusive attitudes towards violence, and we shall show that elements of these three solutions can be found in the contemporary debate about, and practice of, torture. The practice of torture, however, rarely exemplifies either (ii) or (iii) in pure form. It is, rather, the interplay between them that makes torture possible.

I.   Legal humanitarianism: torture as taboo

The state's use of force is supposed to be legitimate in accordance with humane sensibilities because it is used in a parsimonious and humane fashion to protect citizens against violence. If the humane, civilized, use of force is opposed to barbaric violence, then the epitome of barbarism, the thing no civilized official would do, is torture.

Legitimate state violence comes in three main forms, policing, punishment and warfare.[6]

Policing relies on the use of force as an ever-present possibility (Bittner 1981). In theory, in liberal societies, force is only ever used as last resort and to the minimum extent necessary. The craft of good policework consists largely in avoiding recourse to force except as a last resort.[7] Of course, a large literature testifies that the reality is

---

5   A. Burgess, *A Clockwork Orange* (Harmondsworth, Penguin, 1972).

6   H. Steinert, 'The Indispensable Metaphor of War: On Populist Politics and the Contradictions of the State's Monopoly of Force', *Theoretical Criminology* 7 (2003): 265-91

7   Ibid.; W. K. Muir, *Police: Streetcorner Politicians* (Chicago, University of Chicago Press, 1977).

often different;[8] but torture, officially at least, is the antithesis of legitimate police work. The temptation to torture is nevertheless a recognised ethical problem for police officers, as the much discussed 'Dirty Harry problem' indicates.[9]

Punishment involves the deliberate infliction of suffering, but a major penal trend in post-enlightenment societies is away from the infliction of suffering by direct violence to the body.[10] Even the death penalty is supposed to be administered with a minimum of physical pain. Force is used (officially) only to get the offender to comply with the punitive measures. Again, torture epitomizes the barbarous 'other' to modern, humane, penal practices. It is what Waldron calls a 'legal archetype', by which judges and officials assert their civilized credentials:

> The prohibition on torture is expressive of an important underlying policy of the law .... Law is not brutal in its operation. Law is not savage. Law does not rule through abject fear and terror, or by breaking the will of those whom it confronts. If law is forceful or coercive, it gets its way by nonbrutal methods which respect rather than mutilate the dignity and agency of those who are its subjects. The idea is that even where law has to operate forcefully, there will not be the connection that has existed in other times or places between law and brutality.[11]

Waldron observes in a footnote that those who, like the late Robert Cover, believe that the central feature of law is 'that it works its will "in a field of pain and death"' will be unimpressed by his argument.[12] We would suggest, however, that both Cover and Waldron are right: the 'legal archetype' is important precisely *because* of the legitimacy it confers on law's violence.

Warfare, involving as it does the infliction of death and destruction on an immense scale, poses the paradox of state violence in its most acute form. It does not fit easily into a humanistic paradigm, despite being governed by something called 'international humanitarian law'. Even in warfare, however, there is a taboo against intimate, asymmetrical violence. You may kill large numbers of people who pose no immediate threat to you if you do it anonymously, at a distance, by bombing, missiles or gunfire. Or you may kill at close quarters in a desperate struggle, where it's a question of kill or be killed. What you may not do is wilfully to kill or torment helpless prisoners, civilians or wounded enemies at close quarters. Even warfare, in its 'civilized' form, is antithetical to torture.[13]

8   E.g. J. Skolnick and J. J. Fyfe, *Above the Law* (New York, Free Press, 1993); W.A. Geller, and H. Toch (eds.) Police Violence (New Haven, CT, Yale University Press, 1996).

9   C. B. Klockars, 'The Dirty Harry Problem' *Annals of the American Academy of Political Science* 452 (1980): 33-47. See also Steinhoff, Ch. 2 above.

10 M. Foucault, *Discipline and Punish* (Harmondsworth, Penguin, 1977); Spierenburg, *Spectacle of Suffering.*

11 J. Waldron, 'Torture and Positive Law: Jurisprudence for the White House' *Columbia Law Review* 105 (2005): 1681-1750, p. 1720.

12 Ibid., n. 207, quoting R. Cover, 'Violence and the Word' *Yale Law Journal* 95 (1986): 1601-1629, p. 1601

13 The claim of 'civilized' mass killing to moral superiority over 'barbarous' violence against civilians is, of course, debateable: see for example P. Richards *Fighting for the Rain Forest: War, Youth and Resources in Sierra Leone* (Oxford, James Currey, 1996); B. Grosscup, *Strategic Terror: The Politics and Ethics of Aerial Bombardment* (London, Zed, 2006).

II. Bureaucratic instrumentalism: acceptance of regulated torture

Unlike most instances of interpersonal aggression, state violence is commonly depicted as being disciplined and rational. In hierarchical organizations, it is commonly the case that those who calculate whether violence is necessary are not those who carry it out. Thus the agents of violence can differentiate themselves from those who display ordinary aggression, because they do not act on the basis of their own emotions or desires but at the behest of others, and because they do not act for their own ends but for some greater good which their superiors have calculated that their actions will serve.

Systematic and sustained torture practices seemingly cannot exist independently of bureaucratic structures which maintain organizational hierarchies of 'facilitators and perpetrators'. Huggins' work on Brazilian torturers reveals that one of the chief distinguishing features between police officers who became torturers and those who did not – indeed the most important predictor of torture – was 'membership of an elite and/or physically separate and insular police operations or intelligence unit.'[14] No-one could torture routinely unless they were associated with an interrogation squad. It is in this sense that Rejali has argued that 'there is no such thing as "THE torturer"...to speak of the torturer abstracts the fact that the torturers are al situated in an institution known as the State. It disguises a complex institutional and social relationship as a relationship between two individuals.'[15] While accepting Rejali's rationale we nonetheless see value in understanding the psycho-social processes which act upon individuals in the process of dyscivilization.

The experiments of Stanley Milgram indicate the importance of the 'agentic state' in which individuals see themselves as passively carrying out the decisions of those in authority.[16] In such circumstances conscience alone is not enough to dissuade people from engaging in barbarous behaviour. In the face of authoritative commands the temptation to be resisted is in fact to follow ones own humane sensibilities.[17] But obedience to 'authority' as a psychological trait is to be distinguished from 'obedience to violent authority'.[18]

Most torture regimes authorize, through legal means, violence against perceived enemies.[19] Legitimizing state violence in the case of torture also requires the deployment of public justifications which most commonly take the form of utilitarian

14   M. K. Huggins, M. Haritos-Fatouros, and P. G. Zimbardo, *Violence Workers: Police Torturers and Murderers Reconstruct Brazilian Atrocities* (Berkeley, University of California Press, 2002).
15   D. Rejali, *Torture and Modernity* (Boulder, Westview, 1994) p. 9.
16   S. Milgram, *Obedience to Authority* (New York, Harper & Row, 1974).
17   H. Arendt, *Eichmann in Jerusalem* (Harmondsworth, Penguin, 1965), p. 150.
18   M Haritos-Fatouros, *The Psychological Origins of Institutionalized Torture* (London, Routledge, 2003).
19   E. Peters, *Torture* (Philadelphia, University of Pennsylvania Press, 1996); R. D. Crelenstein, 'The World of Torture: A Constructed Reality', *Theoretical Criminology* 7 (2003): 293-318

arguments advancing a greater good. The fact that these have been consistently dis-credited and rejected in case law[20] has not it seems reduced their persuasive power.

In his critique of US legal and academic apologias for torture, David Luban calls the utilitarian approach 'the liberal ideology of torture'.[21] It would be misleading to suggest that *only* liberals embrace this ideology. As Huggins demonstrates, authoritarian Latin American regimes consistently justified their employment of torture in utilitarian terms. The ticking bomb scenario, which Luban sees as the keynote of the 'liberal ideology' and expounded most recently by Harvard Professor Alan Dershowitz, has a long and undistinguished pedigree.[22] But utilitarianism is, Luban argues, the only ideology of torture most liberals could be tempted to embrace.[23] Like the humanitarian solution, it is predicated on a rejection of cruelty. Pain is to be administered parsimoniously, within a rational framework, and only in accord with strict legal rules (e.g. with a torture warrant issued by a judge, subject to judicial review and accountability). It is to be future-oriented, serving the state's highest goal – the prevention of greater violence. Torture is to be highly managed and clinically maintained: while Ignatieff favours what he sees as more 'acceptable' forms involving stress-induced or psychological violence,[24] others from the same utilitarian perspective offer suggestions including the insertion of sterilized needles under the finger nails and dental drills applied to un-anaesthetized teeth.[25] In so-called 'torture lite', direct physical contact is generally to be avoided: the key techniques are sensory deprivation and 'self inflicted pain' caused by standing for hours in stressful positions.[26] Such methods are depicted as 'light years away from real torture and hedged about with bureaucratic safeguards…nothing to do with the Abu Ghraib anarchy'.[27] Those who reject them, we are told, 'have missed at least one half of the humanitarian equation – and the better half at that'.[28]

20   N. S. Rodley, *The Treatment of Prisoners Under International Law* (Oxford, Clarendon, 1999), pp. 80 84.

21   D. Luban, 'Liberalism, Torture and the Ticking Bomb' in K. J. Greenberg (ed.) *The Torture Debate in America* (Cambridge, Cambridge University Press, 2006), p. 36.

22   A. Dershowitz, *Why Terrorism Works: Understanding the Threat, Responding to the Challenge* (New Haven, CT, Yale University Press, 2002).

23   Steinhoff, Ch. 2 above provides an ostensibly non-utilitarian, 'rights-based' defence of torture in 'Dirty Harry' situations, but not of *institutionalized* torture which is what concerns us here.

24   M. Ignatieff, *The Lesser Evil: Political Ethics in an Age of Terror* (Edinburgh, Edinburgh University Press, 2005).

25   Dershowitz, *Why Terrorism Works.*

26   A. W. McCoy, *A Question of Torture: CIA Interrogation from the Cold War to the War on Terror* (New York, Owl Books, 2006).

27   H. MacDonald, 'How to Interrogate Terrorists' in Greenberg, *Torture Debate*, p. 84.

28   L. A. Casey and D. B. Rivkin, 'Rethinking the Geneva Conventions' in Greenberg, *Torture Debate,* p. 211

III. Licensed barbarism: exempting torturers from restraint.

The third solution to the paradox of state violence which posits simply that, in certain situations, agents of the state do not transgress civilized inhibitions on interpersonal violence and cruelty because they are exempt from them. This is not a position one often finds clearly stated in the philosophical and ethical literature; but an honourable exception – in that he states the position only in order to denounce it – is Stephen Holmes:

> To respond to the savages who want to kill us, we must cast off our Christian-liberal meekness and embrace a 'healthy savagery' of our own. We must confront ruthlessness with ruthlessness. We must pull out all the stops. After victory we will have plenty of time for civility, guilt feelings and the rule of law.[29]

For Holmes, this is the subliminal message behind various political and legal arguments of the US administration. Holmes suggests that torture is emotionally satisfying because it mirrors the characteristics imputed to the enemy; to rephrase his argument in anthropological terms, torture is a *ritually,* rather than rationally-instrumentally, appropriate response to terrorism because it is based on the principle of *mimesis*, the re-enactment of the violence it is intended to counter.[30]

For Elias, the civilizing process involves a renunciation of this kind of 'magical thinking' in favour of a more 'detached' attitude which, though less emotionally satisfying, enables human beings to respond to their environment more effectively.[31] Such detachment, however, is much easier to attain in relation to natural phenomena, which can be understood as the manifestation of impersonal forces, than towards acts of violence which are the product of human agency. Even in the most pacified societies, the urge to respond to malevolent human action by revenge or retribution, rather than a calm and detached search for the most effective means of preventing a recurrence, remains strong.[32] Elias feared that the triumph of such emotionally involved responses over rational analysis would bring about nuclear annihilation, and the same risks can be seen in the war on terror.

29   S. Holmes, 'Is Defiance of Law a Proof of Success? Magical Thickening in the War on Terror' in Greenberg, *Torture Debate,* p. 127.
30   See M. Taussig, (2002) 'Culture of Terror – Space of Death: Roger Casement's Putumayo Report and the Explanation of Torture,' in A. L. Hinton, (ed.) *Genocide: An Anthropological Reader* (Oxford, Blackwell, 2002); C. K. Mahmood, 'Trials by Fire: Dynamics of Terror in Punjab and Kashmir,' in J. A. Sluka. (ed.) *Death Squad* (Philadelphia, University of Pennsylvania Press, 2000); Ward and Young, 'Elias, Organised Violence and Terrorism'.
31   N. Elias, *Involvement and Detachment* (Oxford, Blackwell, 1987).
32   D. Garland, *The Culture of Control* (Oxford, Oxford University Press, 2001).

B. Bureaucracy, barbarism and dyscivilization

From the point of view of bureaucratic instrumentalism, the ideal torturer would be thoroughly detached, applying pain without emotional satisfaction or distress in order to achieve organizational goals.[33] It seems psychologically implausible, however, that this attitude could be sustained for long. As Haritos-Fatouros argues, mere obedience to a supposedly legitimate authority may be sufficient to explain why people are willing to inflict torture for brief periods while under the supervision of an authority figure, as in the notorious Milgram experiments, but 'Milgram's model ... does not explain obedient torturing or killing over a long period in the absence of authority'[34]

A method adopted by some torturing regimes to free their torturers from humane inhibitions is to initiate future torturers, suddenly and dramatically, into a secret world in which the rules, expectations and rationality of ordinary life do not apply.[35] Recruits are first broken down by being subjected to arbitrary violence and senseless orders, and then inducted into an elite that obeys no laws except the orders of superior officers. During the period of the Greek Junta, for example, officers within the Special Interrogation Section (ESA) were afforded extraordinary powers. Even low ranking members had the power to stop and arrest military personnel of any rank.[36] A strategy of affording unlimited authority to torturers, training them out of humane sensibilities while dehumanizing their potential victims, instils a sense of extraordinary power in otherwise ordinary people:

'The officers would tell us that the prisoners were worms and we had to crush them, they were Communist, enemies of the state; they told us that ESA men could kill and not be judged by anybody; they said an ESA man was equal to an army major'[37]

Once a torturer has been 'created' what commonly follows is a social – psychological process through which 'perpetrators develop an intense, fanatic commitment to some higher good and supposed higher morality in the name of which they commit atrocities'.[38] Staub argues that this higher moral ideology combines with a differentiated self (in which the torturer is able to exclude targeted groups from his 'moral universe') to produce a person capable of inflicting extreme and inhumane violence.

These psychological insights call into question any attempt to justify the bureaucratic instrumentalist to torture on utilitarian grounds.[39] For a utilitarian, each person's pain counts equally. It seems almost inconceivable that any torturer could do

---

33   J. Wolfendale, 'Training Torturers: A Critique of the "Ticking Bomb" Argument', *Social Theory & Practice,* 32, no.2 (2006): 269-87, p. 273
34   Haritos-Fatouros, *Psychological Origins,* p. 160.
35   Huggins *et al., Violence Workers;* Haritos-Fatouros, *Psychological Origins.*
36   Ibid., p. 34.
37   'A' (former torturer), quoted ibid., p. 34
38   E. Staub, *The Roots of Evil: The Origins of Genocide and Other Group Violence* (Cambridge, Cambridge University Press, 1989), p. 64.
39   See Wolfendale, 'Training'.

his job while accepting the equal moral worth of his victim. For utilitarian reasons – to reduce the potentially overwhelming psychic costs of torture to the torturer – the latter has to learn to regard the former as less than human, or as an evil person who deserves to suffer. But having learned that, the torturer will hardly be motivated to use torture in the parsimonious way that utilitarianism advocates.

Seemingly irrational initiation rites alternating unpredictably between lenience and severity were rationally designed to encourage in cadets obedience without question to orders without logic.[40] Within this framework disturbing, violent and debasing practices may be seen as part of a rational paradigm in which exposure to authoritative, irrational and nonsensical violence delivers the torturer into a world in which previously held norms and sensibilities no longer apply, no longer correspond to the new reality. The torturer enters a bureaucratically defined torturing space where traditional rules of engagement and humane sensibility give way to violence without borders.

Would be torturers are brutalized and humiliated but at the same time they are encouraged to see themselves as superior and elite members of a state which at all costs must be protected.[41] Those who threaten that state are ideologically and systematically dehumanized so that acts of great cruelty against them are diminished in affect for the torturer. There is a tacit recognition by torture trainers of the stress and resistances which accompany the infliction of torture violence and training involves a myriad of social modelling and systematic desensitization techniques to counteract those inhibitions to violence.[42] The apparent irrationality embodied in the training experienced by torturers and their subsequent behaviour is, from the perspective of a torturing regime, brutally rational. To create torturers who will be unrestrained in their delivery of violence against targeted populations is always part of a wider strategy of counterinsurgency and provides a lethal tool in the cultivation of fear and control. Licensed violence exists *within* a bureaucratic-utilitarian strategy, not in opposition to it. Within an Eliasian perspective, Abram de Swaan has captured this synthesis well in his concept of *enclaves of barbarism.*[43]

Torture and other forms of state terror seem to be both rational and irrational;[44] there is a dialectic between the civilizing process and barbarity. Elias argues that state formation leads to a civilizing process which diminishes interpersonal violence (and indeed state violence). The civilizing process also involves the recognition of at least a minimal level of equality, so that in at least limited respects all persons are seen as entitled to protection and humane concern (hence the unacceptability of

40   Haritos-Fatouros, *Psychological Origins,* p. 34
41   Ibid.; Huggins et al., *Violence Workers;* J. T. Gibson, 'Factors Contributing to the Creation of a Torturer' in P. Suedfeld (ed.) *Psychology and Torture* (New York, Hemisphere, 1990);
42   Ibid., p. 85.
43   A. de Swaan, 'Dyscivilization, Mass Extermination and the State', *Theory, Culture & Society* 18(2001): 265–276.
44   Green and Ward, *State Crime,* pp. 111-6.

slavery).[45] But Elias also indicates that sometimes the civilizing process does not accord all citizens equality. Certain groups within society (for reasons relating to state and identity) may be excluded from the protection generally afforded by the state's monopoly of violence. This exclusion exposes these groups not only to higher degrees of interpersonal violence but more significantly to all the violent resources of the state. If we accept Elias's later position[46] that civilization is, in fact, a precarious and reversible process, then 'order *and* barbarism, design *and* impulse, organization *and* wildness'[47] may exist concurrently. Within the civilizing process runs a counterflow, so that while the state promotes civilized modes of behaviour it is also capable of extreme and barbarous violence against those sections of its own population or of other societies not afforded the same degree of protection.

In de Swaan's view, the key feature of the 'bureaucratization of barbarism' is the *comparmentalization* of the target population, the sites of torture or murder, the roles of the perptrators, and their emotional experiences:

> wildness and brutality are let loose, or maybe even instilled, and at the same time instrumentalized, for specific purposes, within demarcated spaces at an appointed time: an archipelago of enclaves where cruelty reigns while being reined in all the while.... [T]he regime creates and maintains compartments of destruction and barbarism, in meticulous isolation, almost invisible and well-nigh unmentionable.[48]

The well-documented practices of past authoritarian regimes like those of Argentina, Brazil and Greece, clearly fit this model, but so in many respects do the practices of the 'war on terror'. There are, of course, very significant differences. Rather than enclaves *within* the society from which torturers are drawn, the American enclaves are physically remote from it, and with a few well-known exceptions the captives are not US citizens. Abu Ghraib was situated not in a pacified society but in the heart of a war zone, though it did constitute an 'enclave' within the command structures of the US military.[49] Perhaps partly for these reasons, the creation of torturers does not appear to require anything resembling the fearsome initiation rites documented in Brazil and Greece. The USA is not a totalitarian state and torture faces serious challenges from civil society and elements of the judiciary,[50] the political class and – perhaps most significantly – from within the military hierarchy.[51] Nevertheless, the use of torture within the 'war on terror' does appear to fit de Swaan's

---

45   T. L. Haskell, 'Capitalism and the Origin of Humanitarian Sensibilities', American Historical Review 90 (1985): 339-361, 546-576

46   See especially N. Elias, *The Germans* (Cambridge, Polity, 1997)

47   de Swaan, 'Dyscivilization', p. 267

48   Ibid., p. 269

49   Maj-Gen. A. M. Taguba, *Article 15-6 Investigation of the 800th Military Police Brigade* <http://www.npr.org/iraq/2004/prison_abuse_report.pdf> (accessed 21 July 2008) pp. 38-44.

50   Notably the majority of the Supreme Court in *Hamdan* v. *Rumsfeld* 126 S. Ct. 2749 (2006), overturning President Bush's decision that Common Article 3 of the Geneva Conventions did not apply to 'illegal combatants'.

51   McCoy, *Question*; P. Sands, *Torture Team: Deception, Cruelty and the Compromise of Law* (London, Allen Lane, 2008).

concept of 'dyscivilization'. It is not a wholesale regression into barbarism ('*decivilization*'), but rather a calculated deployment of barbarism in the service of the state, ostensibly for the purpose of preserving civilization itself.

Violent bureaucracies diffuse responsibility for torture[52] by separating decision from action.[53] At the same time, they create scope for, and may even demand, initiative and inventiveness on the part of low-level operatives.[54] Statements from military police personnel in Abu Ghraib, for example, indicate that intelligence officers gave them instructions such as 'Loosen this guy up for us. Make sure he has a bad night. Make sure he gets the treatment'.[55] Rather than supervision or criticism of the precise methods used, they received positive feedback on the results achieved, so they assumed they were doing the right thing.[56]

In order to exercise the degree of inventiveness required to carry out such general instructions, guards or interrogators must adopt an attitude that resembles sadism at least to the extent that they are able to imagine the effects of their actions in producing pain and humiliation, and desire to produce those effects. The desire may or may not be erotically charged, or its fulfilment pleasurable, but the torturer learns to behave in ways that are outwardly indistinguishable from sadism. One Greek torturer interviewed by Haritos-Fatouros was variously described by his victims as:

'…zealous and unlimited in his variations on torture.'

'He tortured following the whim of the moment and laughed while torturing. He was literally a sadist.'

'…severe but not cruel…he only pretended to be a savage'[57]

The Stanford Prison Experiment provides a classic illustration of 'the ease with which sadistic behavior could be elicited in individuals who were not "sadistic types"'[58] by giving one group power over a group of anonymous others and leaving them to improvise means of maintaining control. Zimbardo, the 'superintendent' of the simulated prison, has noted the parallels with events at Abu Ghraib.[59]

---

52   M. K. Huggins, 'Torture 101: What Sociology Can Teach Us', *Anthropology News* 45, no. 6 (2004): 12-13.

53   Z. Bauman, *Modernity and the Holocaust* (Cambridge, Polity, 1989)

54   See for example McCoy, *Question,* pp. 86-9, discussing US training manuals of the 1980s.

55   Taguba, *Investigation,* p. 19. The chaotic climate in which the Military Police carried out their vague instructions from Military Intelligence is vividly portrayed in P. Gourevitch and E. Morris, *Standard Operating Procedure: A War Story* (London, Picador, 2008)

56   M. Danner, *Torture and Truth: Abu Ghraib and America in Iraq* (New York, New York Review Books, 2004)

57   Haritos-Fatouros, *Psychological Origins,* pp. 69-70.

58   C. Haney, C. Banks, and P. Zimbardo, 'Interpersonal Dynamics in a Simulated Prison,' *International Journal of Criminology and Penology* 1 (1973): 69-97, p. 89.

59   P. Zimbardo, *The Lucifer Effect: How Good People Turn Evil* (London, Rider, 2007), pp. 352-5. As Zimbardo notes, the same parallel is drawn independently in J. R. Schlesinger (Chair) 'Final Report of the Independent Panel to Review DoD Detention Operations' in K. J. Greenberg and J. L. Dratel (eds.) *The Torture Papers: The Road to Abu Ghraib* (Cambridge, Cambridge University Press, 2005), pp. 970-3.

The dynamics of dyscivilization are frighteningly simple. Once pacified public spaces are established – and the process by which they are established is long and complex – people generally abstain from violence because they know it carries high moral cost. It will cause shock and disapproval, damage one's reputation (unless one is among the minority who cultivate a reputation for violence), and possibly bring about public humiliation and the intervention of coercive state agencies. Most of the time we do not need to think about these consequences because we develop a 'habitus' – a term Elias used long before Bourdieu – of peaceable behaviour, and the idea of infringing the ban on public violence simply does not enter our heads. Once we find ourselves, however, in a setting where violence seems to be expected and approved, our unthinking, peaceable habitus no longer allows us to negotiate encounters with others successfully. What the Stanford Prison Experiment, and historical studies of the Third Reich,[60] demonstrate is how is how adaptable most people are to these situations; how rapidly they will develop a new habitus, be it one of conforming to the new rules or of inventive and pleasurable cruelty. The more people around one succeed in shedding their inhibitions against violence, the easier it is shed those inhibitions oneself. Lifton in his work on Auschwitz doctors demonstrated that 'the average person entering' such institutions of violence 'will commit or become associated with atrocities'.[61] And average people can and have entered these institutions of violence, sometimes, at alarmingly high rates. At the most repressive moment in Uruguay's rule of terror (1985) over twenty percent of the country's medical personnel were engaged in torture practices. According to Weschler their sustained involvement could largely be attributed to 'professional ambition and financial reward'.[62] Those who refused to be involved, however, 'disappeared at such a rate that Uruguay's medical and health care programs entered a state of crisis'.[63]

For most people, somewhat reassuringly, there do seem to be limits to this process of easy adaptation to a new social environment. Why else would torturing regimes need such brutal initiation methods? Why did Greek torturers need to be told 'that if a warden helps a prisoner, he'll take the prisoner's place and the whole platoon will flog him'?[64] Why would the Nazis need a special hospital to treat SS men who 'had broken down while executing women and children'?[65] It seems that extremes of physical cruelty and destruction do run up against inhibitions that are more than skin-deep.

The ways to overcome these inhibitions, however, are well understood. The victims must kept at a physical and/or psychological distance; they must be anonymous

---

60 A compelling example is C. Browning, *Ordinary Men: Reserve Police Battalion 101 and the Final Solution in Poland* (New York: Harper Perennial, 1998).

61 R. J. Lifton, *The Nazi Doctors: Medical Killing and the Psychology of Genocide* (New York, Simon & Schuster, 1986), p. 425.

62 L. Wechsler, *A Miracle, A Universe: Settling Accounts with Torturers* (Chicago, University of Chicago Press, 1998), p. 127.

63 E. Scarry, *The Body in Pain* (Oxford: Oxford University Press, 1985), p. 42.

64 Haritos-Fatouros, *Psychological Origins,* p. 58

65 M. Burleigh, *The Third Reich* (London, Macmillan, 2001), p. 604.

and dehumanized, excluded from the class of beings to whom moral sentiments apply.[66] The methods of 'torture lite' are well suited to produce these effects, because they require relatively little direct physical violence and at the same time achieve the anonymization and dehumanization of the victims. Hooding, employed as a means of sensory deprivation, also achieves the effect of concealing the victim's face, reducing him to an anonymous body, and at the same time concealing the torturer from him.[67] As Major-General Fay noted in his investigation of Abu Ghraib, 'The use of clothing as an incentive (nudity) is significant in that it likely contributed to an escalating "de-humanization" of the detainees and set the stage for additional and more severe abuses to occur'.[68] Treating prisoners as dogs – a form of humiliation deemed especially suitable for Arabs – gave a further twist to the spiral of dehumanization. When dehumanization is coupled with intense pressure to get results from interrogation, the dangers of 'force drift'[69] – the escalation of abuse when interrogators encounter resistance – are obvious.

C. Conclusion

We began by outlining three possible attitudes to torture: one which regards it as incompatible with civilized values and absolutely unacceptable; one which regards it as acceptable so long as it is strictly regulated and parsimoniously employed; and one which is willing to throw aside all civilized restraints, albeit only within certain limited spaces. The public and academic debate about torture is almost entirely a debate between the first two positions. Our argument is that the utilitarian case for limited torture is socially and psychologically implausible.[70] The ethical torturer, who scrupulously inflicts the minimum amount of pain justified by the greater good, is as much a myth as the humane executioner averting his eyes from the severed heads on the guillotine.[71] To create spaces where torture is permissible is to create spaces where civilized norms do not apply – enclaves of barbarism.

Moreover, dyscivilization is incompatible with the maintenance of a liberal society. For a state to torture while permitting the existence of a free press, a vibrant

---

66   See H. C. Kelman. and V. L. Hamilton *Crimes of Obedience* (New Haven, Yale University Press, 1989); H. Fein, 'Genocide: A Sociological Perspective,' *Current Sociology* 38 (1990): 1-111; Zimbardo, *Lucifer Effect,* Ch. 13.

67   Huggins, 'Torture 101'

68   G. R. Fay, *AR 56 Investigation of the Abu Ghraib Prison and 205th Military Intelligence Brigade,* <http://www.defenselink.mil/news/Aug2004/d20040825fay.pdf> (accessed 21 July 2008), p. 10.

69   The phrase used by Dr Mike Gelles, chief psychologist of the US Naval Criminal Investigative service and an important opponent of torture and coercive interrogation within the US Military (quoted by McCoy, *Question of Torture,* p. 128 and Sands, *Torture Team,* p. 161)

70   In this we are in agreement with Luban, 'Liberalism' and Wolfendale, 'Training Torturers'.

71   A. I. Applbaum, 'Professional Detachment: The Executioner of Paris', *Harvard Law Review* 109 (1995): 458-486, p. 461.

civil society, a reasonably independent judiciary, and a population part of which has strong feelings of religious or ethnic solidarity for the victims, is not only immoral but deeply stupid – as the more rational elements of the US military and the FBI understand very well.[72] It is therefore likely that the drift towards torture after 9/11 was not the product of rational calculation but an emotionally satisfying response to a crisis which demanded the appearance of resolute action, however uncertain the results.[73] In the words of the CIA's counterterrorism chief, 'After 9/11, the gloves came off'[74] – a phrase perfectly symbolizing the casting off of civilized restraints.

The choice is not between pragmatism and moral scrupulousness; the choice – forgive the cliché – is between civilization and barbarism. It really is that simple.

72 J. Rives et al., 'JAG Memos re: Recommendations of the Working Group to Assess the Legal, Policy and Operation Issues Relating to the Interrogation of Detainees Held by the US Armed Forces in the War on Terrorism', February-March 2003' in Greenberg, *Torture Debate;* McCoy, *Question;* Sands, *Torture Team.*

73 J. Katz, *Seductions of Crime: Moral and Sensual Attractions in Doing Evil* (New York: Basic Books, 1988); Holmes, 'Defiance'; McCoy, *Question of Torture,* pp. 206-9

74 Cofer Black, 2002, quoted ibid., p. 119. Marshall Billingslea, Principal Deputy Assistant Secretary of Defense, introduced new guidance on interrogations to a meeting of military lawyers with the words: 'Guys, wake up, smell the coffee, take your gloves off' (quoted by Sands, *Torture Team.*, p. 166). And (then) Brigadier-General Janis Karpinski, commander of military prisons in Iraq, recalls being told by Major General Miller to 'tak[e] off the kid gloves' and get ,actionable intelligence' from her detainees (J. Karpinski, *One Woman's War,* quoted by Zimbardo, *Lucifer Effect,* p. 336).

11. *24* and Torture

Bev Clucas[*]

A. Introduction

In contrast to the majority of the papers in this collection, this chapter does not examine the permissibility of torture or deal with one of the other more frequent angles on the topic. Instead, I consider the portrayal of torture as an element of entertainment in the Emmy-award winning television series 24 and pose the question whether 24's depiction of torture crosses the boundary between mere entertainment and propaganda.

Many of us are familiar with *24*, the phenomenally popular series from the US, the seventh season of which is due to be aired in January 2009. The formula of each season is the same: 24 hours pass 'in real-time', as we follow the adventures of the protagonists, mainly personnel of a fictional body located in Los Angeles, CTU (Counter-Terrorism Unit). Principal among the characters of the show is Jack Bauer, its hero. Each 24 hours (i.e. 24 episodes) is devoted to defeating some evil terrorist person or group. In each series, people are tortured or killed, in pursuit of a higher goal.

The programme makes repeated use of a device called the 'ticking time bomb' scenario: the good guy has in his power a terrorist or suspected terrorist, against the backdrop of an imminent threat (for example, in *24*'s case, nuclear bombs or biological weapons), which would have, if fulfilled, catastrophic consequences for innocent people. The terrorist refuses to talk – but the hero is convinced that if only he can persuade the suspect to spill the beans, this major catastrophe will be averted. Time is desperately short, so 'persuasion' (if any) quickly turns into a form of torture. In *24*, torture is almost invariably successful as a means of extracting information, which ultimately does prevent the threatened disaster. The only exception to this rule is found in the character of Jack Bauer, who never capitulates, no matter how hard he is pressed.

Despite, or perhaps because of its popular and commercial success, particularly in the context of the US and UK War on Terror and abuse of prisoners in Abu Ghraib, a groundswell of concern about 24 has started to be heard. There is disquiet about the number of torture scenes on television, particularly since 9/11. The Parents' Television Council has crowned *24* as the worst offender.[1] Many people decry the inaccuracies about torture that are promulgated by the show. There is unease about

---

[*] With grateful thanks to all who contributed to the gestation of this paper, particularly Suzanne Uniacke and Christian Twigg-Flesner.

1 J. Shirlen, 'Worst TV Show of the Week'. Available online: <http://www.parentstvorg/PTC/publications/bw/2007/0125worst.asp> (accessed 25 July 2008).

the effect the show may be having on real soldiers' interrogation techniques.[2] Others wonder whether *24* has a persuasive effect that works against the US and its allies – their enemies might themselves be more inclined to believe that torture is widespread amongst Western soldiers, and therefore feel themselves justified in violent action against US and UK soldiers and civilians.

In this chapter, I explore and reflect on the underlying themes concerning torture and legitimate action in *24*. I begin with a short introduction to the TV show itself, highlighting the many different instances of torture, as well as some of the general criticsms levelled at it. I then proceed to consider some of the moral issues associated with the dissemination of information about torture in general, first in relation to factual instances of torture, and then fictional. This discussion informs a more detailed analysis of the depiction of torture in *24*. Having considered the express intentions of the programme makers, I apply a scheme of analysis on 'speech acts' devised by J.L.Austin, and developed by Langton, to argue that the real intention of the programme makers is better understood as pro-torture propaganda: an instance of double immorality, as not only does the show push a pro-torture message, but also, it does so under the pretense of pure entertainment.

B. The show

The series began in 2001, making it broadly contemporaneous with 9/11. The unique selling point of the show is that all the action takes place 'in real-time'. Each hour of an episode on television accounts for an hour in the life of the show. Even breaks for adverts count towards time elapsed. As the action of each series takes part within one 24-hour period, there is urgency to the drama on the screen, which is augmented by the recurrent interpolation of a digital clock, and frequent use of split-screens, enabling the viewer to see the simultaneous activities of different characters.

The good guys of the series, by and large, are the staff of CTU and the American Administration. It is CTU's task to prevent or frustrate threatened terrorist attacks.

The prevention of terrorism requires intelligence. And in *24*, the necessary information is almost always obtained by torture. Unusually, at least at the time the programme was first aired, torture is done just as much by the good people as the bad – if not more.

The types of torture I have viewed on the show include, but are not limited to, the following:[3]

- Hanging a person on hooks
- the application of hot scalpels to the body

---

2   See below.
3   References to specific seasons and episodes where these particular instances occur have not been included for the sake of concision. All are taken from seasons 1-6.

- the application of a sanding machine to the body
- beating someone up or other physical violence
- targeted physical harm (e.g. the bundle of nerves on the shoulder) intended to cause the maximum possible pain
- aggravation of wounds with caustic liquid
- pharmaceutical torture – injections to cause pain (hyocine-pentothal)
- removing the tip of someone's finger with a cigar cutter
- threats to shoot
- breaking a suspect's fingers
- using a power drill on someone's shoulder
- threats with a knife
- shooting a suspect in the leg and threatening to shoot the other one if the information is not revealed
- non-specific threats to 'do anything to get answers'
- threats to kill a loved one
- electric shocks (including at the order of the President)
- electrocution using a hotel lamp
- shocks by taser
- denial of painkillers to someone suffering from a bullet wound
- psychological torture in the form of a fake execution of the wife and children of a terrorist.

Howard Gordon, one of the show's writers who invents many of the torture scenes, describes them as 'improvisations in sadism'.[4] Their source material includes CIA interrogation manuals, but the scenes in the programme are mainly the result of writers' imagination. However, Gordon admits that 'the truth is, there is a certain amount of fatigue. It's getting harder not to repeat the same torture techniques over and over'.[5]

Perhaps *24* is nothing more than a phenomenally successful TV show with a nasty imagination. But various people have been raising concerns about the effects of the show.

I.   Effects of the show

In 2006, there was a visit by US Army Brigadier General Patrick Finnegan, Dean of the United States Military Academy at West point, to meet the creative team of *24*.

4   J. Mayer, 'Whatever it takes: the politics of the man behind '24'' *The New Yorker* 19 February 2007, p. 3. Available online: <http://www.newyorker.com/reporting/2007/02/19/070219 fa_fact_mayer?printable=true> (accessed 11 July 2008)
5   Ibid.

Also accompanying him were persons described as three 'of the most experienced military and FBI interrogators in the country'.[6] This delegation had come to express their concerns about what they saw as the primary political and moral messages of the show – that protection against torture under American law must practically, and morally ought to be, surrendered, in order to preserve security. Apparently, the immoral and illegal behaviour endorsed by the show had already had a negative effect on real American soldiers in training.[7] To this, Philippe Sands adds a description of the way in which *24* provided both the inspiration for interrogation techniques[8] and '[c]ultural sensitisation... that normalised violence and justify aggression.'[9]

Other concerns have been raised about the nature of the entertainment in *24*, as well as this allegedly corrosive effect on the minds and methods of US soldiers. One criticism is that the ticking time bomb scenario hardly (if ever) happens in real life, and that by perpetually presenting this plot device as the case where torture is acceptable or even required, those watching the show become more inclined to accept the permissibility of torture in other cases.[10] And, an important point stressed by real-life interrogators is that torture is not effective – it does not yield reliable information. Yet shows such as *24* send the message that the essential and correct information obtained by torture is what justifies the torture in the first place.[11]

B.   Are bad consequences the only measure?

These consequences, if they do indeed result from the broadcast of shows such as *24*, are alarming and arguably immoral. But consequences are easy to presume and predict, and hard to prove.

In any case, to focus on consequences, on teleological theories as a measure of rights and wrongs (what is morally right or wrong depends on the consequences) is to ignore another important, in my opinion more important, type of moral theory: the type of standpoint from which people have rights and duties, and actions are morally permissible or impermissible, independently of potential consequences – for example in Immanuel Kant's categorical imperative. This latter type of

---

6   Ibid.
7   Ibid., pp. 3-4.
8   P. Sands, *Torture Team: Deception, Cruelty and the Compromise of Law* (London, Penguin, 2008) pp. 73-4.
9   Ibid., p. 272.
10 See Association for the Prevention of Torture, *Defusing the Ticking Bomb Scenario: why we must say No to torture, Always* (Geneva, The Association for the Prevention of Torture, 2007). Available online:
    http://www.apt.ch/index.php?searchword=defusing&option=com_search&Itemid=5
    (accessed 8 August 2008)
11 See below.

position/stance might argue that shows such as *24* are immoral irrespective of whether or not they cause bad consequences.

For the purposes of this chapter, I assume that torture is categorically impermissible in principle (i.e. independently of consequences).[12] Instead, my focus is on this question: if we accept, for the sake of argument, that torture is categorically prohibited, what significance does this acceptance have for our evaluation of *24*? What conclusions ought we to draw about the moral nature of the particular representations of torture in *24*, or the moral status of a television programme that utilizes torture as an aid to dramatic tension?

Before considering these issues, I take a step back to think about the dissemination of images of or portrayal of torture in general.

C. Disseminating torture 'information' – factual and fictional

Information about torture, including allusions to, descriptions or depictions of, and discussions about torture ('information' for short, as an admittedly clumsy shorthand), seems at least capable of being morally neutral in itself. Information may be put to moral use (preventing torture) or immoral use (e.g. the instigation of torture, the encouragement of torture, and the failure to prevent torture). In this view (of at least the neutrality of information about torture), I differ from my colleague, Massimo La Torre, who in his chapter takes the position that even to discuss torture is morally wrong, unless the intention of the discussants is to combat arguments in favour of torture (in which case it is the lesser of two evils).[13]

Whether or not 'information' about torture is real (for example in Abu Ghraib) or fictional (*24*), it is useful to distinguish three sets of circumstances, which will assist in determining the moral status of the publication:

1. the intention or motive of the publisher/broadcaster/disseminator/author (I use the term 'publisher' and 'publication' to cover all of these possible scenarios);
2. the consequences of the publication (broadcast/dissemination/etc), measured by some moral standard;
3. the intention or motive of the recipient (viewer/listener/reader) of the broadcast.

---

12   Space constraints preclude a discussion of this position.
13   Chapter 1 above.

I. Actual torture

First, I consider these three sets of circumstances in the context of information dissemination about real torture.

1. Intention of the publisher

Where the intention of the publisher is to use this information for a morally good purpose, e.g. exposure in order to prevent continuation of the practice, then publication is morally required. (And where someone has knowledge of real torture, it is a least a prima facie moral duty to make this public, not just in order to rescue the victims, but in order that other agents may use this information to guide their choices (e.g. to protest; to lobby against torture; to vote against a government which supports torture)).

2. Consequences of the publication

Even if we assume that the publication of information about real torture is prima facie morally required, there might be thought to be two possible sets of consequences (not the result of any intervening action) that outweigh this prima facie obligation: direct and indirect consequences.

a) Direct

In some circumstances, it might be argued that publication causes a further direct wrong (e.g. a further violation of the rights or dignity or privacy of the person or group against whom the torture was committed). In my view, any such violation could be avoided by obtaining the consent of the person or group involved, or by maintaining anonymity. But even if it were arguable that a violation still persists, any such injustice might be thought to be outweighed by the prevention of more serious wrong (i.e. the continuation of torture; failure to bring a torturer to justice, etc).

b) Indirect

It might be thought that some pernicious, indirect consequences may flow from the publication of information about torture. On occasion, it is argued that, even where activities are not impermissible in themselves, they ought to be prohibited because they make illegitimate activities more likely in various ways.[14] These types of argument come under the umbrella of 'slippery slope' arguments. For example, perhaps it is feared that making it known that torture does in fact occur, or making known the ways in which it occurs, makes it more likely that bad people will use torture in the future, or will give someone inspiration about how best to go about torturing a victim. Or perhaps it is feared that the sight of scenes of torture causes psychological damage to the viewer. Could the force of the slippery slope argument require suppression of factual information?

My answer is a cautious 'perhaps', but this case would need to be made out in full. Beyleveld and Brownsword put it this way, in the context of human dignity:

> [T]hose who argue that intrinsically acceptable activities are unacceptable because they make it impossible effectively to prohibit activities that are contrary to human dignity need to establish their case. This is no easy matter, once it is appreciated that the endpoint 'failure effectively to prohibit activities contrary to human dignity' cannot be broadly defined – e.g. so that it is satisfied by the mere possibility of or even the actual doing of things contrary to human dignity by a limited number of individuals. If such an endpoint is acceptable, and if we accept the argument against cloning of sheep then, in consistency, we must argue that any technological development (or research into it) that provides the means to carry out activities that violate human dignity that ought to be prohibited ought itself to be prohibited. Thus, for example, we should argue that the construction of the printing press (and research and technology that made this possible) should have been prevented, because, for example, the printing press would provide the means for the dissemination of racist propaganda that could (and would, one day, somewhere) be used to aid and abet policies of genocide that are contrary to human dignity. But this logically requires us to argue that all technology, even Stone Age technology and fire-making, should have been prohibited, because such technology could, and would, be used for evil purposes. And it cannot be stopped here; for human beings have, without employing any technology, through using what exists in nature, and by the use of their bare hands, the means to steal, rape, and murder, etc. Hence, accepting this argument requires us to accept that *human beings* ought to be prohibited. In effect, the view that human beings ought not to exist because they have the ability to eat from the tree of knowledge is implicit in the use of a broad endpoint in slippery slope arguments based on empirical claims.[15]

We can apply this analogously to torture. Thus, the indirect consequences are not the responsibility of the publisher, unless and until there is clear evidence that the specific 'slippery slope' scenario is being brought about (e.g. watching news reports about torture invariably causes the majority of viewers to behave with more violence towards other agents than they would have otherwise).

---

14   D. Beyleveld and R. Brownsword, *Human Dignity in Bioethics and Biolaw* (Oxford, Oxford University Press, 2001), p. 166 and S. D. Pattinson, 'Regulating Germ-Line Gene Therapy to Avoid Sliding Down the Slippery Slope' *Medical Law International* 4, nos. 3-4 (2000): 213-222.
15   Beyleveld and Brownsword, *Human Dignity,* p. 167.

3. The intention of the recipient

Where the publication or dissemination of information about torture is morally permissible or required, I would suggest that (fear of) any immoral intention or motive on the part of the recipient does not make the publication immoral. One practical example might be the exposure of the abuses at Abu Ghraib, and the concern that this would invite retaliation (allegedly the impetus for the beheading of US civilian Nick Berg).[16] The wrongdoing is an intervening act which is not the responsibility of the publisher. Many good or neutral things can be put to evil use (e.g. using a pencil to stab someone in the eye), but this does not mean that we should prohibit the thing itself; rather we should attempt to prevent wrongdoing and punish wrongdoers.

To conclude: where the publication of factual information is morally neutral or morally required, I suggest that only a specific and established slippery slope evil ought to override the promulgation of that which is at least morally neutral.

II. Fictional torture

Perhaps we can agree that torture is wrong. We might even agree that torture is absolutely wrong, even where the goal is to save other persons' lives. We might agree that my diagnosis of the moral import of the three circumstances which I have just discussed in respect of real torture.

If the torture scenes depicted in *24* were real, this television show would depict heinously wrong actions, without any noble purpose such as exposure, and without any attempt to bring those responsible for the torture to justice. However, *24* is fiction; entertainment; what's the harm in that?

Entertainment need not be 'mere entertainment'. Educational films, for example, provide a means of disseminating information in a context which is palatable for the viewer. Art of various kinds – whether painting, film, or literature – can prompt the viewer or reader to think, to question, to take part in an ethical enterprise, or at least to discover, in Milan Kundera's words, 'the various dimensions of existence'.[17] These instances will all seem to fall within the category where the intention or motive of the publisher is good. And, as discussed earlier, I suggest that where publication is morally neutral or morally good, only a specific and established slippery slope evil ought to override the promulgation of that which is morally neutral.

Popular television programmes, although not part of the high culture that we normally think of as providing a doorway to the ethical world – what Roger Scruton

16   B. Branford, 'Berg father "had to let son go"'. Available online: <http://news.bbc.co.uk/1/hi/world/americas/3853607.stm> (accessed 25 July 2008).
17   M. Kundera, *The Art of the Novel* (rev. ed., London, Faber and Faber, 2005), p. 5.

calls 'the secular path to the ethical life...which teaches us to live *as if* our lives mattered eternally',[18] need not be excluded, surely, from categories of fiction which may have morally good or morally neutral status. In March 2000 the soap opera *Hollyoaks* broadcast an episode in which a young man was raped by a group of youths, aiming to raise awareness of the fact that rape is not simply a wrong that is practised against women.[19] Perhaps some perverted individuals were titillated by in this, but I do not think, if this was the case, that the intervening acts or motives of the recipient of the broadcast detract from the morally good aim of the programme.

According to the scheme outlined above, the depiction of torture may be permissible where the intention of the publisher is not immoral, and the publication neither causes direct harm nor leads to a demonstrable 'slippery slope' situation. This would tend to suggest that fictional TV series which include scenes of torture may be broadcast, so long as they avoid harm. However, the assumption that a programme with the express intention of entertainment is not immoral requires further investigation.

D.   The morality of 24

In the case of *24*, has the series stepped out of the category of programmes which we might accept as pure entertainment? Is it arguable that there is some other, discernable, implicit message?[20] If so, might this change our view of the legitimacy or moral permissibility of the intention of the publisher? In order to address this question, I consider the quantity of torture in the programme; the portrayal of torture as a necessary and valuable means of extracting information; the dodging of questions regarding legal permissibility; the clear implication that heroes torture as part of their duty; the suggestion that torture does not have serious physical or psychological consequences for the victim; the role of the repeated 'ticking time bomb' scenario providing support for the necessity of torture; and the lack of any convincing dramatic challenge to these points.

18   R. Scruton, *Modern Culture* (London, Continuum, 2000), p. 14.
19   BBC News, 'The Drama and Crisis of Soaps'. Available online: <http://news.bbc.co.uk/ 1/hi/entertainment/tv_and_radio/1574982.stm> (accessed 25 July 2008).
20   At various points during the gestation of this chapter, I worried that I might have set myself the mammoth task of pronouncing on the moral status of all films, TV series, and books, containing violence that lacked an overarching moral, educational, purpose. I'm thinking in particular about films such as the *Terminator*, or Steven Segal movies with their high violence and body counts. But I do not think it is necessary, for this paper, to come to any verdict on this type of entertainment, though this is a very important question. (Though we should not forget that even if such programmes are morally permissible in themselves, they arguably ought to be prohibited if a serious slippery slope case can be made out.)

I. The quantity of torture

The Parents' Television Council, a non-partisan watchdog group, reports that the first five seasons of *24* (120 hours' of viewing) contained 67 torture scenes – 1 torture scene per 1.8 episodes, or an average of 13 per series. The *New Yorker* reports that Melissa Caldwell, the Council's senior director of programmes, said, '*24* is the worst offender on television: the most frequent, most graphic, and the leader in the trend of showing the protagonists using torture'.[21]

I counted a similar prevalence of torture in season six – 13 scenes or types of torture. In so counting, I restricted myself to instances where physical or psychological distress was inflicted in order to force one of the characters to reveal information (e.g. the location of the remaining nuclear bombs), or perform an action under time pressure (e.g. programme a trigger for the remaining nuclear bombs). These were in addition to various other instances of threat, blackmail, beatings, shootings, and killings.

We tend to think that frequency has some correlation with an agent's attitude towards something. A man who once, in an unusual state of emotional distress, lashes out and hits his wife, is not necessarily branded a perpetrator of domestic violence (which implies a person who believes it is permissible to behave violently, in this case towards women). However, the husband of a woman who ends up in hospital on multiple occasions is likely to be identified as a wife-beater. If *24* had used torture as a device to break the ticking timebomb deadlock on one occasion or perhaps twice throughout its six series, we would not necessarily diagnose a pro-attitude towards torture on the part of *24*'s creators. But 70 times in six series is too frequent to make plausible the equivalent excuse of 'I walked into a door/fell down the stairs'.

II. Torture is necessary

24 continually reinforces the message that torture is necessary (whether or not it is a necessary *evil*). When faced with the ticking time bomb scenario, or other shortness of time, *one is required* to torture.

This requirement, this necessity, is a practical necessity and, particularly when practised against (suspected) terrorists, a moral necessity. Time and time again, characters, especially Jack Bauer, are portrayed as being backed into a corner by circumstances, the only solution to which is torture.

And no one is safe. In Season Four, the Secretary of Defence orders the torture of his own teenage son by sensory deprivation, in order to make him reveal the names of his associates, who, it was feared, had used information he had innocently

---

21   Mayer, 'Whatever it Takes', p. 2.

disclosed in order to kidnap the Secretary and his daughter. Later in the same series, the daughter of the Secretary of Defence, Audrey, is herself subject to intimidating interrogation by Jack (who is her lover), and then pharmaceutical torture by Burke of CTU, in order to reveal information about the same terrorists who had earlier kidnapped her and threatened her life. (Happily, Jack discovers that the information CTU possesses about Audrey – which mandated the decision to interrogate and torture her – has been planted by another of their prisoners. He holds a gun to this woman's head and threatens to kill her, until she confesses that the evidence implicating Audrey is a fabrication.)

Joel Surnow, co-creator and executive producer of *24*, has said this about fighting terrorism: '[t]here are not a lot of measures short of extreme measures that will get it done'.[22] Could he have stated his view more plainly?

III. Torture is valuable

24 assures us that not only is torture necessary; it is valuable. It yields useful information, the majority of the time (though sometimes a suspect will die before confessing).[23] There are rare instances where a terrorist will endure torture rather than reveal a plot, but even this unusual stoicism can be overcome, as in the case of Sayyid Ali in the second series. Jack beats him, breaks his hands, and threatens unbearable pain, none of which measures is successful. Eventually, Jack stages the fake execution of Ali's wife and children, shown to Ali via a remote satellite link. When Ali's son is 'killed', he finally breaks, and reveals vital information about the nuclear bomb.

Tony Lagournais, former interrogator for the US Army in Iraq, told the show's creators:

> In Iraq, I never saw pain produce intelligence... I worked with someone who used waterboarding... I used severe hypothermia, dogs, and sleep deprivation. I saw suspects after soldiers had gone into their homes and broken their bones, or made them sit on a Humvee's hot exhaust pipes until they got third degree burns. Nothing happened... [confessions] just told us what we already knew. It never opened up a stream of new information... physical pain can strengthen the resolve to clam up.[24]

In 2006, a letter and *Statement on Interrogation Practices* was sent by 20 former[25] US army interrogators and interrogation technicians to the Committee on

---

22   Ibid.
23   See D. P. O'Mathúna, 'The Ethics of Torture in *24*: Shockingly Banal' in J. Hart Weed, R. Davis and R. Weed, *24 and Philosophy* (Oxford, Blackwell, 2008), pp 100-101 for a discussion of the efficacy and effects of torture.
24   Ibid., 5.
25   The names of interrogators on active duty were deliberately not included, in order to avoid open conflict with public statements by the US Secretary of Defense, his officials, and the Vice President and his office.

the Armed Services. The interrogators included the Army's most senior interrogator at the time of his retirement, and veterans from conflicts ranging from Vietnam to Iraq. These documents denied that 'coercive interrogation techniques' and torture are necessary tools in the War on Terror, and in fact stated that 'experienced interrogators find prisoner/detainee abuse and torture to be counter-productive to the intelligence countering mission'.[26]

Interestingly, the statement itself uses the following phrasing: 'Prisoner/detainee abuse and torture are to be avoided at all costs, *in part* because they can degrade the intelligence collection efforts by interfering with the skilled interrogator's efforts to establish rapport with the subject'.[27] This suggests that this instrumental reason is only one aspect of these seasoned interrogators' objections to torture.

IV. Torture is legally permissible

The show gives the erroneous impression that torture is legally permissible, but this ignores both domestic provisions[28] and international agreements (such as the UN Convention against torture) outlawing the use of torture. The only concession to the question of permissibility of torture in the course of duty are occasional references to internal CTU protocols on the limits on the use of pharmaceutical torture.

> **2:12 P.M.** Buchanan shows Jack the toxicology reports on Graem. The coronary was caused by hyocine-pentothal used in the interrogation. The field reports show that Jack exceeded protocols, even after Burke warned him about the dangerous levels of serum.[29]

Yet despite having cavalierly ignored operational limitations, Jack is portrayed as a hero, not a criminal or a liability. Some oblique reference to the dubious nature of his intended actions can be inferred from the occasions on which Bauer resigns from CTU in order to remove procedural constraints from his actions. On one occasion, after discussing his planned illegitimate activities with the President, he resigns in order to ensure that the President has formal deniability.

V.   Heroes do torture as part of their duty

The depiction of torture in *24* leads us to understand that Bauer takes no pleasure in inflicting pain;[30] rather he does these unpleasant things, again and again, because it is necessary and dutiful.

26   P. Bauer, *et al.*, *Statement on Interrogation Practices* 31 July 2006. Available online:
      <http://www.amnestyusa.org/denounce_torture/statement_on_interrogation.pdf> (accessed 10
      November 2007).
27   Ibid. (emphasis added).
28   However controversially interpreted – see la Torre, Ch. 1 above.
29   Fox, Series 6, Episode Guide.

For US army Brigadier General Patrick Finnegan, one of the military experts who protested to the creators of *24* about its pernicious effect on American soldiers, this equation of torture and duty is particularly distressing: 'the disturbing thing is that although torture may cause Jack Bauer some angst, it is always the patriotic thing to do'.[31]

This message of *24*'s resonates with the words of Dick Cheney, speaking shortly after the terrorist attacks of 9/11:

> We also have to work, though, sort of the dark side, if you will. We've got to spend time in the shadows in the intelligence world. A lot of what needs to be done here will have to be done quietly, without any discussion, using sources and methods that are available to our intelligence agencies, if we're going to be successful. That's the world these folks operating in, and so it's going to be vital for us to use any means at our disposal, basically, to achieve our objective.[32]

Joel Surnow, co-creator and executive producer, puts it this way:

> Isn't it obvious that if there was a nuke in New York City that was about to blow – or any other city in this country – that, even if you were going to go to jail, it [torture] would be the right thing to do?

And

> America wants the war on terror fought by Jack Bauer. He's a patriot.[33]

Surnow also claims that soldiers in Iraq and personnel in the Bush administration are partial to the show: 'it's a patriotic show. They *should* love it'.[34] Cannily, this juxtaposition of torture and duty makes those who protest about Jack's actions not just weak, but also – one of the greatest of American sins – unpatriotic.

VI. What differentiates heroes and villains?

There is little differentiation between heroes and villains in terms of their actions.[35] It seems that the main thing that marks Jack and his colleagues apart from the terrorists is the nature of their goal: Jack *et al* want to save CTU/Los Angeles/the USA: the terrorists desire to destroy CTU/Los Angeles/the USA. Yet without any independent means of weighing the relative worth of these opposing goals, the series is left with nothing more than a conventional prejudice in favour of the US, or its

---

30   Cf. T. Morris, 'Philosophy? If you don't know *24*, you don't know Jack' in J. Hart Weed, R. Davis and R. Weed, *24 and Philosophy* (Oxford, Blackwell, 2008).
31   Mayer, 'Whatever it Takes', p. 4.
32   T. Russert, NBC News' Meet The Press: interview with Dick Cheney. Available online: http://www.fromthewilderness.com/timeline/2001/meetthepress091601.html (accessed 10 November 2007).
33   Mayer, 'Whatever it Takes', p. 2.
34   Ibid., p. 1.
35   The lines are blurred still further in Series 6 with a sadistic CTU agent, Doyle.

power. It would be overly simplistic to say that *24* promotes the idea that might is right. However in all of the series, it tends to be the case at the mightier (the US) is more right than its opponents.

VII.   Torture doesn't have serious (physical or psychological) consequences

Jack Bauer is almost superhuman in his ability to rise from the dead (literally, in one scene in which his heart was stopped by electrocution), or recuperate from less lethal damage, for example athletically escaping Fayed and his men after being tortured, and carrying on with active duties even whilst suffering from fragmented ribs in Series 6.

His colleagues also display remarkable fortitude. Two examples taken from the same series provide a brief snapshot. Morris, after having a steel bit power-drilled into his shoulder in order to compel him to do a task for some terrorists, returns to CTU and work at a computer. The only ill effect he seems to suffer is the impetus to start drinking alcohol again. Men are not the only heroes: Nadia, after suffering credible and frightening threats from her sadistic co-worker, Doyle, returns to work (and shortly afterwards even takes the role of Acting Director). Far from resenting or fearing Doyle, she seems to feel gratitude to him later in the programme.

These examples seem to suggest a rather flippant attitude on the creators' parts, denying the real aftermath of torture. This is the corollary to the 'sane and somewhat sanitized'[36] presentation of torture on *24*.

VIII. The ticking timebomb situation is a real threat to the US

Mayer quotes Bob Cochran, one of the show's co-creators, saying 'most terrorism experts will tell you that the 'ticking time bomb' situation never occurs in real life, or very rarely. But on our show it happens every week'.[37] The sympathetic presentation of Bauer and CTU's mission has been described as 'a weekly rationalization of the 'ticking timebomb' defence of torture'.[38]

The Association for the Prevention of Torture describes the ticking time bomb scenario in the following terms:

> [It] operates by manipulating the emotional reactions of the audience. It creates a context of fear and anger. It artificially tilts the circumstances to evoke sympathy or even admiration for the torturer, and hatred or indifference towards a torture victim...

36   O'Mathúna, 'The Ethics of Torture in *24*', p.99.
37   Mayer, 'Whatever it Takes', p. 1.
38   J. Poniewozik, 'The Evolution of Jack Bauer' 14 January 2007. Available online:
      <http://www.time.com/time/magazine/article/0,9171,1576853,00.html> (accessed 8
      November 2007).

[T]he intended effect of the ticking bomb scenario is to create a doubt about the wisdom of the absolute prohibition of torture. This doubt, in turn, is usually designed to lead the audience to accept the creation of legal exception to that prohibition, or at least to accept non-application of the criminal law against torture in particular cases. The true aim of proponents of the ticking bomb argument may be to create a broad exception while seeming to argue for a narrow one. By trying to force torture opponents to concede that torture may be acceptable in at least one extreme case, proponents of the ticking bomb argument hope to undermine the very idea that opposition to torture must be absolute as a matter of principle and practice. As such, the scenario has been given prominence lately by those who seek to end the taboo against torture, to make its application to prisoners suspected of involvement in terrorism seem acceptable, and to provide legal immunity for themselves and others who authorise, tolerate, order, or inflict it.[39]

What does it say about the goals and political sympathies of the show's creator(s) that they repeatedly portray the ticking time bomb scenario as real, with the concomitant message that torture is necessary to frustrate these attacks?

IX. These messages are unambiguous

There are occasional points in the programme at which the acceptability of torture might be thought to be questioned. For example, in the most recent series, Jack loses his nerve: there is a moment when he took can no longer force himself to 'do what is necessary.'

Bauer has been returned to the US after 18 months of secret detention and ceaseless torture in China (he was captured at the end of Series 5). However, his return is not to safety: Jack learns that his superiors and the President have agreed to exchange him for a wanted terrorist, Assad, believed to be planning an imminent attack on the US. The compatriot who is betraying Assad wants to possess Jack Bauer in order to exact revenge for some encounter in their mutual past in Beirut. Bauer, whilst accepting with stoicism that it is legitimate for the President to use him as a pawn, to trade his life in order to thwart a major terrorist attack (accepting the universalization of the principle he lives by), manages to escape.

In one of the plot twists characteristic of the series, Assad turns out to be a sympathetic character, now resolved on peaceful political action, and it is in fact his compatriot Fayed who is planning the terror attack.

Bauer discovers that there is a mole within Assad's organization, who may have information the US security services need. He pursues this spy. An hour and a half into Series 6, Bauer has the spy in his power; circumstances require Bauer to extract information from the terrorist spy by inserting a knife into his open wound:

7:35 A.M. Jack aggravates Omar's open wound but Omar claims to be unaware where Fayed is. Suddenly, Jack stops. He is oddly reluctant to inflict any more pain on the man. This

39   Association for the Prevention of Torture, *Defusing the Ticking Bomb Scenario*, pp. 2-3.

uncharacteristically disturbs him. He tells the puzzled Assad that he could see it in Omar's eyes that he wasn't going to talk.

7:36 A.M. Assad sticks his knife into Omar, who gives up that he knows where Fayed's men are going to meet. After Omar gives him the address, Assad kills him. Assad goes to leave but Jack is frozen. 'I don't know how to do this anymore,' Jack whispers.[40]

Jack is so traumatized by this and other happenings at the beginning of the latest series (he was 'forced' to shoot and kill Curtis, his colleague, in order to protect Assad) that he resigns from CTU.

However at 9:58 a.m., Fayed's group detonates a nuclear bomb in Los Angeles. Jack's qualms are dissolved by the impetus to do his duty, which in this case involves torturing his own brother (who has been implicated in the supply of the nuclear weapons), just under an hour later:

10:56 A.M. Jack slugs Graem and knocks him out. He ties Graem up in a chair. Jack grabs him by the throat and threatens to hurt him if he doesn't give up information. Graem says he is already hurting him. 'Trust me, I'm not,' Jack says intently.[41]

A few moments later, Jack suffocates his brother (non-fatally) with a plastic bag.

Jack's reluctance to torture the spy a few hours earlier is shown to be a momentary weakness, which is overcome when he comprehends the depravity of the terrorists. He is soon back on message after this epiphany: gung ho, efficient, and determined.

This is not the only occasion where opposition to its torture is shown to be weakness. In an earlier series, a suspected terrorist named Joe Prado is released from CTU just before interrogation, thanks to the efforts of a lawyer working for 'Amnesty Global', who had received an anonymous tipoff. Jack resigns from CTU in order to avoid implicating the organization in his actions. Prado is handcuffed in a parked car outside the CTU building. Jack enters the car, breaks Prado's hands, and is rewarded with crucial and accurate information. Earlier, the audience had been shown that Prado's lawyer's tipoff came from a terrorist source. This undoubtedly accentuated the predominant message of that storyline: 'regardless of good intentions, those seeking to protect suspects' rights risk abetting terrorist activities, to catastrophic ends.'[42]

The pro-torture message of the series is unambiguous. Any derogation from the position that 'torture is a necessity; it is my duty to torture' is shown to be frailty: psychological or political weakness; rather than a reasonable and rational position to take.

---

40   Fox, Season Six Episode Guide.

41   Ibid.

42   A. Green, 'Normalising Torture on "24"', *New York Times* 22 May 2005. Available online: <http://www.nytimes.com/2005/05/22/arts/television/22gree.html?_r=1&oref=slogin&pagew anted=print> (accessed 12 November 2007).

In the counterterrorist world of '*24*,'...torture represents not the breakdown of a just society, but the turning point – at times even the starting point – for social relations. Through this artistic sleight of hand, the show makes torture appear normal.[43]

E. Intention(s) of the programme makers

What meaning do the programme-makers aim to convey?

I. One message?

A complicating factor is that different people are involved in various aspects of the creation of the programme. The writers on the show are described by Surnow as a mixture of liberals and conservatives.[44]

Squarely on the conservative side is Joel Surnow, co-creator and executive producer, and as such most clearly the author of the show.

Surnow is quoted as saying that the series is

> '... ripped out of the Zeitgeist of what people's fears are – their paranoia that we're going to be attacked... [it] makes people look at what we're dealing with...'[45]

Suzanne Fields, in the *Washington Times*, reports Surnow to have said 'Every American wishes we had someone out there neatly taking care of business'. She relates his response to a question – whether he would show waterboarding as one of the techniques used to produce a confession – 'Yes...But only with bottled water — this is Hollywood'.[46] This response in isolation might simply be viewed as tasteless, but Surnow clearly isn't joking about justice and heroism when he discusses the character, Jack Bauer: 'There's nothing left but to do the right thing... He's come to symbolize this sort of pure killing machine that all of us secretly want to unleash on the bad guys... [Bauer] really represents just justice'.[47]

And, as he told The Washington Times,

---

43 Ibid.
44 A. Cusac, 'Watching Torture in Prime Time' *The Progressive*, August (2005). Available online: <http://www.progressive.org/?q=mag_cusac0805> (accessed 12 November 2007).
45 Mayer, 'Whatever it Takes', p. 2
46 S. Fields, 'Tortured by compromise' *Washington Times* 15 October 2007. Available online: <http://www.washingtontimes.com/apps/pbcs.dll/article?AID=/20071015/EDITORIAL02/11 0150006&template=printart> (accessed 12 November 2007).
47 R. S. McCain, '"24" producer: Hilary as president is "nuts"' *Washington Times*, 11 November 2007. Available online: <http://www.washingtontimes.com/apps/pbcs.dll/article? AID=/20071111/ NATION/71111001/-1/RSS_NATION_POLITICS&template=printart> (accessed 12 November 2007).

'[i]f there's a bomb about to hit a major U.S. city and you have a person with information . . . if you don't torture that person, that would be one of the most immoral acts you could imagine.'[48]

Surnow is reported to have said that *24* does not 'try to push an agenda,' but is 'committed to being non-PC'.[49] It is unlikely that many readers would accept a commitment to being 'non-PC', with all of the negative connotations a conservative such as Surnow places on 'being PC', as a *neutral* position. But even if it were, Duncan Kennedy could have told Surnow that a commitment not to act ideologically is in itself an ideological position.[50]

Bob Cochran, co-creator with Surnow (and a law graduate), is reported by Jane Mayer in *The New Yorker* to have said that he:

...supports the use of torture 'in narrow circumstances' and believes that it can be justified under the Constitution' [in the case of necessity, i.e. ticking timebomb].[51]

So here, we can clearly see that the two most important individuals driving the series – whose imagination and inspiration provides the overarching flavour of the show – accept torture, at least in ticking time-bomb situations. And perhaps unsurprisingly, this is the message one derives from *24*.

II.   'Just entertainment'

On the liberal flank of the writing team is Howard Gordon, who describes himself as a moderate Democrat. He also writes many of the torture scenes. He is concerned when:

'...critics say that we've enabled and reflected the public's appetite for torture. Nobody wants to be the handmaid to a relaxed policy that accepts torture as a legitimate means of interrogation... I think people can differentiate between a television show and reality'.[52]

This is frequently the cry of those who are involved in *24* and don't support torture – it's just a television show; it's just entertainment; it's not real.

One of the most vocal proponents of this view is Kiefer Sutherland, the actor who plays Jack Bauer, who in addition to being executive producer of the show, is left-wing and anti-torture.

In a TV interview with Charlie Rose, he is reported to have said:

'Do I personally believe that the police or any of these other legal agencies that are working for this government should be entitled to interrogate people and do the things that I do on the show? No, I do not'[53]

48   Cusac 'Watching Torture'.
49   Ibid.
50   D. Kennedy, *A Critique of Adjudication* (Cambridge (Massachusetts), Harvard University Press, 1998).
51   Mayer, 'Whatever it Takes', p. 4.
52   Mayer, 'Whatever it Takes', p. 3.

In *People News*, Sutherland said:

'24' is absolutely not – categorically not – a justification for torture. I think the whole thing has been taken out of context. We are interested this has become a debate on a very public level. That's what is fantastic about entertainment – it brings certain subjects into people's conversations...'We are a television show, we use some of the torture sequences as a dramatic device to heighten tension. We are not saying, 'This is the way the world should be, and we are condoning this.[54]

On the other hand, there is the following description by David Danzig, a project director at Human Rights First, of an encounter between interrogators visiting the set of *24* and Kiefer Sutherland:

Sutherland was 'really upset, really intense' and stressed that he tries to tell people that the show 'is just entertainment'. But Sutherland, who claimed to be bored with playing torture scenes, admitted that he worried about the 'unintended consequences of the show'.[55]

III. The true message – more than mere entertainment

O'Mathúna argues that 'the banality of torture in *24* should shock us into realising how easily and quickly torture becomes acceptable.'[56] However, I argue that the effect on the viewer is not shock, but acceptance. In *24*, there is a constant, dramatically unchallenged repetition of the message that torture is necessary; valuable; morally (and legally) permissible; that a hero has the duty to torture; that America is under constant ticking time bomb threat. The way the programme is constructed, with action taking place against the clock; the repeated recourse to torture as 'the only option available', required in the circumstances (averaging 13 instances of torture per series); the fact that the torturer-in-chief is the 'hero' with whom we are meant to identify and sympathize – all these things are much more than 'mere entertainment'. The eminently watchable – what some people call 'addictive' – nature of the content makes the ideological message more powerful.[57]

These qualities convince me that *24* is more than merely entertainment with a right-wing slant. Certain characteristics of the series are more than amusement and rather akin to propaganda. For present purposes, we can borrow the OED's definition of propaganda as 'the systematic dissemination of information, esp. in a biased or misleading way, in order to promote a political cause or point of view. Also: information disseminated in this way; the means or media by which such ideas

53   Cusac 'Watching Torture'.
54   People News 'Kiefer Sutherland's 24 Defense' 18 March 2007. Available online: <http://people.monstersandcritics.com/news/article_1279058.php/Kiefer_Sutherlands_24_defense> (accessed 12 November 2007).
55   Mayer, 'Whatever it Takes', p. 5.
56   O'Mathúna, 'The Ethics of Torture in *24*', p.103.
57   See also S. Žižek, 'The depraved heroes of *24* are the Himmlers of Hollywood', *The Guardian*, 10 January 2006.

are disseminated'. Specifically in *24*, there is a repeated and systematic dissemination of material which favours the cause of a particular right-wing, pro-torture viewpoint. This may or may not be consciously done by (all) the show's creators, but the utterances of Joel Surnow, co-creator and executive producer of *24*, suggest that thoughtlessness at least is not one of the factors in his part of the show's gestation.

Even if we accept that the express intention of *24* is to entertain, we may believe that the meaning of the programme goes further, giving it an altogether different, and worrying, significance. It is therefore neecessary to identify what this more extensive message might be.

F. Subordination and Silencing

The question of more extensive messages is precisely the point considerd by Rae Langton in the context of pornography. She discusses whether there may come a point at which the speech of one person subordinates and silences another, depriving them of effective speech, and reflects on the two feminist claims – often regarded as confused or problematic – that pornography, in addition to depicting subordination and causing subordination, is itself a form of subordination, and that it silences women. I explore her arguments before applying them to the context of torture in *24*.

I. Subordination

In her examination of pornography *as* subordination, she draws on J. L. Austin's categorization of words as 'speech acts' in *How to Do Things with Words*.[58] If a first man tells a second man to shoot the woman standing next to them (and the second man does so), the act of uttering 'shoot her' is the performance of a *locutionary* act – the utterance of a sentence with a particular meaning. But this does not exhaust the description of the scene. Additionally, part of the *perlocutionary* act involved is the shock generated by such an utterance; as is the persuasive effect of saying 'shoot her'.[59] And this is still not a comprehensive description:

> ... if you stop there you will still have left something out. You will have ignored what our first man did it saying what he said. So you go on. *In* saying 'shoot her', the first man *urged* the second to shoot the woman. That description captures the action constituted by the utterance itself: it captures what Austin called the *illocutionary* act.[60]

58   R. Langton, 'Speech Acts and Unspeakable Acts' *Philosophy and Public Affairs* 22, no. 4 (1993): 293-330, p. 295 *et seq.*

59   Ibid.

60   Ibid., pp. 295-296.

Austin's account of this additional dimension of speech acts encompasses the idea that speech has some kind of illocutionary power when certain 'felicity conditions' are satisfied, usually specified by written or unwritten conventions, which characteristically require intention on the part of the speaker.[61] Examples Langton gives of such illocutionary acts include warning, promising, and marrying.

However, as a type of action, speech acts suffer from the same weaknesses as action in general: sometimes we do something other than that which we aimed to do – the recipient of our speech may have understood our words as an order rather than advice, for example. Alternatively, the intended illocution may simply fail.[62]

Langton considers that Catherine MacKinnon's claim[63] that speech can subordinate makes sense if the illocutionary aspect of speech is taken into account, in addition to locution and perlocution. In the context of pornography, its illocutionary force is subordination.[64]

Where subordinating speech is uttered by someone in power (for example 'Blacks are not permitted to vote' said by a legislator enacting legislation which underpins apartheid),[65] the illocutionary power of the utterance

> ... *unfairly* ranks blacks as having inferior worth; they legitimate *discriminatory* behaviour on the part of whites; and they *unjustly* deprive them of some important powers.
>
> ...Actions of ranking, valuing and placing are illocutions... labelled *verdictive* by Austin.[66]

Other types of illocutions – those which order, permit, prohibit, authorize, enact, or dismiss – may confer on or deprive of powers and rights. These are called *exercitive* by Austin. Crucial to both these types of illocution is the fact that the speaker is in a position of authority (formal or practical), which gives such speech a power it would otherwise lack.[67]

Can it correctly be said that pornographic speech acts have the authority needed to be verdictive, without which they cannot *subordinate* women? After all, pornographers tend not to be legislators, statesman, etc. Langton considers that

> what is important here is not whether the speech of pornographers is universally held in high esteem: it is not – hence the common assumption among liberals that in defending pornographers they are defending the underdog. What is important is whether it is authoritative in the domain that counts – the domain of speech about sex – and whether it is authoritative for the hearers that count: people, men, boys, who in addition to wanting 'entertainment,' want to discover the right way to do things, want to know which moves in the sexual game are legitimate. What is important is whether it is authoritative for those hearers

---

61   Ibid., p. 301.
62   Ibid., pp. 301-302.
63   C. MacKinnon, 'Francis Biddle's Sister' in *Feminism Unmodified* (Cambridge (Massachusetts), Harvard University Press, 1987), p. 176, as cited in Langton, 'Speech Acts', p. 294, n. 2.
64   R. Langton, 'Speech Acts', p. 302.
65   Langton, 'Speech Acts', p. 302.
66   Ibid., p. 304.
67   Ibid., pp. 304-305.

who – one way or another – do seem to learn that silence is sexy and coercion legitimate... in this domain, and for these hearers, it may be that pornography has all the authority of a monopoly.[68]

Authority, then, may be practical and subjective, rather than formal, and need not follow the conventional social order.

II. Silencing

Langton proffers a threefold classification of silencing that corresponds to Austin's scheme. First, persons or a group may be literally silent due to intimidation or hopelessness. Here, they do not perform even a locutionary act. Second, despite speaking, the group or persons will fall short of their intended goal – their perlocutionary act has been frustrated, for example when one's vote for a particular party is part of the minority. The third silencing goes to the heart of the illocutionary action intended:

> ... one speaks, one utters words, and fails not simply to achieve the effect one aims at, but fails to perform the very action one intends. Here, speech misfires... Silencing of this third kind we can call *illocutionary disablement*....[69]

Not having authority in a relevant field may constitute illocutionary disablement.[70] This kind of silencing, in Langton's terms, has made the actor's speech *unspeakable*. Langton goes on to consider instances of illocutionary disablement in the context of pornography, and concludes that pornography may silence women by making it impossible for them to achieve the effect they wish to achieve – for example, if one of pornography's messages is that sexual violence is permissible, it is a corollary that pornography may prevent a woman's genuine refusal of sex from being taken seriously: 'the felicity conditions for refusal, for protest, are not being met. Something is robbing the speech of its intended force'.[71] What is preventing a woman's refusal from being understood in this type of case?

For Langton, the diagnosis is stark:

> *The felicity conditions for women's speech acts are set by the speech acts of pornography.* The words of the pornographer, like the words of the legislator, are 'words that set conditions.' they are words that constrain, that make certain actions – refusal, protest – unspeakable for women in some contexts.[72]

Whilst pornography does not usually prevent women from uttering words at all (performing locutionary acts), Langton wishes us to take very seriously the claim that pornography literally silences. If women are merely able to use words, but not

68   Ibid., p. 312
69   Ibid., p. 315.
70   Ibid., p. 316.
71   Ibid., p. 323.
72   Ibid., p. 324.

achieve their aim – if the illocutionary import of an utterance has been neutralized or disabled, they fail to perform a speech act.

> On Austin's view, locutions on their own are nothing. Locutions are there to be used. Words are tools. Words are for doing things with. There is little point in giving someone tools if they cannot do things with them. And there is little point in allowing women words if we cannot do things with them. That, at any rate, is not free speech.[73]

III. *24* as speech acts

Having set out Langton's analysis, we can now consider whether *24* contains an important illocutionary message.

In *24*, the locutionary aspect of the torture scenes, the 'speech act' in question, is the depiction of torture. The effect this depiction has on viewers – including the potential encouragement of torture as an interrogation method in real life – would be a perlocutionary aspect of the series' speech acts. What illocutionary message might the programme hold?

To misquote Langton:[74] not all explicit depictions of torture promote torture. Locutions that depict torture could in principle be used to perform speech acts that are a far cry from torture promotion: documentaries, for example, or investigative reports, or government studies, or books that protest against torture, or perhaps even legal definitions of torture. It all depends, as Austin might have said, on the use to which the locution is put.

What does *24* do in its depiction of torture? *In* repeatedly portraying torture as necessary, valuable, legally and morally permissible, and the proper remit of the hero, the series *urges* both the public and the interrogator to accept torture as a good tool, and to disregard any qualms we may have about its legitimacy and efficacy, and the subordination and dehumanization of any person suspected of terrorism. This is *24*'s illocutionary aspect.

Again, substituting '*24*' and the theme of 'torture' for Langton's references to pornography:[75] torture promotion is first, verdictive speech that ranks victims as inferiors, and second, exercitive speech that legitimizes violence interrogation. Since torture is not simply harm, not simply crime, but discriminatory behaviour, torture promotion subordinates because it legitimizes misbehaviour... for these two reasons, then, *24* is an *illocutionary* act of subordination.

The verdicts in its message are unfair, giving undue weight to one side of the argument; are discriminatory against anyone suspected of possible involvement in terror, and the illocutionary message of *24* unjustly deprives terror suspect of important safeguards. In its own world as well as the real, the verdictive force of *24*

---

73   Ibid., p. 327.
74   Ibid., pp. 305-306.
75   Ibid., pp. 307-308.

is also exercitive, as those suspected of terrorism are deprived of power and rights, and those suspecting terrorism are permitted frightening latitude in their interrogations.

A television show that depicted positive messages of torture in a debate about diverse interpretations of 'right action' and different criteria of morality would not have this illocutionary force. Debate is valuable in its own right; not least to expose the weaknesses of any argument. The existence of alternative, credible points of view would negate the overwhelmingness of one illocutionary message, and undermine the verdictive power of one standpoint. But in *24*, there is no debate. Any divergence from the orthodox message is quickly portrayed as pathetic and insubstantial. The verdictive illocutionary effect remains.

How important is this illocutionary message? If we agree that *24* has a pro torture message that subordinates the interests of anyone suspected (reasonably or not) of terrorism, is this a real cause for concern? The answer to this question depends on whether the verdictive and exercitive messages of *24* are taken seriously by its recipients. In other words, does *24* have practical, subjective authority for (at least a significant part of) its audience?

Before addressing this, we need to pause to deal with one potential objection: it might be thought, when referring back to my three sets of circumstances in the context of information dissemination, above, that I am attempting some sleight of hand. Why is the subjective authority of the speaker important, when I have already stated that the intention of the recipient of (torture) information cannot make a publication immoral? However, in that instance, I was referring to situations where the publication or dissemination of information about torture is either morally permissible or required. This present discussion relates to practical considerations in the instance where the intention of the publisher is (at least arguably) *impermissible*.

Joel Surnow, as principal creator of *24*, has broadcast his views on torture and legitimate interrogation quite extensively. As the creator and director of a popular television series, and the personality in his own right, he may be seen as authoritative person for at least some of *24*'s audience. However, I suspect that the principal person giving voice to the speech acts of *24* is someone else: Jack Bauer.

Jack's views are, unsurprisingly, coextensive with his creator Surnow's. Jack is the hero, the man who always does the right thing, the character with whom we are invited to identify and for whom we are expected to feel admiration. When we suspend our critical faculties and enjoy the entertainment on offer, the internal logic of the series makes eminent sense, and we, too, feel that Jack has no real option *but* to torture, even with the most slender grounds for suspicion of a particular individual. Kiefer Sutherland's contribution to this message is the way in which he convinces the audience that his character is admirable rather than abhorrent.

Is it implausible to think that interrogators who want to discover the right way to do things, want to know which moves in the interrogation game are legitimate, may use *24* as their guide? It is reported that Sutherland agreed to talk to cadets at West Point military academy, at the invitation of the US military, in order to teach recruits that torture is wrong.[76] Sutherland's commitment indicates that he thinks that this is at least plausible.

Is it not possible that the illocutionary message of *24* has contributed to the illocutionary disablement of suspects in the war on terror? It seems that there is at the least the danger of illocutionary disablement. If we accept that pornography may make women's protests unspeakable, we should be concerned that *24* may silence victims of torture and other interrogation abuses by making it impossible for them to achieve the effect they wish to achieve; by frustrating the felicity conditions for the arguments against it.

But it is important not to overstate the case against *24*. Although the TV series sends a message that purports to have authority and is plausibly subjectively received as such, and does seem to have had some very regrettable effects on the actions of soldiers,[77] it is not the only culprit. Nor is the popularity of *24*, although extensive, comparable with the pervasiveness of pornography and other means of subordinating women.

Moreover, my objection is not simply that *24* sends an immoral illocutionary message. I object to the context in which it does so.

IV Propaganda, lies and disguise

24 is not simply entertainment. *24* is a vehicle with a pervasive ideological message. It is propaganda.

Propaganda generally involves some element of persuasion, if not deception.[78] We may agree that deception is prima facie wrong, but I doubt that many people would claim that deception is always wrong. There may be circumstances in which the purposes of a lie justify its telling: where the wrong done is outweighed on the moral scales. Examples might include lying to the victim of a car accident about the extent of their injuries, with the intention of inculcating hope and therefore promoting survival, or disseminating untruthfully positive information about Allied military successes during World War II, to avoid despair and therefore defeat.[79]

In this chapter, I have assumed, rather than established, that torture is morally wrong. If we continue to accept this, we may be willing to categorize the message of *24* as an untruth, relevantly similar to the factual untruths in the above scenarios. As such, it it would be prima facie wrong.

Perhaps we may consider that telling lies about the permissibility and efficacy of torture is justifiable in some circumstances. If so, it may be possible to generate an

---

76   Mayer, 'Whatever it Takes'.
77   See e.g., P.Sands, 'Stress, hooding, noise, nudity, dogs' *The Guardian* 19 April 2008.
78   Cf. Paul Taylor's neutral definition of progaganda: P.M.Taylor, 'Perception Management and the "war" against terrorism' *Journal of Information Warfare* 1(3) (2002): 16-29.
79   'Information warfare' as per Taylor. Ibid.

argument that justifies the broadcasting of *24*. I am unable to think of one, it is true – but even my outrage at the wrong of telling lies about torture does not seem to exhaust the iniquity of *24*.

Let us consider another scenario: an alternative show, with similarly entertaining storylines, but which promoted a (stereo)typically liberal position in a comparably repetitive, simplistic, didactic and authoritative manner.

Per series, this imaginary show (working title *9 Months*) depicts an average of 13 instances of abortion, because:

- it is the right thing to do;
- it's what a woman needs to do in those circumstances;

and

- any squeamishness on the part of those involved needs to be overridden, because it is their duty to choose/perform abortions;
- in the face of the imminent threat of population explosion/global warming/food shortages, abortion is what's necessary.

Would Surnow, and *24*'s creative team be satisfied with the excuse that *9 Months* is just entertainment'? Rightly, I suspect they would not. The verdictive, illocutionary aspect of such a show would shift the programme outside the category of mere entertainment – as is the case with *24*.

But the 'just entertainment' excuse is not simply an inaccurate description of such a programme. 'Just entertainment' is part of *24*'s disguise.

24 is propaganda by virtue of its illocutionary force. Moreover, it is *surreptitious* propaganda which masquerades as entertainment; whose existence is 'justified' as entertainment. Its very existence as a television programme is a lie, irrespective of its ideological content. Here, we have a double lie: content and concealment.

Moreover, *24* stealthily, seductively convinces us that torture is a serious option, in fact a necessary, mandatory and inevitable right response to suspicion and time pressure and the need for information, and does so *in the guise of entertainment*.

G. Conclusion

The programme *24* is immoral in its exclusively pro-torture message, which has a disturbingly verdictive force, and in the way this message masquerades as entertainment.

Torturers deny the humanity of their victims. Torturers violate our most important moral and societal norms. *24* violates these standards, in the name of entertainment, and it also abuses the norms of entertainment. It is part of the poison of the programme that we are persuaded to suspend disbelief and witness repeated

201

inflictions of extreme physical or mental violence. To return to my third point about the intention of the recipient: we suspend our humanity by watching uncritically.

Contributors

Francesco Belvisi is Professor of Philosophy and Sociology of Law at the Law Department of the University of Modena and Reggio Emilia. His scientific interests include the German legal culture (researches on Jhering, Simmel, Weber, Schelsky, Luhmann), philosophy and sociology of constitutional law and of fundamental rights (immigration and asylum law, citizenship, the European Charter of Fundamental Rights) and the legal problems related to the integration of the (European) multicultural society. Among his publications are *La teoria delle istituzioni di Helmut Schelsky* (2000), and *Società multiculturale, diritti, costituzione* (2000). He was the editor of J. Raz, *I valori fra attaccamento e rispetto* (2003), co-editor of *Diritto e filosofia nel XIX secolo* (2002), and is Associate editor of *Ratio Juris*.

Hauke Brunkhorst studied German Literature, Philosophy, Education and Sociology at the Universities of Kiel, Freiburg und Frankfurt in Germany. He obtained his doctorate in 1978, and took his 'Habilitation' in Education in 1982 at the University of Frankfurt, followed by a 'Habilitation' in Sociology in 1985, also at Frankfurt. Between 1985 and 1997, he held chairs and visiting chairs at the Universities of Vienna, Frankfurt, Duisburg and the Free University Berlin. Between 1995 and 1997, he was Research Fellow at the Institute for Cultural Sciences for North-Rhine Westphalia. Since 1997, he has held the Chair of Sociology at the University of Flensburg, and in 2005, he was a Research Fellow at the Maison des Sciences de l'Homme, Paris. His publications include *Solidarity. From Civic Friendship to a Global Legal Community* (2005) and monographs on Marx's *Eighteenth Brumaire,* Habermas and Hannah Arendt.

Susan Benedict teaches the ethics of research and international health at the Medical University of South Carolina in Charleston, SC, USA. Her research is focused on the ethics of nurses during National Socialism and has been funded by the Greenwall Foundation of New York and the National Institutes of Health, USA. Professor Benedict completed a post-doctoral fellowship in Medical Ethics and the Holocaust at the United States Holocaust Memorial Museum in Washington, DC. She is the author of articles on the Nazi 'euthanasia' program and the roles of nurses in the medical experiments of the concentration camps. She is a collaborative partner with Professor Linda Shields of the University of Hull.

Patrick Birkinshaw is Professor of Law at the University of Hull. An experienced and widely published public lawyer, he is an authority on secrecy and access to justice, freedom of information, European public law in addition to government and economic regulation. He has acted as a special adviser to the Commons Select Committee on Public Administration in that Committee's inquiries into Freedom of Information legislation and Political Memoirs. He is the author of *Freedom of*

Information: the Law, the Practice and the Ideal (4th ed 2008); *Government and Information: the Law Relating to Access, Disclosure and Regulation* 3rd ed.2005) and European Public Law (1st ed. 2003).

Bev Clucas is Lecturer in Law at the University of Hull. Her research inte rests have included jurisprudence and children, and her PhD thesis was concerned with a modified application of Alan Gewirth's moral theory with respect to the rights of children. She was supported by the AHRB Research Leave Scheme for the project *Children's rights: autonomy and the welfare/best interests tension. A Welsh perspective,* a study on the practice of the first Children's Commissioner for Wales. She has published articles on jurisprudence; medical ethics, particularly conjoined twins; human rights, and children's rights and welfare.

Penny Green is Professor of Law and Criminology at King's College London. She has published numerous papers on state crime, state-corporate crime, natural disasters, Turkish criminal justice and politics, transnational crime, illegal logging and environmental harms, asylum and forced migration, and dealing in stolen antiquities. She is the author of six books including *The Enemy Without: Policing and Class Consciousness in the Miners' Strike* (1990); *Drugs, Trafficking and Criminal Policy: the Scapegoat Solution* (1997), *Drug Couriers* (1991) and, with Tony Ward, the first European monograph on State Crime, *State Crime: Governments, Violence and Corruption* (2004). She was formerly Professor of Law and Criminology at the University of Westminster and prior to that Senior Lecturer at the University of Southampton and Research Fellow at the LSE.

Gerry Johnstone is Professor of Law at the University of Hull. He is the author of *Restorative Justice: Ideas, Values, Debates* (Willan, 2002); *Medical Concepts and Penal Policy* (1996) and editor of *A Restorative Justice Reader: Texts, Sources, Context* (2003) and (with Daniel Van Ness) *Handbook of Restorative Justice* (2007). He has also written numerous journal articles on therapeutic interventions into criminal justice, participatory justice, and critical legal education.

Tsvetana Kamenova has held a number of academic posts, including Dean of the Law School, Plovdiv University, Bulgaria; Director, Institute for Legal Studies, Bulgarian Academy of Sciences (BAS) (1995-2006); Professor of Law, Plovdiv University (1992-2006); Professor of International Law, New Bulgarian University (1997-2005); and she was Visiting Fulbright Senior Scholar, Columbia University School of Law, NY, USA (2000-2001). Her publications include 11 books and more than 100 articles published in Bulgaria and in Germany, USA, The Netherlands, France, Hungary, Russia. She has undertaken judicial work since 1973, as Junior Judge, Sofia City Court, and acted as consultant for the United Nations Human Rights Field Presence in Tajikistan (2002-2003). Judge Kamenova has been an ad litem Judge at the International Criminal Tribunal for the Former Yugoslavia since 27 June 2006.

Marina Lalatta Costerbosa is Lecturer in Moral Philosophy and Bioethics at the University of Bologna (Department of Philosophy). Her main research interest is in the theory of practical reasoning and applied ethics. Her recent books are *Law as Moral Reasoning. Contemporary Natural Law Theories and Bioethical Applications* (Soveria Mannelli 2007) and *Wilhelm von Humboldt's Political Thought* (Milan 2000).

Massimo La Torre has studied law and political science and has taught at the University of Bologna and at the European University Institute in Florence. He is now Professor of Philosophy of law at the University of Catanzaro, Italy, and Professor of Legal Theory at the University of Hull, England. His latest book is *Constitutionalism and Legal Reasoning* (Springer, 2007).

Agustín José Menéndez is senior researcher at the Universidad de León (Spain) and research fellow at ARENA, the European Studies centre of Universitetet i Oslo. His main research interests concern European constitutional law, the normative theory of taxation and wicked legal systems. His publications include *Justifying Taxes* (2001); *Developing a Constitution for Europe* (co-editor, 2004) and *Arguing Fundamental Rights* (co-editor, 2006).

Alison Jane O'Donnell is currently a Lecturer in Nursing, University of Dundee, Dundee, Scotland, UK. Her background interest in her current PhD studies originated from an initial MSc in Nursing dissertation completed in August 2000 at Queen Margaret University College, Edinburgh, Scotland. The purpose of her present PhD studies is to explore and expand this original thesis in more depth, but from a different stance.

Linda Shields is Professor of Paediatric and Child Health Nursing, School of Nursing and Midwifery, Curtin University of Technology, Perth, Western Australia. She was formerly Professor of Nursing at the University of Hull and held the Foundation Chair in Nursing at University of Limerick in Ireland. She is an Honorary Professor at the University of Queensland, Australia and Northumbria University in the UK and a visiting fellow at Örebro University in Sweden. Her research interests include the care of children in health services and ethical issues surrounding nursing such as nurses' roles in the euthanasia programmes of the Third Reich. Linda maintains a small clinical load in paediatrics.

Uwe Steinhoff is Assistant Professor in International Political Theory at the University of Hong Kong. He was Research Associate in the Oxford Leverhulme

Programme on the Changing Character of War, and before that he taught philosophy at Humboldt University, Berlin. He has published numerous articles and three books, among them *On the Ethics of War and Terrorism* (Oxford: Oxford University Press, 2007). He has recently finished a further book on the ethics of war, focusing on non-state actors.

Tony Ward is Reader in Law at the University of Hull and previously taught at De Montfort University, Leicester. His main research interests are in state crime (including torture) and the law, history and epistemology of expert testimony. He is co-author with Penny Green of *State Crime: Governments, Violence and Corruption* (London, Pluto, 2004) and with Gerry Johnstone of *Law and Crime* (London, Sage, forthcoming).